The
Essential
Partnership

Also by Stanley Greenspan

First Feelings
(with Nancy Thorndike Greenspan)

Infants in Multi-Risk Families
(co-editor)

Psychopathology and Adaptation
in Infancy and Early Childhood

The Clinical Interview of the Child
(with Nancy Thorndike Greenspan)

Intelligence and Adaptation

A Consideration of Some
Learning Variables in the Context of
Psychoanalytic Theory

The Development of the Ego

The Course of Life
(co-editor)

The Essential Partnership

How Parents and Children Can
Meet the Emotional Challenges
of Infancy and Childhood

Stanley I. Greenspan, M.D.
Nancy Thorndike Greenspan

Viking

VIKING
Published by the Penguin Group
Viking Penguin Inc., 40 West 23rd Street,
New York, New York 10010, U.S.A.
Penguin Books Ltd, 27 Wrights Lane,
London W8 5TZ, England
Penguin Books Australia Ltd, Ringwood,
Victoria, Australia
Penguin Books Canada Ltd, 2801 John Street,
Markham, Ontario, Canada L3R 1B4
Penguin Books (N.Z.) Ltd, 182-190 Wairau Road,
Auckland 10, New Zealand

Penguin Books Ltd, Registered Offices:
Harmondsworth, Middlesex, England

First published in 1989 by Viking Penguin Inc.
Published simultaneously in Canada

1 3 5 7 9 10 8 6 4 2

LIBRARY OF CONGRESS CATALOGING IN PUBLICATION DATA
Greenspan, Stanley I.
The essential partnership.
Includes index.
1. Child rearing—United States. 2. Emotions in
children. 3. Child development—United States.
I. Greenspan, Nancy Thorndike. II. Title.
HQ772.G674 1989   649'.1   88–40291
ISBN 0–670–81279–X

Printed in the United States of America
Set in Baskerville
Designed by Kathryn Parise

To our essential partners:
Elizabeth, Jake, and Sarah

Contents

Contents

viii

=VII=
Negative Emotions:
Separation Anxiety, Fears,
Sadness, and Competition

=VIII=
Intelligence, Perception, and Movement

=IX=
Peer and Group Relationships

Conclusion

Index

Preface

In *First Feelings*, we formulated six predictable stages in emotional development, beginning at birth. We explained these milestones in order to help you observe, enjoy, and participate in the complex unfolding of your baby's emotional life. Just as parents have traditionally followed their babies' physical development, we wanted you to come to appreciate the steps by which your baby becomes a reasoning, feeling, caring, emotive child.

But, as many parents have stated, "This is the *ideal.*" They ask, "What happens in real life? How can we tell if there are problems? How can we solve problems and facilitate healthy development?"

Historically, parents have been offered vague platitudes for advice: "Be supportive"; "don't overexcite"; "don't be overly punitive"; "find the right balance between frustration and indulgence"; "don't spoil, but don't deprive." . . . No wonder many parents feel confused. "Sounds good," one parent said, "but when I'm in the trenches with my child, the vague generalities don't make sense."

At the other extreme, parents are inundated with highly specific advice—advice which, in overlooking the child's unique abilities and sensitivities, often undermines his or her overall emotional development. Some of this specific advice also challenges parents' instincts and common sense. For example, for sleeping problems, the advice "Tough it out," or "Let your baby cry it out when he wakes up at night," may ignore the needs of the child.

Similarly, for aggressive or impulsive children, the maxim, "Never reinforce (reward) aggressive behavior with attention; always punish it with time-outs or isolation," often ignores the larger social and emotional context of the child's development and may in fact undermine the very goal that one has for that child in the first place—to teach him how to care for others.

In *The Essential Partnership* we respond to parents' questions in a detailed way that is neither too specific nor too general. We focus on the ingredients of the Essential Partnership, showing you how it will encourage emotional health and teach your child how to cope with and turn problems into opportunities for growth. We divide the baby's emotional world into the areas you are most concerned with—those that form the cornerstone of a healthy personality. These are:

- mood and self-esteem

- sexuality, pleasure, and excitement

- anger and aggression

- such seemingly negative emotions as separation anxiety, fears, sadness, and competition

- the capacity to concentrate, process information, and learn

- peer and group relationships

For each of these areas, we describe healthy development and how you can foster it. For example, we discuss how expressing pride in your toddler's unique talents, even in potentially negative ones, can bolster his self-esteem; how helping your preschooler to express rather than repress her anger through the "ideas" of pretend play and conversation will help her develop her reason, judgment, and sense of empathy; and how cautiousness in pre-school group relationships—which is often falsely identified as problematic—may in fact be a sign of special sensitivities and comfort with intimacy.

We also discuss the most common obstacles encountered by children and parents (or other caregivers such as relatives, teach-ers, day-care staff, babysitters) in each phase of the child's emo-tional growth, and present concrete steps for turning a "problem" into an opportunity for healthy development. Each problem, if identified early enough, becomes a window of opportunity.

For example, a twelve-month-old who persists in waking up at night may be acting upon his need to work out power struggles that crop up during the day; a three-and-a-half-year-old's nightmares may offer insight into his anxious curiosity about the human body; an eight-month-old's stubborn anger at being left may reveal her preferences for gradual—rather than hurried—reconciliations. Such realizations may change the nature of your relationship for years to come and open the way for you to gain an even deeper understanding of and compassion for your baby and child.

You may find yourself or your child in a situation similar to one in this book. We hope that what you learn will deepen your understanding of your child's emotional life and development, and help you to face one of the most important challenges of parenthood—your role as the emotional partner, teacher, mentor, and guide—with success.

S.I.G.

N.T.G.

The Essential Partnership

I

Parenting Responsibilities and Opportunities

Today the responsibilities of child rearing create big and small challenges on all fronts: Can both spouses have careers and be good parents too? How much time, aside from physical caregiving, does a baby need? What is having and raising a child really about anyway? When the realization sinks in that we parents are ultimately the ones responsible for our babies' development and well-being, these basic questions can begin to seem overwhelming.

Perhaps the most perplexing and controversial issue is gauging the importance of the "parent factor" in a baby's development. How important are you to your baby's healthy emotional growth and development? What role does your relationship with your baby play in his developing his own special emotional traits? How much do you contribute to your child's ability to overcome the many emotional challenges he will face—challenges that range from early separation anxiety to issues of control and aggression, to night wakening and sibling rivalry, and, later on, to issues of sexual identity, the complexity of relationships, sharing, competition, envy, and jealousy, and of self-esteem? Though you may quickly recognize the importance of the parental role in all of these, just how or what kind of commitment from you is needed to help your child learn his or her emotional ABCs may be less clear.

There are basic experiences everyone needs in order to grow and develop emotionally. Picture a pyramid divided into three levels. At the foundation of the pyramid is good physical care. This includes proper medical care, nutrition, protection from abuse and neglect, and adequate nurturing. In many families, these basics go without saying, but in some they do not.

At the second level of your pyramid is the need for ongoing, constant human relationships characterized by positive feelings. This is not to say you should never get angry with your child or that you should never have separations. The overall feeling, however, needs to be positive. For the long haul in both good and bad times, your child needs to be able to rely upon stable, available adults. After all, he is just learning to form relationships, and intimacy can't occur when you or your love is ephemeral, inconsistent, or spread thin, or when there are too many losses or changes of the primary people in his life. One hour here and there and/or a new caregiver every six months just won't do.

Even in many intact "traditional" families, positive relationships between infants and caregivers are not always easy. When you begin to think about single parents, two-parent working families, day care—and the various babysitting experiences we provide for our children, not to mention marital or personal problems and divorce—the difficulties of providing the second level of emotional well-being are all too apparent.

Above levels one and two is the third level of the pyramid—the need for specific emotional experiences. At each stage of his or her development, your child has different emotional needs. For example, your four-month-old needs wooing into a relationship, but your three-and-a-half-year-old must learn to symbolize feelings and practice reasoning. Pretend play and "floor time," where you're right down there with him, engaging in make-believe play, or, like a lawyer, discussing the merits of an eight o'clock versus an eight-thirty bedtime, is what teaches your young child about emotional ideas and reason.

Our first book, *First Feelings: Milestones in the Emotional Development of Your Baby and Child*, discusses what your baby requires to meet each of his or her *emotional* milestones. These include:

0–3 months:	Protection, comfort, and interesting sights and sounds to *feel regulated* and *interested in the world*;
3–7 months:	Wooing and loving overtures to *fall in love*;
4–10 months:	Sensitive, empathetic reading of cues to foster *purposeful communication*;
9–18 months:	Admiring, organized, intentional interactions to foster *a complex sense of self*;
18–30 months:	Pretend play and functional use of language to foster *emotional ideas*;
30–48 months:	Effective limits and use of logic in pretend play and language to foster *emotional thinking*.

So, physical care and protection, a constant loving human relationship, and specific emotional experiences are all necessary for proper emotional growth. It's a tall order, especially when, in addition to Mom and Dad, day-care staff, babysitters, or live-in help come and go.

It's no easy task either to get all the adults in your child's daily world to operate like a team, an "extended family" tied together by common goals and feelings. Yet cultivating a sense of "extended family" is essential. By knowing the sequence of emotional development and observing when your child is progressing or stumbling, you will be able to take the responsibility for, as well as the opportunity to encourage, your child's healthy emotional development.

Parents may feel overwhelmed when they can't provide all the ingredients. "How do I know what's going on at the day-care center or with the babysitter?" When there is an "extended family" type team, parents have no choice but to orchestrate or manage the team. This requires an intimate relationship with the day-care staff, conversations at the transition times to find out how the baby is doing, continuing assessments of the personalities involved, and a fair amount of hand-holding and teaching. Teachers, day-care staff, babysitters, and relatives have ample opportunities to foster a child's emotional growth. Knowing what a baby needs and when he needs it is the first step.

Children's Emotional Goals

The experiences we have been describing help a child meet his/her early emotional goals, which in turn are the foundation for the most important personality functions. These are briefly reviewed below.

Four-year-old children should be capable of:

1. Forming healthy, warm, and trusting relationships with others—peers as well as adults.

2. Experiencing self-esteem, feeling good about themselves and what they do.

3. Using good impulse and behavioral control.

4. Exhibiting a rich, emotional imagination and using words to express needs and feelings.

5. Separating make-believe from reality and beginning to adjust to reality's demands.

6. Beginning to deal with loss and beginning to show empathy and concern for others.

7. Concentrating, focusing, and planning as a basis for learning in both informal and formal educational settings.

In this chapter we have outlined parenting or caregiving responsibilities and the early emotional goals to which they contribute. Fortunately, for most parents their parenting responsibilities rapidly become a labor of love. This labor of love evolves into an ongoing parent-child relationship, the Essential Partnership. In the next two chapters, we describe why this partnership is so important and how it contains within it the critical ingredients for healthy emotional growth and for overcoming challenges and problems.

II

Stages of the Essential Partnership

Feeling part of a relationship, being fully involved with another person, is an important childhood experience. It is the cornerstone of the child's initial sense of security. It encourages healthy emotional development and helps the child deal with emotional challenges and problems. Especially in the early years, we parents are the perfect partners in this experience.

Emotional learning is based on shared emotional experiences. For babies to learn about intimacy, for example, requires a responsive, trusted partner who can read the baby's signals for closeness and provide the requested hug. Mechanical, cold holding from one of a sea of faces cannot create the same confidence or security that a warm, tender hug from a valued person does. Both the emotions and their quality depend on an essential partnership.

Recall the last time you were upset or had a problem. What helps more than having your spouse or best friend listen patiently and sympathetically while you elaborate your pain and anguish? It is through such a process that one can come to an understanding of the main issues at stake: what the problem is really about, what part you played, what solutions there may be. With warmth and support, problems become more tolerable.

People can't grow emotionally if they don't have a sense of

secure, empathetic connection with others. You know yourself in part through the eyes of another. And the extent to which you trust others reflects your level of comfort with yourself, your ability to experience new feelings, to progress from one emotional state to another, and to solve problems by seeing how feelings relate to one another.

In this chapter we describe how your partnership with your baby will develop as he encounters each new emotional milestone, and how play can facilitate such progress. We also explore the vital connection that exists between emotional security and intellectual growth.

The Building Blocks

As important as building a close relationship with your child may seem, it is not always easy. We only have to look at our adult relationships to see why. Much of our adult activity is structured around particular tasks: the club meeting, the sports outing, a party. As an alternative, many of us unwind by entertaining ourselves with a favorite hobby—maybe puttering around the house or doing a crossword puzzle. But while these activities are great for relaxing, they don't do much for building relationships.

Even under the best of circumstances, parent-child relationships can be difficult. And even when parents don't see any problems, children often do. Children old enough to do so often complain that their parents don't know how to talk or listen to them. They think their parents have their own agenda and don't really want to know what is happening with them.

These feelings often come as a surprise to the parent who has just taken five-year-old Billy to two movies, the video arcade, a football game, and a museum. When confronted, the parent quite naturally exclaims, "What do you mean I don't want to be with you? Look at all the things I bring you to." And Billy retorts, "But we're always doing things you think of."

"Didn't I read you a book last night?"

"Yeah, but I want you to do some of my things with me."

A scene from a TV show maybe, but it illustrates a challenge that is often unacknowledged. How can two people, especially an adult and a very young child (smaller than the five- or six-year-old who is verbal) learn to be together in a way that is mutually satisfying and enjoyable?

Mrs. Worcester complains that she is bored with the endless puzzles her three-year-old enjoys. Mr. Hartley finds his four-year-old's cowboy games tiresome. For others, it's the horsy rides or the baby dolls that prove uninspiring. Given the repetitive nature of most children's play, parents may find it difficult to maintain the sincere and spontaneous interest that fuels a close and pleasurable parent-child relationship, which is in turn the cornerstone of emotional growth and development.

We can usually count on one hand the moments in a week when we have that special spark of mutual connectedness and joy, whether it's with adults or children. And here we're not talking about just a quick spark—a smile and a few friendly words. We mean a spark sustained by a warm, steady fire—soothing, empathetic words that nourish emotional growth and help to solve challenges. Couples can go through years of marital therapy trying to discover where they lost it. Friends spend hours aggrandizing old relationships that had it. If these moments could happen a little more frequently, how much more fulfilled each of us would feel!

The elements of this elusive state of mutual pleasure and connectedness can be easily missed or avoided. As relaxing and pleasant as it may be, engagement is not two people sitting together listening to music through separate earphones. Simply looking and listening is not empathy. Engagement is two people wrapped up in a conversation, establishing a rhythm, responding to each other's feelings, ideas, and basic patterns, transcending their separateness. If one establishes engagement and empathy with children, then sharing needs or wants and interests—first through gestures and later through words and play—also becomes possible. How do we develop this elusive state?

Relationship Through the Stages

The stages of emotional development described below will outline how infants, children, and parents develop their unique essential partnership. These stages also form the structure for most of the other chapters. Each chapter follows a particular emotional idea, such as self-esteem or aggression, through the six phases of development and addresses common obstacles to healthy growth in each instance.

In the early stages of life, mutual pleasure and connectedness is already evident. We see special moments of contact when the baby looks into Mommy's or Daddy's eyes, Mommy vocalizes to maintain the baby's attention, and the baby, for a few seconds, is absorbed by Mommy's every sound and expression, maybe even imitates Mommy's facial movements. After the first few moments of the baby's intense, pleasurable engagement and Mom's sense of the baby's recognition and attachment, the baby may take time off to suck her fist, nurse, or snuggle. These moments, lasting for seconds at first, and stretching out to a few minutes by two to four months, are among parents' most memorable. For infants, such moments are their first sense of being involved in the world in a mutually satisfying way.

Achieving this stage is easier with some babies than others, and each new child will require different responses from parents. A baby who is overly sensitive to high-pitched noises, to light touch, or to certain holding positions can definitely be a challenge. To gain his attention, you may need to experiment with different vocal tones, different kinds of touch, or different positions. Similarly, the baby who seems to take little interest in the world needs you to make a little extra effort. If his muscles are a little on the loose side or his attention wanders to nothing in particular, moving him in rhythmic patterns or talking more and with greater animation may help him to stay alert and attentive to you for more than a fleeting glance.

With a challenging baby, you may feel that you are putting in more than your fair share of the work. At first you may find the relationship disappointing—but patience and modified expectations can be rewarding too. Because your very few, short moments of connectedness must count for a lot, your initial satisfaction may have to come from the glance that Susie can now sustain for three seconds, and in the promise of more that will come with time and patience.

By the time your baby is two to four months, she can engage not only with her eyes and ears but also with glowing smiles. She becomes very sensitive to your joyful interest in her and responds with her own joy. These moments, as memorable as the earlier ones, bring a sense of synchrony. As before, only now more clearly, Susie is enraptured with Daddy's every word, gazing into his eyes and beaming, moving her arms and legs in rhythm to his looks and words. And as before, Susie's moments alone are still precious to her but maybe less frequent. In general, she may enjoy looking around more or watching her older brother or sister, but special moments with Mom or Dad are the key to her budding relationships.

By four to ten months, parent-child togetherness and pleasure take on a more complex, more interactive quality. Johnny not only simply gazes into his parents' responsive eyes; now he puts his fingers in Mommy's mouth, smears up Daddy's glasses and tries to pull them off. Similarly, Molly sits on the floor, reaches out, and gurgles as though to say, "Pick me up," and Mommy gives her a big hug and nuzzle. Johnny and Molly now experience heightened pleasure, engagement, and comfort with a loved one. Through their gestures and sounds, four- to ten-month-olds are able to let their parents know even more about their needs, interests, and frustrations. Specific, purposeful communication is the new vehicle for mutual pleasure and engagement. Empathy and shared meanings reach a new level.

Again, children will respond to new emotional stages in their own unique way. It is the parents' responsibility to learn to identify, interpret, and respond to their child's particular approach to the world. For instance, some babies appear to be uninterested in their parents. They look every which way but at Mommy or Daddy; they reach out for the toy but not for Mommy or Daddy; when Mommy or Daddy reaches for them, they seem to turn away. Here, the baby may not fully understand Mom's verbal tones or Dad's non-verbal gestures. His inability to decipher communications could lead him to be non-responsive or, on the other hand, overwhelmed. Getting into a rhythm of mutual engagement may not be easy with an infant who is offering confusing signals.

Another baby could have difficulty with muscle control. We mentioned babies with loose muscles in the previous stage, but by now loose muscles are more apparent because the baby will try to gesture to you. Conversely, babies may have tight muscles, which can cause them to overreach and hit you in the eye when they are really intending to explore your mouth. If you can decipher your child's intentions, mutual engagement will become that much easier. If there are delays in motor development, you should consult your pediatrician and if necessary a specialist.

Emotional moods—the family's or the baby's—can also interfere with establishing connectedness. Tensions, fatigue, and anxiety create strains that can dampen the glow on both sides. When babies sense stress, they often react in kind, becoming fussy or withdrawn.

But babies' moods can change even when the family is harmonious. Some babies are fussy at specific times of the day. If your time for relaxing with your baby happens to coincide with her "fussy time," involving her may be quite a challenge. Likewise, babies' moods will sometimes respond to the disruption of a pattern. If you are away for more time than usual, the baby may sense your absence and be angry upon your return. Such reactions are not the product of conscious thought; rather, they reflect the formation of intentional behavioral patterns.

The parent's task at this age is obvious but not necessarily easy. You must pinpoint the baby's individual needs, figure out the family's emotional patterns and circumstances, and then try to create a sense of mutual rapport and engagement, as Mrs. Wiley did. Mrs. Wiley came home from work every day around 4:00 p.m. Her daily routine was to get dinner organized so that she could then relax and have some play time with Billy before his father came home.

Now Billy was an active nine-month-old who spent his day with a babysitter. He had no patience with his mother's bustling kitchen routine—especially after being absent from her all day. He clearly communicated his annoyance to her by being irritable, pulling at her, and then ignoring her when she responded.

Mrs. Wiley didn't take too long to come to an understanding of this behavior. She learned that spending time with Billy before getting organized made both their lives fuller. So she changed her routine and got down on the floor with him soon after walking in the door. Billy would initially crawl around and play with his toys for a few minutes, but then he would warm up, bringing her into his world and becoming secure again with her before the babysitter left. Pretty soon, he would be pulling her hair, squeaking her nose, and playing a crawling game. A few bounces on the tummy and he was totally engaged with Mom. Sometimes she would put something in her mouth and he would take it out, look her in the eye, giggle, and give it back to her so they could play the game again. Their half hour together established a wonderful quality of mutual engagement that satisfied them both. They became connected with each other in an organized way, using looks, words, and gestures.

After about half an hour, both of them were tired. Billy could now play by himself for a little while. He did not resent his mother's cooking. Frequently he would crawl near her in the kitchen; she would talk to him while he babbled back and crawled between her legs. From this experience Mrs. Wiley evolved a new cardinal rule, "Billy first, everything else in time."

In the next stage, at ten to eighteen months, a complex sense of self emerges, concomitant with organized complex behavior. Your toddler is now a little person who is both dependent and independent, who begins to understand himself and others as whole people, and who begins to combine his loving feelings with his angry ones. Such complex toddlers can now tease and joke, provoke and taunt, as well as cooperate in remarkable new ways.

But, of course, all these wonderful new abilities increase the stakes. An angry, negative toddler can be very, very difficult to engage. A toddler who is confused by the rhythm and emotional tone of her father's words may be quite dismayed. All of a toddler's negative emotions, from fear to belligerency to confusion, become more powerful as he or she acquires the ability to organize them in a focused or intentional manner.

Emotions are now communicated through a critical, often ignored, aspect of human communication—*intentional non-verbal gestures*. These include facial expressions, sounds, posture, arm and leg movements, and so forth. From the middle of the first year of life through adulthood, people are always using gestures to communicate. How important is this pre-verbal system? Perhaps more than one might think. The basic emotional messages of life—safety versus danger, acceptance versus rejection, approval versus disapproval—are communicated in this way. Words enhance this more basic communication, but, interestingly, we all form quick, split-second judgments regarding a new person's dangerousness or safety or rejection or acceptance of us before the conversation even gets started. In fact, if the person looks dangerous and says, "You know I am quite safe," we tend to believe the gestures and disbelieve the words. People can fool us, to be sure, but that doesn't change the fact that we all rely on gestural communication. Gestural communication also informs us what aspects of our own emotions are being accepted, ignored, or rejected. The looks and head nods as we are communicating about closeness, curiosity, anger, or excitement quickly tell us how the person feels about our message. More importantly, our emerging definition of the uniqueness of our very self is dependent on how others react to our pre-verbal gestures. How is our mischievous behavior and smile responded to? With a smile and grin of acceptance or a head-shaking frown of disapproval?

This gestural system, which is so important in human development, is perhaps the one aspect of communication most frequently ignored. For example, in the understandable eagerness to teach new words or even numbers and letters to a child, we often focus on the child repeating the word or letter or number. We feel frustrated if the child looks dazed and feel satisfied if the child, after five minutes, says the magic "word." We may miss the fact that this same child marches to his own beat, floats in and out of the room, does not respond to facial expressions with his own facial expressions or to sounds with his own or to arm and hand gestures with his own.

This gestural capacity is the foundation for language, reasoning and the use of ideas in relationships. As it develops, what is communicated in the intimacy of a relationship naturally becomes more complex.

Little Joanie, no longer satisfied with looking into your eyes and cooing with you, now wants you to meet her on her own terms. If there is a guiding principle at this stage, it should be, "Meet your child at his/her level, not at a level convenient to you or at a level coincident with an earlier developmental stage."

The Horners used to come home exhausted from a long day's work. They would pick up seventeen-month-old Eddie from the day-care center, fix dinner, then all would cuddle up and listen to music. Little Eddie, an agreeable child who gave his parents no trouble, was quite willing to sit in their laps and relax with them. During the day he was equally complacent. He would go off to day care without a fuss and was orderly once there. Hearing stories from friends about their rambunctious toddlers, the Horners were pleased with Eddie's relaxed, undemanding style.

One day the director of the day-care center told the Horners that Eddie seemed "spacey" and isolated from other children. He didn't participate in simple activities; he didn't fuss when some other child took his toy away; he just went about his own business. The Horners became concerned.

The Horners were unaware of their lack of engagement with Eddie; to them, Eddie seemed to enjoy their evening relaxation time. He would put his head on Mom or Dad's shoulder and listen to the music, not fussing at all. Since the Horners enjoyed this quiet activity with each other, they assumed Eddie derived the same benefits. What they didn't realize was that as a small piece of his day, this activity was fine, but as their main activity with Eddie, it offered no opportunity for engagement, no exchange of complete information, no tuning in at his developmental level.

Eddie was capable of many toddler activities, such as deciphering his parents' emotional tone from word patterns or facial expressions, soliciting their help by taking their hands and guiding them someplace. But the Horners' lack of interaction provided little support or practice for these abilities. When it was suggested to Eddie's parents that they engage him at a more complex level than just holding, they began to explore and experiment.

They discovered that Eddie loved to toddle around in different rooms and to play his own version of hide-and-seek, especially when he was the seeker. Another favorite game was riding on Daddy's back, sometimes wearing the cowboy hat that Dad had bought for him. He also liked to sit on the floor with Mommy and play with pots and pans. Trying to imitate Mommy, he would bang around and relegate Mommy to assistant chef. When his mother clapped and said, "You're a terrific chef!" he would look at her with a big smile. When she asked for a taste and showed him how to put the spoon to her mouth, he was soon offering her frequent tastes, with loud giggles to show his pleasure at his successful recipes. This complex, gestural, and imitative play, beginning to take on the quality of make-believe, was mutually enjoyable to both parents. It had a sense of warm pleasure and joint satisfaction. Playing with Eddie involved much more activity than they were accustomed to, but the joyous hugs and babbling of words and sounds made their newfound games fun.

Soon Eddie began using these same skills in school and became more involved with his peers. No longer did he appear isolated and "spacey," as he could now imitate, interact, vocalize, and even begin some make-believe play. Eddie's newly discovered need for intimacy demanded that his parents be quite active in the evenings and that they engage Eddie on his terms rather than at their own level of quiet, passive harmony.

When children reach the next stage, of emotional ideas, and then the stage of emotional thinking—in the eighteen-month to four-year range—they evolve in even more remarkable ways. During these stages they create new opportunities for involvement by expressing their emotional ideas in make-believe play and in words. Such play starts off as simple repetitive sequences of, perhaps, putting a doll in a car and rolling it back and forth. By the time children are three, it graduates to an intricate series of actions as the doll goes to have lunch with a friend or maybe runs away from two monsters. Their make-believe play begins to take the form of complex dramas.

The ability to enact complex dramas develops along with the ability to express wishes in terms of words, starting with such expressions as "Good girl" or "More cookies." At two and a half or three, they aren't yet able to logically string together different ideas. But, eventually, by three to four, they add logic to the expression of emotional ideas, with such comments as "I don't want to eat that because it looks yucky," or, "If you get to stay up late, why can't I?" In addition, their interactions become more spontaneous, taking on elements of curiosity and interest in almost all aspects of life. As the dramas go from simple repetition to epic novels, so communications go from simple expressions of need to legalistic negotiations arguing the merits of certain foods or bedtimes.

Sometimes, as we saw with little Eddie, the child's journey through these stages is diverted. Instead of the three-year-old who plays out wonderful fantasies with his friends, there is a three-year-old who appears to be a loner. He seems shy and introverted. His parents feel there is no spontaneous synergy with him, no rhythm to the relationship. Was the child like this at three or four months of age? Did he never tune into a relationship with his parents? Or did it only happen after age two? Or is this a pattern that is more isolated and only seen in certain settings? It is very important to answer these questions because your response to the child can vary accordingly.

Everyone wants to be with someone who is warm and accepting. Who wants to talk to a person who listens for ten seconds and then partly turns away? Social situations offer many opportunities for encounters where people engage and then disengage or change the subject, as though they had not been listening at all.

With an adult, the only way to reengage that person (should you have any interest) is to try to roll with the situation and woo them back when they seem ready. Children, fortunately, are more flexible and open to direction. Even if a child has a history of chronic avoidance, you can slowly reengage his attention and try to evoke his warm emotions.

His mother says, "Sam was different from other children. Even when he was a baby, I could never hold his attention. He always shifted his gaze from me to one of his toys." At twelve months, Sam still preferred toys to people. As a two-year-old, he would acknowledge Mommy and Daddy but basically he liked to practice running or do puzzles, an activity at which he was very gifted. Because Sam was adept at doing puzzles and building with blocks as well as being good with language, his mother and father assumed that he was just different from other children. In nursery school he followed this same pattern, going off by himself and playing with his blocks and puzzles.

For his own idiosyncratic reasons, this little boy never became sold on people. Even though his family was very well intentioned, he never mastered the intimacy of a two-person relationship and at the age of three and a half still needed to learn how to be intimate.

It's so easy for parents to become discouraged and rejected by a child who tunes them out. These particular parents both acknowledged later on, "You know, I felt much more rejected by Sam than I did by my other two children." Parents have different ways of handling rejection. Often they say that the child is "just independent and doesn't need me." Sam's parents felt this way and left Sam to follow his own interests.

Nursery school made Sam's parents rethink their response to his "independence." After observing him for a month or so, the teacher told them that Sam's isolated play was not good for him. So, confused and a little worried, they decided to seek professional help.

Through a few consultations they became aware of Sam's needs. They learned that every child wants to learn about relationships, even if he does not come to them spontaneously. In particular, they learned that Sam needed his parents to woo him, to *show* him that people are more interesting than blocks and puzzles.

Sam's mother and father used his interest in toys as an entry to a closer relationship. Individually, they spent part of every day playing his favorite games with him. At first this meant just admiring his abilities. When he became comfortable with this limited involvement, they played a more active but still secondary role. They started to participate, mostly following his lead but occasionally making comments. For example, they would talk out loud about whether the puzzle pieces went here or there; they wondered if the dog in the puzzle was a happy, sad, or angry dog.

Gradually, fleeting sparks of intimacy flew between them. Mommy smiled and Sam, being pleased at her interest, smiled back. Daddy clapped at a particularly complicated building scheme and Sam giggled. These first moments were very brief, very little, really, compared to other children at this age, but with great patience on his parents' part, they grew and multiplied. His parents made it their goal to expand these moments day by day. To minimize their frustration and give themselves some measure of success, they sometimes even remarked upon moments of contact.

Another part of the solution was encouraging Sam's relationship with a neighborhood child. Joey, who lived around the corner, enjoyed the same pastimes as Sam but was more nurturing and could reach out to friends. The two were able to sit side by side and build castles, but they didn't interact much.

One day Dad decided that it was time to see if he could help them get more involved. First he acted like an admirer of both children, comparing techniques and chatting just a little. Through each child's separate enthusiasm and a little encouragement from Dad (his suggesting, "Let's build together"), Sam and Joey combined their efforts and excitedly designed a "neighborhood." Little by little, Sam allowed the human world to come to him. Dad had helped by gradually and patiently fostering "collaboration" between the two builders.

Your child's ability to pretend-play and express herself verbally gives you a vast new arena in which to engage her. The level of understanding developing in this area bolsters healthy emotional development. This development, in turn, becomes the cornerstone for almost all approaches to solving problems and understanding challenges. Now when your child is troubled with nightmares, or is being provocative or belligerent or bossy, she can help you find the answer. Of course, her answer will not be in a well-formulated, logical dialogue—it may not even be completely verbal. Through what we call "floor time," your child can use her new tools—words, gestures, and make-believe—to communicate with you.

Once a child is three or four, parents can engage him or her simultaneously on several levels suggested by the developmental levels just described. Shared attention and engagement is always the first and most essential level. It should never be skipped over in one's eagerness to communicate at a higher level. Intentional gestural communication is an integral part of this basic human connection. The use of emotional ideas and ultimately the capacity for shared meanings and symbolic conceptualization is based on the level of security, safety, and intentionality established in early life.

At every stage, parents can tune into their child's natural interests to nurture mutual engagement, mutual empathy, and mutual understanding. It is these elements that shape the Essential Partnership. Different developmental levels, of course, demand different approaches to foster it; but with special times set aside, you can form a close, intimate relationship with your baby.

=====III=====

Floor Time:
From the Ground Up

=======

Floor time is a special play time that you set aside for yourself and your child. During this period, play is a spontaneous, unstructured activity when you get down on the floor with your child and try to follow his/her lead. Your initial goal is to tune in to *whatever* motivates or is of interest to your child.

Together with you, your child can smile and coo, roll a ball back and forth, build blocks, race cars, "read and discuss" a book, or produce any number of fanciful dramas—all activities where two people have the opportunity to be involved in an emotional way. Passive activities, such as doing a puzzle *for* a child, or reading a book *to* a child, where the child is the observer, do not serve as floor time. These activities, instructive and important as they are, should not be overlooked, but they are not interactive, with the child taking the lead, and should not replace floor time. To be sure, some children, for various reasons, will need to be wooed into this special time. But once there, they will want to return again and again.

Why do you need to set aside special time for this, you wonder? Ideally, you don't. It just happens spontaneously. But for many families, time is strictly budgeted, and time alone can get lost in the shuffle of each person's hectic day. It is easy for us as parents to take advantage of our child's budding independence and begin to get on with our own business. We don't think twice as we spend Saturday taking care of chores while three-year-old Johnny either stays with a neighborhood babysitter or follows us around in the stores all day. So, reserving special *daily* times, of 25 to 35 minutes or more of floor time, can be especially meaningful. This time with your child allows you to reaffirm that rhythm and sense of connectedness that you established at the beginning stages and enables you to elaborate your growing empathy and shared meanings.

Floor time is not always easy, especially for the parent, whose goal is to become a good and active play partner. It may be more intuitive for some parents, but for most of us difficulties do arise some of the time. If you watch parents, teachers, or even child psychiatrists try to become play partners, we all fall into the same pitfalls. Some of us get too passive and just watch the child. Our thoughts drift as she gets involved in a theme that is not very compelling to us. If you're too passive, the child will just go off on her own because your physical presence is not enough. The child needs your emotional presence as well.

Others of us get overly controlling and bossy. We are all energized, wanting to make the most of the time taken out of our busy schedule. We start asking questions about the child's play and helping to direct the action, stepping up the pace whenever possible. In the extreme, your bossiness can lead to the child becoming negative and rebellious. Even as early as eight months of age your child wants to be the main director of his or her own play.

Children engage and, at the same time, make their emotions known through their spontaneous chatter and their make-believe play. Your job is to let the child set the emotional tone and then join in on that level. You may want to describe what the child is communicating. The stories might contain fighting, or car crashes, or people cooperating and helping each other. The theme may be an adventurous search for missing toys or hidden treasure. Curiosity, assertiveness, closeness, dependency, the human body, separation, rejection, learning about the world—all of these themes may characterize children's pretend play and verbal communications.

Some children prefer you to read them a story or rearrange their blocks in an undramatic way. Go with your child's interests and build on them. As you read, wonder out loud what the dog in the story is going to do next or what you will find behind the tree. Help your child actively use her imagination. Transform the one-way activity into a two-way one. Pretty soon, she may be telling you stories or asking the questions. Similarly, over time, your block arranger may be building cities. And, after all, cities need someone to deliver food, provide security, and make sure the monsters don't get inside. You can be the assistant architect and then promote yourself to city planner. Be patient, however. This process is usually very gradual.

Repetitive play without an obvious drama may not appear to be as worthwhile as dramatic play for your child, and maybe it wouldn't be, except that you're there. Your gestures—pointing, smiling, frowning, and vocalizing ideas ("The truck is fast," or "That door is open")—all add an interactive component and complexity and depth to the play. When your child becomes repetitive, he needs more, not less, floor time and more, not less, patience. As we will discuss later, much more than you would imagine is going on even when the play seems repetitive or undramatic. The children are the coaches; you are an active partner, always trying to expand the activity further than they would on their own, but without taking charge.

Let's say Johnny starts out with He-Man attacking some bad guys. You get involved by saying, "Boy! Look at those good guys get the bad guys. The bad guys must have been really mean. Wow!" You are simply saying the obvious but with enthusiasm and pleasure. Your interest will spur Johnny on. If Johnny decides to continue with the theme of anger and aggression, you don't interfere by saying, "Why is he so mad? Why doesn't he behave nicely?" Instead you say, "Gee, he really wants to bomb those bad guys. He's going to destroy them in a hundred different ways. He must have a good reason for that." You acknowledge both the range of anger that Johnny is portraying and the fact that he must have good reason for it. Your empathy makes Johnny feel that you are on his side in the drama rather than a proponent of your own agenda, which may be, "How do I keep my child from turning into an aggressive monster?" (As an aside, keep in mind that your acknowledgment does not imply approval. In fact, recognizing a child's "pretend" agenda will strengthen your ability to set relevant limits on his aggressive behavior at a later point in time.)

Surprisingly, your acknowledging these "negative" feelings may eventually help Johnny to introduce the opposite theme. Most children have a balance of feelings. Dependency, love, and concern will spontaneously emerge alongside aggression, setting the stage for them through empathy. But if your child senses that you don't accept him, his frustration will cause him to polarize his feelings and opt for aggressive themes.

At this point, don't worry about the balance of emotion in your child's drama: different emotions will emerge with time. For example, a child playing Mommy or Daddy is taking care of the baby doll, hugging the baby, changing the diapers, putting the baby to sleep. (This scene actually occurs frequently when the mother really is pregnant.) Although the child is only mechanically caring for the doll, your empathizing with her focused interest lays the groundwork for the introduction of greater complexity into this scenario. For now, you want to contribute to a sense of mutual pleasure and empathy and, most importantly, to help the child feel understood.

You can enhance the depth and complexity of your child's play drama and conversation in several ways.

— Help your child take initiative by being patient. As you follow his lead, capture his gestures and emotional tone with your own expressions. Share his smile or pout.

— Help your child elaborate on the theme of his play. For example, your child may explain that "the bear is mad." In response, you can try to find out exactly how mad the bear is by asking, "Very mad?"

CHILD: "Yes."

YOU: "What does he want to do?"

CHILD: "Throw you in the garbage."

YOU: "And then?"

CHILD: "Put you in the ocean and make sure the pieces never come back together again."

YOU: "Sounds like a big anger."

CHILD: "It is!"

— Help your child switch back and forth between his feelings on the one hand and the details of the drama or event on the other. For example, after watching his action figures fight for a few minutes, you may say, "They look angry." Or after listening to your child complain, "I hate everyone in my class," you could suggest, "They must have done something you didn't like."

— Help your child amplify each side of a theme that involves conflict. If the play theme is "the cat hates the dog, but the dog insists on playing with the cat," it may relate to a child's insistence on playing with the one person in his class who is mean and rejecting. Here, your learning about the 100 ways the cat shows his hate for the dog or Timmy shows his hate for your child would elucidate one-half the problem posed by the theme. Discussing how the dog must have his way—that is, he can play with anyone he wants to irrespective of the cat's feelings—would amplify the other half of the drama. Often negative feelings and all-powerful feelings go hand in hand, even though one or the other initially may be more prominent.

— Help your child explore the reasons for his/the teddy bear's feelings.

YOU: "You must have good reasons for being so mad."

CHILD: "I have at least ten. Want to hear them?" (It should be this easy!)

— Help your child expand the theme by placing it in different contexts. For example, if the child is talking about competition, explore different scenarios involving rivalry at home, at school, etc.

— Help your child to summarize and expand upon his theme by summarizing it in your own words, and then encouraging him to follow suit.

These suggestions are only illustrative, but they may help with problem-solving discussions (to be explored shortly) as well as pretend play.

You may think that floor time is only effective for three- and four-year-olds because they are capable of carrying on a conversation; actually, verbalization is only *one* of the components of floor time. Let's look at floor time with an eighteen-month-old. A lot can go on at a number of different emotional levels in what, at first, may appear to be a simple (some parents even say boring) encounter. You are lying on the floor, helping your child—let's call her Susan—roll a little car back and forth. She pushes the car in one direction and you, smiling proudly, emphatically say, "Boy! What a good push." She looks at you and gives you a big grin, then pushes the car back toward you. You say, "You push the car so straight. It went right into the garage," as you cup your hands on the rug, making the garage. She gives you another big grin, grabs the car, and goes on rolling it.

It is a simple encounter, but much is happening that doesn't meet the eye. First, your child is experiencing a sense of closeness and interest. It's as though she says to herself, "As simple as rolling a car is, Mommy and Daddy are really excited about what I can do." Your child feels your pride in her and in her ability to be coordinated.

Unfortunately, the simplicity of this play often elicits an alternate response from parents—that is, to sit on the floor preoccupied and uninvolved. Now Susan, not being a dummy, feels your lack of interest. If a seemingly out-of-control car hits you in the nose, don't be surprised. Susan figures that since you are not interested in coordinated focused play, maybe you are interested in chaotic, rambunctious activity.

Second, in simple games like this, Susan is learning about acceptance and security through gestures and simple words. She is reading your gestures, pointing at her car, looking impressed. Every time you say, "Gee, that's terrific!" she is getting practice at understanding words in context. She is learning to connect the happy expression on your face with your saying, "That's a great push." All of this further enhances her sense of being an important person who is in a relationship. Through having a sense of mutual understanding, Susan realizes the world makes sense. Security, acceptance, and a sense of order are present even without words, because many of life's most important communications occur through looks and gestures.

Third, she is experiencing a feeling of closeness inspired by your words and gestures while, at the same time, remaining independent. She's running back and forth, pushing the car to you, gesturing to you to send it back. She is not just sitting in your lap, cuddling and hugging. She is having a great time: practicing and coordinating her fine and gross motor skills, receiving information through language, experiencing closeness and relatedness, experiencing positive self-esteem. All of this and being assertive too.

Fourth, Susan is learning that human relationships can be characterized by a quality of connectedness that allows for a great range of feeling and exploration. For example, it's as though she says to herself, "I don't have to hug Mommy or Daddy and sit in their laps to feel loved. I can be myself. I can push the car at them a little too hard sometimes and still feel warm and tender. They can feel warm and tender to me. Love and assertiveness can go hand in hand. I don't have to have one *or* the other. I don't have to be passive and compliant to be loved. If I'm independent, I'll still be loved."

Many adults separate these two basic feelings of closeness and dependency on the one hand and assertiveness and curiosity on the other. They struggle with feeling that if they are assertive and successful, they won't be loved. To be loved, they feel that they have to be passive and compliant. They may, as do some children, give up feeling lovable and decide to be provocatively independent all the time, daring you to love them. Your involvement with Susan's simple interaction can teach her a valuable lesson.

Finally, Susan's physical, intellectual, and emotional patterns are all being coordinated in the context of warmth, closeness, and respect. As with two adults who meet, establish a rapport, and share spontaneous ideas and activities, nothing is quite as comforting as feeling that "you" are understood. Floor time can be meaningful at each level of development. Communicating through gestures is every bit as important as communicating through ideas. Remember, it is the process of communication and involvement, not the specific topics, that is most important.

Sometimes children make it difficult to relate to them. *The more difficult it is, the more the child needs it.* The child who is open and engaging is probably getting lots of practice in the stages of relationship building. The child who is withdrawn, negative, or provocative, the child who prefers to play with things rather than people, the child who throws a tantrum as soon as you do something that's not exactly to his way—*all* need this shared experience, this sense of pleasure and mutual understanding. Understanding and empathizing with the child will not always be easy, but the situation that arises because you don't won't be easy either.

Let's look at little Mark. He tends to be withdrawn and sullen. His parents worry because he is now three and, although he is talking and walking, he doesn't seem to enjoy time with them very much. Mom and Dad are energetic people who like to do things quickly, often getting to the point rather abruptly. To counteract Mark's lack of interest, they talk rapidly, hoping to capture his attention. Failing at this, they become frustrated and do something more structured, such as reading to him. He is a reluctant participant and, by the end of the story, looks sad and disengaged.

Exasperated, they seek professional help and soon realize that they need to try more flexible approaches. If Mark doesn't respond to one approach, it's best to try another. First, they try to tune into his rhythm—in his case, to sit beside him for five to ten minutes, letting him take the initiative. When he doesn't do much, they give him a little "push," making gentle overtures like putting an arm around him or extending an invitation to play with some blocks that are on the floor. This little warm-up, without any demands on him other than their enticing presence, is an important step.

Slowly, his curiosity emerges. He criticizes his mother and father for putting the block and the doll in the wrong place. Over time, however, he invites them to share his play ideas—which turn out to be plentiful. Donald Duck and Mickey Mouse become active participants in his play, as well as the baby doll that had been neglected in the corner for many months. Surprisingly, as play develops, he becomes most enthusiastic about the baby doll, casting himself as a caregiver who has a sick baby to attend to. His parents empathize with him, "How wonderful it is that you want to take care of a sick baby. What's the matter with your baby, anyway?" Explains Mark, "My baby is always hungry. She wants more milk all the time. I have to feed her all day and then she is happy."

In metaphorical terms, Mark was telling his parents that he needed lots of emotional filling up. That he expressed this theme in his play meant that his parents were beginning to fulfill this need. Mark's parents understood that caretaking was an important issue for Mark, and they could see that their new approach was working because he was becoming a much more engaging, warm, and related child.

It is hard to think of any childhood problem that is not partially helped through special floor times. Floor time increases security, trust, warmth, initiative, and a sense of being understood. It creates opportunities to make vague, "private" feelings—whether they are needy, scary, anxious, or angry ones—part of the world of ideas and relationships.

It perhaps goes without saying that some children, as they become older, will want to engage in floor time without toys or props. Their minds become their only tool of imagination. Here, you follow your child's verbal productions just as you did with his combination of play and words. "Floor time of the mind" or daily chitchat about seemingly uneventful things—school, friends, TV shows, a new pair of shoes—can give you the key to your child's thoughts, fears, and wishes.

How Emotions Emerge During Floor Time

Floor time encourages your child to spontaneously tell you about his emotional interests through pretend play. He can practice using ideas and communicate all his emotions. Let's say you have been away recently and your child has some fears of separation (a topic covered in chapter VIII). During your floor time together, your child's initial reaction may be to show his general feelings toward you (warm, aloof, irritable, demanding, solicitous). Then even without your prompting, "Gee, do you think you had your nightmare last night because I have been away?," he might introduce some aspect of separation into his play. He might play it out with animals leaving each other or with one animal being mad at the other. If he is troubled by the separation, he might also incorporate themes of devastation, for example, hurricanes or earthquakes, to show how he feels about your leaving him. Or he might be especially undramatic in his play—only building a block tower as though to say, "I have no special feelings about you. I'm only interested in my tower."

Your job is very simple. You want to respond to your child's overall emotional tone—being respectful if he is being formal, warm if he is being loving—and encourage him to communicate all his feelings in an understanding atmosphere. So, part of your role is to make comments that help you understand the play more and help the child elaborate more. You could say, "Oh! What will the pig do when the hurricane comes? How does he feel?" These questions help the child to elaborate his feelings. They help him add one more piece to his play. Or better yet, you could just comment on his drama, "Oh, the pig sees the hurricane coming." You are expanding his drama just a little, by summarizing the action and by empathizing with the child's interests.

Being a participant is another part of your job. Often the child will want to assign you a role. Sometimes you can gently offer. In the above example, the child might reverse the actual roles and have you be the one who is left. He may even direct you to cry and fuss like a baby, while he gives you a kiss and starts to leave, saying, "I'll miss you. Be a good girl." Upon returning in a few seconds, he gives you a hug and solicitously inquires about your obvious distress. He probably won't mind and may, at this time, even want you to play his accustomed role, the aggrieved child. You fuss a little more, say you are mad, and don't let him engage you too easily, but finally you come around to being loving. Of course, one episode of make-believe may not completely dispel his separation fears, but it helps him to know that you understand these fears and to know what being in charge of the situation feels like.

Occasionally you will misjudge the child's clues and do the

wrong thing. Maybe he wanted you to welcome him with sunshine and smiles when he "returned from his trip" and your feigned fussiness ruined his secret scenario. His annoyance may make you feel like a bad play partner. Here you have been spontaneous, tried to further the drama, and instead have caused a rupture in the play. At such a juncture, go with the flow. Try a new drama around the theme of "Mom is always doing things wrong." Perhaps this is really the main issue. The key is to see his rejection of you as part of the drama. The drama is not only the content of the plot but also the process surrounding the plot. If the child insists on being alone, empathize with his wish while remaining available.

Reasons for nightmares, anger, and provocations often emerge during floor time: let's take a child who fears that the witch who lives under his bed will attack him during the night. Worries like this often reveal a struggle between security and anger—and nothing will make him feel better than an increased sense of connectedness with Mom and Dad, especially when the interaction occurs on his level rather than on the babyish one of just being held and cuddled. As his witch attacks or scares you in pretend play, he learns that you are still there for him, and are tolerant of his "witchlike" feelings.

Or take the little girl who, on starting nursery school, becomes slightly withdrawn—fearful of the separation from Mother and of the hubbub of activity emanating from the other children. Special floor time with Mom or Dad can help her feel grounded in her new experiences. It will increase her sense of security, and provide her with an opportunity to express some of her fears: her chaotic play scenes may reveal the stress of having so many new children around.

Parents need not try to be psychologists or psychiatrists or even attempt to understand the "unconscious" elements of the child's play. They don't need to say, "I can tell you're scared about that." But, as part of your intuitive skills, you should be able to characterize the child's communication much as you would the communication of an adult. It's a little more difficult with a child because he or she is communicating indirectly through play and is not saying explicitly what is on his or her mind. But then, most adults don't say exactly what is on their minds. You learn to read between the lines.

Just as some emotions are difficult for children to handle, so they are for most parents. It's the rare human being who is completely comfortable in all the emotional themes and dramas of life. Some of us will become anxious over aggression; others are unnerved by curiosity and sexuality; and still others feel uncomfortable with dependency and closeness.

As you pinpoint the emotions you enjoy most, watch for those you ignore, deny, or find boring. These are the ones you are more uncomfortable with. By becoming aware of this, you give yourself a chance to grow emotionally, along with your child—and you can use such information to ensure that you do not undermine your child's play in that emotional area.

To twist a child's plot away from his intent is so easy. A mother uncomfortable with sexuality and bodies may say quickly, "Let's put a different dress on the doll," when her child wants to undress it. A father uneasy with themes of closeness may shift the focus from the joy of taking care of a baby doll to the mechanics, such as making sure the diapers are clean; he will miss the child's real excitement in being a caregiver. The parent anxious about separation may decide it's time for lunch just as the mama and papa bears are leaving the baby bear. The parent who is anxious about aggression may wonder how to make the soldiers happy so they won't fight each other.

One mother was very anxious about rejection. One day her little boy was playing with a toy walkie-talkie and wanted her to get on the other end. He started a typical dialogue: "Hi, Mommy. How are you?" He even decided to have his toy cow talk on the telephone to Mom too. After a minute of this conversation, he said, "We don't like you. We want to talk to the bear." As part of the pretend play, he was introducing separation and rejection. But unfortunately, Mother responded, "You don't like me! Then I don't like you," and she threw the walkie-talkie on the floor. A couple of seconds later he tried to resume the dialogue, but his mother wouldn't be wooed. The situation deteriorated into a power struggle in which finally, out of frustration, he began jumping on her new coffee table because he couldn't woo her back.

This mother generally entered into all her son's play, but anxiety over rejection made her react personally and withdraw. If she had been comfortable, she might have said, "You're sending me away. Woe, you're banishing me to the bad kingdom."

Upon reading this scenario, you may think, "I would never do that. The child was obviously just playing." But everyone who is sensitive to certain emotions sometimes loses perspective and inadvertently interferes with the child's intent.

We have discussed following your child's lead and being a good play partner. We have cautioned about suddenly changing the theme of the child's play. It would appear that the rule is not to interfere with whatever theme the child is developing. *But*—just to confuse the issue—in certain situations you may need to compromise this rule in order to further your child's emotional flexibility.

Some children become fixated with one theme. An example is a little boy who struts around with a macho air, issues commands to his parents, and only plays games involving war and fighting. Any one of these forms of self-expression is fine in isolation, but when a child's entire repertoire consists of only one role, parents need to create an opportunity for balance in the kinds of emotion the child is comfortable with and able to express. You don't change the issue. You only create an opportunity to look at related issues.

For example, if, after playing with your child for a month or so, you realize that she is playing out only aggressive scenes, you should try to introduce some emotional balance. As the bombs explode on your war-torn rug and the soldiers are annihilated, you could say, "Oh, gee! Don't the soldiers need a doctor?" A few gentle pushes may help her to introduce nurturing themes.

If the child does not become nurturing at the first hint, roll with the punches so she can continue to elaborate her true feelings. As she says, "Okay, bring in the doctor," and then proceeds to have the doctor break the soldier's leg, you see she really wants to keep aggression as the main theme. So you comment, "Huh! Even the doctor is mad. How come? What happened to his nice side?" Over time you will hear about "why the nice doctor is mad." Maybe, "People hit him." Eventually, you will probably hear why "it's scary to be nice." Often she will relate themes of being taken advantage of or hurt. Including some nurturing feelings in her play will frequently follow these revelations.

Maybe your son plays out only very superficial and seemingly compliant themes where everyone is lovey-dovey. Assertiveness and conflict never surface. You can muse aloud, "I wonder what makes the doll ever get mad." You might also deliberately provide opportunities for the child to assert new sentiment. When setting the table for him and his "friends," you "accidentally" drop some of the plastic play dishes and say, "Jimmy, I dropped the plates and I think I broke some. Are you going to be mad at me?" In this way you are being responsive to the child's intent but are also helping to insert a balance of emotion into the drama.

Helping your child elevate behavior and feelings to the world of ideas through pretend play will, in the long run, enable her to reason about feelings, not just feel them and act them out. A five- or six-year-old with an internal sense of emotional ideas will usually realize that when she gets mad at a school friend, her angry feelings can be expressed in words rather than hitting. Labeling and expanding feelings in pretend play creates this sense.

Floor Time with Children Who Make You Work

THE PASSIVE CHILD

A passive child who is very reluctant to assert his will, even in gesturing, using words, or doing pretend play, can be frustrating to even the most patient parent. It is hard to resist doing too much for this child. But instead of overdoing, you need to woo or entice the child into activity. When stuck on the floor with passive Jack who only wants to be read to, wonder out loud if Jack will (pretend to) read to his Teddy bear. As Jack angrily says, "No! You read me," try to enjoy Jack's assertiveness and say something like,

"Oh, so you're the boss." "Yes," says Jack. "But Teddy wants to be the boss also," says Dad. "No, me," says Jack.

Here, Jack's father has already enticed passive, "bossy" Jack into a nice verbal exchange. After all, Jack assertively stated his position. And eventually, these bits and pieces will lead Jack to joyfully play teacher and order Dad around the room in an active, rather than passive, manner.

Often a child may need to manifest aggression through gestures and behavior before he can express it with words. Engage your child at all levels.

THE ACTIVE CHILD

The very active child provides a different challenge (and is further addressed later under the heading Concentration). How do you woo him into an attentive state where he will interact and play with you? How do you keep him from getting too excited and disorganized? Here your task is twofold. (1) Go with the flow and build on *his* natural interests; but (2) hold his attention and help him elaborate rather than flit from one thing to another.

Jane liked to run, jump, and move about. Stationary tea parties were not for her. Mother harnessed Jane's natural interest in activity by playing a game that pitted Jane as queen against Mother as evil witch (alternating with being a fairy godmother). In both instances, Mother chased Jane, and vice versa. They argued. They cast magic spells. Jane and Mother played throughout the whole house. Mother's ability to harness Jane's interest in big spaces and movement helped Jane focus on an organized theme. If not engaged in this flexible way, Jane might have been active and unfocused rather than active and organized. Interestingly, with this drama in mind, Jane could sit for 15 minutes with Mom to make a better crown for her queenly head.

THE NON-VERBAL CHILD

The non-verbal child, of course, needs extra practice in using words. But just repeating Mommy's words is not the best solution for this. Pretend play, where he is naturally motivated to talk for his dolls or action figures, is better. Trying to chit-chat with him when he wants something helps, too. Natural situations are always best.

Michael pointed, grunted, and banged, but was reluctant, in part because of difficulty in articulating, to use words. During floor time he would get excited about his truck. Seizing this opportunity, his mother put another truck on the road and said, "Drive carefully. We don't want them to have an accident." Michael slowly learned to say, "Stop! Danger! Watch out!" Feeling the excitement coming from the pretend play, he began experimenting more and more with words.

THE EASILY OVERWHELMED/ SENSITIVE CHILD

Some children, as discussed earlier, are sensitive to light touch, to sounds, to bright lights, or to their own movement. In floor time such children may be very cautious, wanting lots of time to adjust to anything new. They may also need to be the boss and control you. After all, their barrier to the world (i.e., their skin) may be very sensitive, so naturally they want to go into the waters of life one toe at a time and with great control.

These children need to be wooed into pretend play gradually. Respect their need to be in charge. Let them use the play to eventually experiment with assertiveness.

Robbie would sit in his corner and either cry or demand to be picked up rather than play out interesting dramas. To draw him out, his Dad learned to sit next to him, making himself available. If Robbie didn't make an overture to him, Dad would pick up on whatever Robbie was doing. When he played with the toy telephone, Dad would say, "Calling Robbie." If Robbie then gave him a dirty look, Dad would say, "Sorry. Okay, tell me what to do." Sometimes Robbie would say, "Sit over there," pointing to a spot ten feet away. Dad would dutifully do this. The master-slave drama had begun.

Seeing that Robbie enjoyed being the boss, Dad would gently encourage him to express his wishes assertively. "What next, boss?"

Dad would ask. Robbie would sometimes put his father in his fort and lock him up. As time went on, Robbie was shooting Dad with his laser gun as Dad "made mistakes." Dad became the "bad boy" who acted out the feelings that Robbie struggled with inside himself. This, coupled with themes of anger expressed in violent storms or bombs exploding, helped Robbie verbalize how he so easily felt overwhelmed.

While always cautious, Robbie gradually, through floor time, became more assertive and confident. He began elaborating his ideas and feelings with play and words.

THE AGGRESSIVE CHILD

Some children who get carried away with the excitement of pretend play may end up pushing and biting. They seem to be saying that having fun and feeling close is too much. It is almost as though they want to hurt the other person before that person hurts them. Here, extra practice in playing out both anger and love, accompanied by firm limits, is important so that feelings of anger and love are not confused and expressed inappropriately.

Gail was one such child. She was scared of closeness and seemed to operate according to the philosophy, "I'll bite the hand that feeds me before it bites me." While there were many reasons for this, she needed to learn that she could be close without being hurt or hurting someone else.

Gail would often hug her doll and hug her mother but then begin excitedly to pull Mom's hair. Her mother worked to prolong the loving part with, "Oh, hugging feels good. What happened?" At one time, Gail even replied, "Scared of hugging." Mom suggested that instead of Gail's pulling hair, her dolls should pull each other's hair when "scared and mad." As Gail learned to include love and anger in pretend play, she became less impulsive.

Of course, limit setting was essential while Gail was learning to use ideas to express love and anger. Mother tried to prolong any moments of closeness and refrain from getting caught up in Gail's provocativeness. But when Gail would go too far, Mother would combine quick firmness with an effort to reestablish closeness.

Expressive and Receptive Language

Many children enjoy practicing speech, concentration, and motor skills in the excited fun of floor time. Children who are lagging in any of these areas require extra practice. Interestingly, because floor time can combine the child's natural pleasures and interests with developmental skills, it is much more effective than structured teaching as a way to practice these skills. Because the child enjoys them, floor-time exercises are likely to inspire him to practice on his own.

There's nothing more fun for children than to practice using words as part of a heated drama, whether it's Bert and Ernie arguing, the perfect tea party, the caring for a baby doll, or the princess going to a ball. Encouraging children to narrate their own dramas, with you as their co-narrator, allows them tremendous practice in talking. They naturally experiment with many words and sounds. If a child has trouble with a particular sound, the play partner can encourage its use in the drama by saying phrases with that sound or giving a character a name incorporating the sound. Children's attempts to express whole thoughts in words and gestures are exciting for them, especially if you are there to help them out.

The receptive language abilities of children are as important as the expressive ones, but less obviously so. One of the biggest challenges for the one-and-half- to five-year-old is to comprehend what is said to them. Frequently it is very hard for parents, as well as professionals, to know whether two-and-a-half-year-old Jessica is being negative because she happens to be angry or because she is frustrated from not understanding what someone wants from her. I see many children in my office where the latter case is the problem.

I have found "Simon Says" a useful tool in teasing out the problem. Often, when Simon says, "Touch your head," the child touches his head; when Simon says, "Touch your knees," the child will do so; but when Simon says, "Touch your head, touch your knees, touch your nose," the child immediately stops playing the game and starts pulling on the phone, messing up the books, and generally being negative and provocative.

With this type of response I replay the game, again starting with one simple command and moving on to compound ones. If the child gets disruptive again, I immediately go back to "Touch your head," and the child usually complies while giving a big smile. This series of reactions is a strong indication that the child has difficulty taking in and sequencing three thoughts together—meaning that the child needs extra practice in this area.

Parents often receive indirect hints of this problem. One sure clue is when you feel reluctant to place too many demands on your child. Maybe you find that when you play with him, you shrink from offering suggestions. If asked about this, you say that he gets fussy when you make suggestions or ask questions. Because it's easier to go along with the child, you become a follower rather than an active participant in his games. Take your hesitancy as a sign that your child may have a problem with auditory-verbal sequencing.

Sometimes children who are slower in one type of learning are quicker in another. Nature can balance our strengths and weaknesses. So the child who is having trouble with understanding complex verbal sequences may have extraordinary potential in visual-spatial domains and in such subjects as physics or mathematics. This child will need more practice in verbal symbols as well as a show of pride and admiration for his considerable talents in other areas.

Pretend play can give children tremendous opportunities to practice receptive language skills. Your goal is to gently challenge the child's verbal skills. As you participate in the drama, gradually increase the complexity of your verbal contributions, from simple sequences such as "Is he going over here or there?" to "Is the train going to New York, Boston, or Philadelphia?" Your involvement during pretend play makes the experience more rewarding.

Take a little girl who is telling her mother to put the teacups on the table. This is a perfect opportunity for Mother to ask a question that challenges the child. She can say, "Do you want me to put them by the fork, the spoon, or in the middle?" Her question does not change the flow of the drama or interfere with the child's leadership. But the child must work with the choices in order to respond.

Or maybe you and your child are playing G.I. Joe. G.I. Joe has just been captured by the bad guys. That's you. You can't quite remember the name of your character and you say, "Oops! I need your help. I forgot if I am supposed to be Zartan, Cobra Commander, or Destro." (Now, how could you forget that!) Here, you are challenging the child's verbal skills while at the same time showing interest in him and his ideas. The child is receiving information and processing it while telling you what role to play.

Another tactic is to give the child a choice of activities to perform in the service of the drama. Still being the bad guy, you say, "While I tie up this good guy, do you want to bring the good guys to rescue him and have them surround the fort and shoot at it?"

For children who have difficulty with receptive language, such verbal challenges may provoke a negative reaction. It's often too difficult for them to follow you if you list a number of activities. In this case, you'll need to simplify and build up. Go back to presenting one idea and, if that is accepted, try two.

Concentration and Focus

Play can be important in helping your child learn to concentrate. In the first four months of life, your infant's focused attention, usually aimed at your smiles and noises, may only last for a few seconds. At eight months, your infant may look and examine something for 40 to 60 seconds. By fifteen months, he can spend 15 or 20 focused minutes, and by two-and-a-half or three the span may stretch to a half hour.

Children with a high activity level often have trouble being that focused. If your child is very active, you may need to put in more effort to capture her attention. Once you have it, she may focus on the activity for a long time.

For some active children, however, sheer effort doesn't seem to pay off. They spend one or two seconds with you and boom, they are off to something else. Just as children differ in their athletic, musical, or language capabilities, so they differ in their ability to focus and concentrate. Through play you have a wonderful opportunity to enhance your child's attention span. If your child is gifted in this area, practice will occur naturally; children, like the rest of us, are drawn to activities they do easily. But if your child is easily distracted, now is the time to work with him. Remember that by age five, the brain has grown to three quarters of its adult size. Take advantage of this tremendous growth and maturation as it is occurring.

When you first sit down with a highly distractable child, he may tend toward disjointed play. He may pick up a doll for two seconds, then get up and run around, then roll his cars across the floor without developing a sense of continuity between these activities or maintaining much eye contact with you. So, the question is, how do you develop a rapport with this child? What do you have to do to engage him?

One family that I saw had a two-year-old who was very active and would involve his parents for only one or two seconds at a time. Most of the time he would buzz around the room, pulling everything apart. Every time he was about to grab a book off my shelf or spill the toys from their container, one of his parents would jump up, grab him, and bring him back to their chair. Once released, he would zip around the office seeing what else there was to get into. His parents had given up using words and only used physical methods to gain his attention.

We tried an exercise. I explained to the parents that they were not allowed to move. In order to teach him to respond to gestures and words, they had to use their voices—not physical restraint—to get his attention. They could yell as loud and energetically as was necessary. They responded, "Are you sure you want to go through with this? It's your office that's at risk." I said I was willing to take that risk.

Following my guidelines, they put energy into their voices as their son propelled himself around the room. They even yelled. First, they said enthusiastically, "Come. Let's play with the car." With no reaction on their son's part, they declared forcefully, "Stop pulling the books out," followed by a loud and emphatic, "Come here *now*." It only took a couple of minutes to get his attention. He stopped what he was doing, stood still, and cried. Quite angry, he then walked over to his parents and started pummeling them.

Unhappy as his engagement was, he did stay involved with them for 30 or 40 seconds. In other words, they had finally caught his attention with just the emotion in their voices. He didn't like it, but it was clear that he could relate to them if their voices insisted.

Many parents do not like to experiment with using voice and emotion, and yet this is often critical for a child who is having trouble focusing his attention. You have to find the right level, the right pitch of voice. In fact, contrary to this example, some children do much better with gentle persistence and a soft tone.

Once you have the child involved with you, you have a completely different relationship. Now you need to see how long you can keep the child's attention and you need to build upon this foundation. No matter how little time you start with, it's imperative that you strive to add a few more seconds.

The first step is finding activities of interest to the child. Some children will stay more involved if you are being very physical, maybe jumping and hopping. Others will be caught up with fine motor projects—drawing, cutting, painting. Others enjoy certain emotional themes—maybe ordering you around or being taken care of.

Just as a child with receptive language problems needs to be challenged, so does the child with attention problems. And play is the perfect medium for teaching your child to become involved rather than shifting from one activity to the next.

Fine and Gross Motor Abilities

Some children don't even like to hold a crayon or pencil. Their hands are uncomfortable with holding; their fingers can't grasp. Any number of reasons can account for a child who shies away from fine motor tasks.

Using floor time is a great way to practice such skills painlessly. For a child who has trouble with fine motor tasks, organized exercises, such as sitting at a table and writing the alphabet, may be akin to torture. But working on a sign together to go over the "grocery store" can cast the exercise in a different light. So, too, can drawing puppet figures for a play. Use your ingenuity.

Gross motor activities can be treated similarly. Clearly, hopping, skipping, and dancing can all fit nicely into a lively drama. Chase scenes and discos are tailormade. If these activities are too difficult for the child with gross motor problems, maybe a few minutes of being a one-legged pirate—standing on one leg and then the other—will give a little subtle practice.

"Closing the Circle"

During floor time, you follow your child's lead with empathy and encouragement for his interests and ideas. But your partnership with him needs another element. Your child must use your information; he must close the circle.

Some children readily make communication and interaction a two-way street. Eighteen-month-old Harold would always vocalize and make gestures whenever his father spoke and motioned to him. If Harold were moving his truck back and forth, going, "Zoom!," and Dad said, "Boy, that's moving fast. Is it going under my tunnel [made with his hands]?," Harold would almost always move his truck under the tunnel, look at his father, and make a joyful sound such as "Beep-beep."

Three-year-old Lynn did the same. Often she would comb her doll's hair and say, "Pretty doll." Mother, across from her on the floor, would smile and chime in, "Yes, you are making her very pretty." Lynn would then either ask her mother to help by holding the doll so she could better comb her hair or seek her assistance in changing the doll's dress.

In both these examples, the children "closed the circle." They initiated an action, Mother or Father responded, and *the children, in turn, responded to these actions or words.* It is this latter ability, to tune into their partner and build upon their response, that makes communication truly interactive. Even when a child's response is simply "No" or "Quiet," he is closing the circle. In other words, the child is responding to his partner in a logical manner.

Most children, when communicating with someone, naturally close circles. But there are children who find it difficult. These children tend to ignore their parent's contribution and only elaborate upon their own ideas.

Three-and-a-half-year-old Charlie is an example. Charlie was very creative. He set up complex play sequences where rocket ships were going to the moon. Having a great sense for spatial relationships, he carefully laid out cars, trucks, and space-launching equipment. Dolls were put in just the right compartments and every step for the visit to the man in the moon was well designed. But when Dad would say, "Wow, the rocket looks powerful," or, "Who is going to drive the rocket?", Charlie would respond, "Now the little lambs are going on the ship," or, "Let's put the fuel truck here."

Charlie never used Dad's comments or, for that matter, even acknowledged them. Because he had good hearing (he never missed a call for cookies or ice cream), and was quite bright and verbal, his parents just assumed that he "liked to do his own thing." But one day, Charlie's preschool teacher told his parents that he did not interact very much with the other children and often ignored their comments. At this point his parents decided that it was time to try to understand Charlie's tendency to take in only his own information.

Charlie and his parents came to see me. While playing with Charlie in my office and observing him with his parents, I could see that almost no circles were closed. Charlie only did what was on his mind.

Now, Charlie was a nice, warm child. He was careful not to be aggressive or impulsive and he concentrated very well, but he refused to accept others' input. I wanted to figure out why he didn't close his circles. Was he just stubborn? Was he not interested in others' opinions, or was he simply inattentive to people? When playing with him, if I kept my comments simple with lots of gestures, he would respond.

To find out if he had a problem with receptive language, I tried him on "Simon Says." Here he responded to "touch your nose," and "touch your shoulders," but compound commands such as "touch your nose, touch your shoulders, touch your waist" were ignored in favor of his rocket.

It was clear that Charlie's remarkable ability to *express* complex information was not matched by his ability to take it in. His mother, in fact, recalled that even as a four-month-old, he responded more to her facial gestures than to her sounds. So Charlie was going with his natural strength and minimizing his problem with receptive language. He was creative, verbal, and organized, and chose to ignore what was hard for him to understand.

I explained to Charlie's parents how to help him close the circles, given his particular difficulties: to start with simple comments and lots of facial animation and gesturing, and persist until given a response. For example, when Charlie ignored his father's comment, "Should I hold the moon over by the lamp or by the window?", and went back to "vrooming the ship," Dad did not drop the issue but simplified the comment. He gently and supportively attracted Charlie's attention until his comments were acknowledged in some way. He would say, "But what about my moon?" If ignored, he might add, "You are vrooming but not looking at my moon. How did you get from my moon to vrooming the rocket?" If still ignored, "I can tell you don't want to hear me or look at me." Often by this time, Charlie would say, "Be quiet." And by saying this he had closed the circle. The response need not be positive, only logically responsive. "I don't want to do it your way" is a fine way to close a circle.

Over time, Charlie began taking his parents' behavior, words, and gestures into account. Soon his play became more interactive. He would rev up his rocket and Dad would say, "I'm here on the moon waiting for a landing." And Charlie would happily say, "Landing soon." He was indeed no longer lost in space.

Children sometimes seem to close a circle, but instead say something only partially related to the subject at hand. Three-year-old Peter, for instance, responded to his parents' comment, "Gee, you seem to want to call someone," with "Telephone . . . talk," and descriptions of the color of the phone. Peter was quite intentional and focused, but because of a severe auditory-verbal processing problem, he only comprehended one word in his parents' long sentence. He then tried to be as conversational as he could by using words he associated with the telephone. His parents, confused over Peter's pattern of verbalization, sought consultation. In this way, they learned to simplify their comments so Peter could understand them. As Peter learned to respond more logically they gradually began to increase the number of words in their sentences.

Some children who have trouble closing the circle also tend to be inattentive and impulsive. Often their inability to comprehend and respond to other people's ideas and feelings intensifies their inattentiveness. This challenging situation requires a parent to patiently build from two or three seconds of attentive interaction with one closed circle to a two- or three-minute interaction with ten closed circles until half-hour play sessions are the norm. Patience and slow work are necessary. All learning depends on a child both taking in and giving out information.

It is through a logical interactive relationship with another that a child learns how to balance his own ideas with the world of reality. The logical sharing of information in a drama—no matter how fantastic—is one of the building blocks of your child's approach to reality. While the rocket is going to an imaginary planet, the child's ability to respond to your comment about the power of the rocket ties the child to an external reality—you. Without the ability to take in your information, the child can become lost in his own thoughts. When children close circles, they feel close, connected, and reality bound. They can communicate wishes and ideas, feel loved and understood, and create a vital balance between fantasy and reality.

Problem-Solving Time

So far, your main tools for achieving a successful partnership are following your child's lead in floor time and helping him to close circles. Now add time for problem solving. More relevant to the verbal child (ages three to five), it provides an opportunity for you two to discuss daily events and figure out, or even "negotiate," differences and difficulties.

As most parents know, practical conversations with children are not always easy. Typically, Drew always responds, "Nothing," when Mom asks, "What did you do in school today, Drew?" At this point, it's easy for Mom to back off and rationalize, "He needs his privacy." Stay in there, Mom. To be sure, he does need privacy, but not to the exclusion of your involvement in his daily events. To initiate some reaction, you can gently work with him by having a one-way conversation:

MOM: "I guess not much happened . . . I guess you didn't draw or sing songs or play with other kids," or "I bet that the teacher/Sally/Dan was so nice [or so mean] . . ."

By the third day, when Mom surmised incorrectly, Drew was ready to chime in to correct her.

DREW: "Sally was mean today. She didn't let me play with her."

MOM: (empathetically) "Oh, I can tell you didn't like that."

DREW: (with feeling) "No, I didn't."

MOM: "Well, what happened?"

DREW: "She was playing with Mark and they wouldn't let me play."

Now you are off and running.

Mom's success came through a persistent curiosity, not through withdrawing, acting rejected, or being too intrusive. Her curiosity expressed itself with cues that could serve as reminders for the events of the school day. Do not expect to succeed at first. You may not strike gold immediately, but with daily persistence your child will eventually decide that your patient interest is worth some sharing.

To add variety to your persistent curiosity, you could also try to help your child talk about wanting to keep things to herself. Some of the answers can be very enlightening: "You don't really care." "You like Joanie [little sister] better than me." "You never tell me your secrets." Whatever the answer, if you get one, you are on your way.

Daily chitchats are only a first step. With some success here, you can move on to initiating special times for problem solving.

Here, *you* can sometimes set the agenda—anything from waking at night, to toilet training, hitting other children, throwing food on the floor, temper tantrums, being mean to a sibling—and you set the time, ideally not during the crisis but at a calm time, when you are both relaxed.

Persistence over a period of days rather than a "one-shot" big discussion is most helpful, with 15 to 30 minutes or more devoted to each discussion. If your Johnny or Sally is strong-willed, he/ she will spend the first ten minutes ignoring you, changing the subject, or saying, "I don't want to talk about it."

Some parents complain of being bored after five minutes, especially with minimal responses. We can't emphasize enough that it takes a minimum of 15 minutes for each discussion for the child to see your interest. Of course, not every child is this difficult. Some can talk for an hour.

Once you bring up the subject, try to listen to your child and to empathize with his perspective. "I can tell you enjoy pinching your brother and you do it even though Dad and I punish you." Sam may grin and be silent. You persist and continue to emphasize that Sam must have what he feels are good reasons. Eventually he may tell you his list of complaints: "He gets into my toys and you always take his side," and so on.

As you understand Sam's perspective, you can then try to solve the problem. You agree to do a better job of keeping little brother away from Sam's toys; Sam agrees to tell you his complaints rather than "take the law into his own hands." To be sure, limits are often necessary to enforce your "negotiated" plan. But the better you understand where Sam is coming from, the better chance you have of obtaining emotional growth and a resolution to the problem.

So, to work things out, listen to your child's perspective and then share your point of view. Remember you always have the prerogative of "pulling rank." But understanding your child's viewpoint and giving her a chance to verbalize complaints, fears, or wishes can only be helpful. Do not assume you know what children think and feel. And even if you do, *they need to say it.* Make sure they, not you, talk for more than half the time. Nodding or mumbling yes or no to your questions is not helpful.

Not only does this approach solve problems, but consider how much receptive and expressive language and logical thinking is practiced with each discussion or negotiation. Even if you have to pull rank, the process of negotiation is one of the best learning opportunities your child will ever have in logical thinking. Remember, the child who likes to talk the least needs to practice this skill the most.

You may notice that your child has difficulty seeing the "big picture." Some highly verbal and emotionally sensitive children fall prey to this syndrome. For example, Janet felt, "Mary hates me" and "Sally won't play with me . . . I have no friends . . . I feel so lonely." She often became overwhelmed with her feelings of the moment and tended to "miss the forest for the trees." In such a case, focusing on your child's particular approach to problem solving can help her to see the larger issue at hand. Through a series of conversations, Janet's mother was able to help her to see that she liked to be the boss—and often insisted that "anyone I like must like me and behave toward me as I see fit." Implicit in this is the assumption that "if someone else tries to be the boss then they must hate me." Janet learned that her feelings of loneliness were only one little, yet painful, part of a larger pattern sustained by her unrealistic expectations.

Other children are fully capable of seeing the big picture but have a hard time describing the details or the shades of their feelings. Here your job is just the opposite of the task that confronted Janet's mother. To help your child focus on detail and nuance, pursue every hint of detail in your conversations with great interest: "Your friends don't like you? Which ones? Tell me what happened with Sam; I have lots of time." Your interest in the particular aspects of his feelings will help your "big picture" child avoid overgeneralization.

A PROBLEM-SOLVING ATTITUDE

To make problem solving work, value your child's perspective. To give his perspective relevance, provide him with enough information to participate (but be careful not to overwhelm him). Frequently, for instance, parents enmeshed in power struggles over eating hide the facts. They are prepared to offer Johnny an alternative to his mashed potatoes, but they don't give him the choice up front.

Second, within your child's ability to be responsible, allow joint control over some decisions. Let your fussy, hard-to-please four-year-old participate in creating the family menu, picking out foods at the supermarket, and selecting clothes at the store. You can always overrule a bad choice, but a sense of initial collaboration will make it easier when you do have to set limits. Third, always increase self-sufficiency. For example, for the child who forgets which day it is, make a long stick with the days laid out so she can check each one off. Use colors or shapes to help. Then, let her tell you which day it is. Most battles seem like they are over issues of dependency, "You do it for me," but they really involve power and competition—"I am the boss," "You have to tie my shoes." If helplessness arises, recognize it as a disguised form of competition and harness your child's assertiveness to solve problems, not create them.

To help your child win the competition constructively, always break down the task you are working on into its smallest parts. Your child needs to try to get his socks on for a week before he progresses to pants and shoes. His first success will spur him on. His failures will discourage him.

When using reward and punishment to further motivate him, set up the requirements for a reward in such a way that he gets more rewards than punishments. If you are giving him stars for putting away toys, make sure his chart doesn't stay blank for very long. If it does, you haven't broken the task down into small enough steps. Remember, respect and engage your child's problem-solving ability.

FROM ONE-WAY STREET TO
TWO-WAY STREET

Many parents, especially those whose children tend to be pensive or distractable, inadvertently allow floor time or problem-solving time to become a one-way street. They wind up doing most of the directing and/or talking and miss opportunities to help their children take charge and be assertive. Often children require an extra second or two—or even five—to figure out their next step. Accustomed to the natural rhythm of adult conversation, the parent moves in too quickly and takes over. One very competent mom who came to see me was so intent on getting a drama going that she wouldn't give her four-year-old son, Sam, a chance to develop the story. He was playing with a dollhouse and looking at several little bears. Before Sam had a chance to decide what story, if any, he wanted to tell, Mother quickly shot in with "Let's put all the bears together." Later on, as he was beginning to place the bears in different rooms, perhaps to develop a family drama of sorts, Mom enthusiastically said, "Let's see who is visiting the bears." Each time Mom suggested activities, Sam would turn his back on her and "tune out" for a few seconds. As he tuned out, Mom became more impatient and began asking questions that only required "yes" or "no" answers. "Is the aunt visiting?" "Are they going to serve his visitor food?" Sam grunted "yes" or "no" each time and the one-way dialogue continued.

After a few minutes, we worked on a different approach, the goal of which was to help Sam be assertive and in control: *adding only as much help or structure as was needed.* To do this, the mother had to be more patient. As he was setting up his bears again, Mom stayed engaged with eye and verbal contact but gave him time with comments like "Gee, each bear has his own room." Sam nodded and methodically set up eight bears in eight rooms. "I wonder what's going to happen," his mother said quietly. (An open-ended question is best when a question is needed. Often just describing what the child is doing is sufficient.) Sam looked around the room; he was deciding. Mother looked at him with anticipation, but with respect for his rhythm. She waited as he thought and thought. To show interest she said, "I can tell you are thinking hard."

Many children at this point would come up with something on their own, like "The wolf is visiting or attacking the bears," but Sam wasn't able to develop this next step. Instead of asking yes/no questions, Mother now tried to provide the minimal support needed by commenting on each alternative Sam entertained. For example, as Sam looked at the big monster doll and then over at the space ship and then at a big truck, Mom said, "Gee, I wonder what's next. Maybe a visit from the space ship or the monster, or the big truck?" By providing alternatives that were obviously of interest to Sam, his mother, although helping, was leaving the decisions to Sam. Sam then smiled and brought the space ship over, saying, "Bears going to the moon," and they were off on a moon adventure.

Another family illustrates these points even more strikingly. Three-year-old Susan was delayed in her language abilities and was highly distractable. Father, trying to interact and engage her, started talking and wouldn't stop. "Susan wants to put the doll in the house; put the car in the garage. Good girl, Susan! Now, put the hat on the doll. . . ." Dad, in his efforts to help Susan, didn't even break to take a deep breath. Needless to say, even though Susan complied with a few of his requests, it was hardly a two-way communication.

I asked him to be a little more patient and see where Susan's interests took her. She began jumping aimlessly around the room. Father looked at me as though to say, "See, this is what she does if I let her." In keeping with the principle *Follow the child, but then engage them in their own interests*, I suggested that Dad jump with her to see if she was interested in a jumping bunny dance. Dad jumped with her and then Susan smiled gleefully and hid her face on the floor. I wondered out loud if Susan was interested in an "I hide, you hide" game. Dad quickly hid behind a chair. Susan found him and said, "Find you!" Dad laughed, saying, "You got me." Then Susan hid and Dad found her. They exchanged grunts, giggles, gestures, and even a few words—a first for Susan. Within five minutes, they had closed over thirty circles and were clearly engaged in a two-way dialogue. Prior to this, Susan never closed any circles. At best, she was thought only able to respond to simple commands, cuddle, or tune out.

It was critical for Dad to give Susan some room to express her interests. Even though her interests were initially not interactive, Dad built on these and made them so.

The principles for a two-way street are:

1. Be patient and follow your child's lead;

2. When your child gives you some clues, accept them and be interactive;

3. Provide the minimum amount of support or structure needed with descriptive comments, open-ended questions, alternatives based on the child's cues, and alternatives based on your own imagination if the child is not providing any cues.

Sometimes these same issues come up in routine chitchat or problem-solving chitchat. One father introduced his son to a friend by commanding, "Say hello to the doctor," a clearcut order. I suggested that if his son is ignoring someone, he should generate interaction, question him about it, or offer a series of alternatives, such as, "Do we know who this man is?" This type of kidding will usually elicit a smile and a greeting of one sort or another.

Another not-very-verbal boy would point to the water and say, "Boat on . . ." and Mom quickly supplied the word "water." I suggested that, if her son wasn't able to think of the word with time, she should act a little confused but very interested, like the TV detective Columbo, commenting, "What's that?" or, "Let's see. I know the word. It's that stuff you swim in or drink. What's it called?" By this time, the child will often smilingly say, "Water." Cues are helpful, but they should not take over. Always be patient and help your child do the talking. Remember, if he is only saying "Yes" or "No," it's your dialogue, and he isn't learning to talk, think, or interact.

Limit Setting

Of course, floor time does not replace discipline—it supplements it. When a child is misbehaving, floor time can sometimes help reveal what's on the child's mind, why he's so angry and provocative. But most three- and four-year-olds worth their salt will not give up aggressive and provocative behavior just because they are now expressing their feelings in pretend play. This special time for building a relationship has to be coupled with firm, solid, consistent limits that have resolve behind them. There must be a balance. The golden rule says, *Every time you set firm limits to help impulsive Frankie become more obedient, increase the floor time. Never increase limits without increasing floor time. When you eliminate one avenue of expression—provocative behavior—give him another way to express his concerns.*

Successful limit setting, an ever-present challenge for parents, merges warmth and empathy with a "bricklike" resolve. Add an instructive rather than a punitive attitude to a respect for the child's underlying needs, and you will have a child who understands limits.

MOBILIZING RESOLVE

Frequently, parents explain that little Tommy just won't listen. The usual litany goes: he hits his brother, won't clean up his toys, and throws his food on the floor. At this point, I often wonder out loud about the difficulty of repainting the living room each week to cover Tommy's drawing on the wall. "Oh no!" they respond, "he would never do that! He knows we wouldn't stand for it." The question then is, "How come Tommy doesn't feel the same resolve when it comes to throwing food on the floor?"

Intuitively sensing their parents' resolve and intensity, most children pick their spots carefully. They usually misbehave where they think they can get away with it. Some children do write on the walls repeatedly, but they are in the minority. So the first step in limit setting is deciding that the limit is really important to you and developing resolve. Resolve can be communicated through your gestures as well as words. Some parents and children, however, have not learned the gestural system. The importance of gestures in communication cannot be overestimated, especially when it comes to setting limits.

A TEACHING ATTITUDE

Limits are taught, not dictated. Transgressions provide that "learning opportunity." Eighteen-month-old Molly wants to grab

Mommy's favorite lamp—a perfect learning opportunity. Mommy, aware of Molly's developmental level, knows that Molly understands gestures and a few words. Mommy (unless she is in a hurry and needs to leave teaching for another time) gets in front of Molly, indicates "No" with hand and facial gestures as well as verbally, and attempts to redirect Molly like the corner policeman, helping Molly to associate word and gesture. (Eventually this integration will allow Mommy just to say, "No.") Molly tries to get around Mommy and eventually cries in frustration, but not before ten minutes of good learning have taken place. Mom, using clear graded gestures, has been firm and persistent and has refused to give in. Over time, Molly learns what Mom's words and gestures mean. If Mom picks Molly up because it is easier, Molly only learns that being picked up means "I can't do something."

Every parent is familiar with the helpless feeling of trying to set limits in the store while Jane is grabbing a toy and ignoring your command to "Stop it!" Many parents, after yelling, physically limiting, or giving in to their preschooler, repeat the whole process the next time they are at a store. The issue is not the store. It's the fact that Jane does not pay attention to, or respect, her mother's wishes. There are at least a hundred opportunities each day to teach "respect" for Mom's and Dad's words and guidance; the store is the last place you want to do your "tough" teaching. It's like trying to prepare your quarterback during the Super Bowl rather than before. Teach on your own turf at home, not in a store where you will be embarrassed either by your own yelling or your child's. At home, you have almost infinite opportunities—when you ask Jane to pick up her toys, come to the dinner table, eat with a spoon and not her hands, get ready for bed, share her toys with a friend, or please put on her coat because you have to go home. Don't gloss over these opportunities or—conversely—be too concerned with trying to win a power struggle. Instead, be concerned with the process of learning. Ask yourself these questions:

1. Do I have my child's attention?

2. Does my child understand that I want her to pick up her

doll (for example)? Are my words or gestures clear and simple enough?

3. If she is paying attention and understanding, but is not obeying, then why? Am I motivating her enough with positive regard, including respect? Am I prepared to motivate her with punishment if needed?

4. Do I cultivate regular opportunities for empathy and dialogue through daily floor time and problem solving?

5. Am I willing to be more persistent and firm, and prepared to add physical restraint to my words and gestures?

If the answers to these questions are all yes and if, as indicated above, you make firm commitments to the issues you want to deal with, then limits should be readily learned by your toddler.

MAINTAINING EMPATHY, INVOLVEMENT, AND DIALOGUE

The natural human tendency is to decrease empathy and closeness when involved in angry exchanges, power struggles, or limit setting. "How can I empathize with his desire to be spoiled?" asked one perplexed mom. The answer is, "Set the limits firmly," and empathize with how hard it is for Johnny to learn his new lessons.

To repeat the Golden Rule—whenever increasing the limits, always increase the floor time, and with older children, the problem-solving time. The floor time provides empathy and warmth, as well as a sense of connectedness. The problem-solving time lets the older child discuss his perspective and helps the parent and child "negotiate" the difficulty. Only through both limit setting and empathy will children eventually "wish" to please. After all, your goal in setting limits is to teach greater empathy and respect for others. And children learn from what *you do*, not what you say.

ESCAPE VERSUS TAKING CHARGE

While struggling to be empathetic, many parents find that they can't resist their desire to escape from their whiny, angry children.

One mother said, "I can't stand her nagging and whining. I just want to get away!" But the escape pattern only leads the child to feel more rejected, vulnerable, angry, and frightened. Your best approach is to take charge and reestablish a sense of security and control with extra floor time and problem-solving time. After a few weeks of reaffirming these special moments, your setting firm limits on the angry whining is both appropriate and helpful to the child. Empathy, rather than escape, will permanently reverse the cause of your distress.

PICKING YOUR SPOTS AND FOLLOWING UP

Perhaps the hardest part of setting limits is deciding what to limit. This should depend on your values and attitudes. Our suggestion is to pick your spots, set your boundaries wide, and then enforce them. In other words, it is better to win a few battles with sound teaching than to lose lots of little ones out of exhaustion. Take a few key issues at a time. Work on table manners and leave cleanliness for later, or vice versa. Don't make the tactical mistake of waging a war on three fronts at once or setting very narrow categories.

For example, do not punish Joey for hitting Jane one day and spitting at Tom the next or pinching Harold on yet another. Instead, discuss a large *category*, "respecting other people's bodies and therefore not hurting." The issues of "respect and not hurting" will cover any ingenious twists your child can create to defy you, such as in this example: "Don't hit." "I didn't hit, I pushed." "Well, don't push then." Next day, "I didn't hit or push, I just leaned on him hard." You want to deal with the forest (general principle) rather than the trees (specific behaviors).

In this way, you won't get lost in endless debate over definition and your child will learn general principles rather than concrete behaviors. In short, he will learn to respect other people's bodies.

WHAT ARE REASONABLE PUNISHMENTS
OR SANCTIONS?

What do you do to set limits though? What about the three- or four-year-old who won't pick up her toys or come to dinner when you ask? Sanctions or punishments are often necessary to reinforce the resolve. Try to select punishments that are not developmentally detrimental. Do not, for instance, restrict playing with friends; it is too developmentally useful. Consider things like no TV, no computer games, earlier bedtime, KP duty. Remember, children need sanctions that challenge them. As one four-year-old said in response to 15-minute time-outs, "That won't work. It's too easy for me." And while time-outs and isolation have become popular, they raise important questions.

Isolation or time-outs can suggest to a child that you are not able to withstand her anger. Going eyeball-to-eyeball with her or even asking her to think quietly in your presence about what she did may communicate greater resolve on your part.

More importantly, some disobedient children have maturational lags, including receptive language problems. They are already "tuned out," often getting lost in their own fantasy world. The last thing they need is social isolation where they tune out more, further undermining their already fragile reality testing. In addition, children who tune out often find isolation easy. As one child told me, "I daydream a lot on my own anyway." He asked me not to tell his parents that not being allowed to watch TV would be far more painful to him.

One of the rationales for isolation and time-outs is based on behavioral or operant learning theory. The reasoning goes—when a child misbehaves, one should try to avoid any inadvertent reinforcement or reward for his misbehavior. Therefore, any contact with a child, even scolding him, may be secretly reinforcing to him and actually increase his unwanted behavior. This logic quickly falls apart when one realizes that for many children, especially some of the most inattentive or aloof, the isolation itself may be pleasurable or reinforcing. More importantly, from a developmental context, we know that only the ability to balance intimacy, trust, and respect with anger will lead to self limit-setting. Methods of punishment should never be cold, mechanical, or lack the very human traits you are trying to teach. Constructive punishment must always be in the context of an empathetic, respectful relationship.

OVERPROTECTIVE PARENTING

Parents who are overprotective are often too pained by their child's discomfort to set meaningful limits. One mother couldn't bear to seriously punish her four-year-old after he punched a little girl in the nose. She took away TV for one day. Mark later confided to me: "That didn't bother me much. One day of no TV was no big deal. I'll hit her again if she doesn't let me be the boss." When I asked him what punishment would make him consider alternatives for dealing with his frustration, he said, "Probably a week of no TV because then I would have to miss my favorite cartoons."

Children at this age will often tell you about what they consider a "meaningful punishment." Sometimes it comes out humorously or indirectly. One child said, "If I must be punished, make me go to bed early, but don't take away my late afternoon G.I. Joe cartoons. They are my favorites." (Hopefully he's not taking lessons from Brer Rabbit.) When Mark told his mother that he didn't consider one day of no TV sufficient punishment to deter him from hitting kids at school, she tearfully but stubbornly told me "I couldn't bear to take away a whole week of TV. He would be so unhappy and would feel I'm mean."

Fear of the child's discomfort or anger is a major reason why limits are hard for some parents. (Parents need to discuss these feelings with each other and explore the roots of such feelings in their own backgrounds.) But instead of watering down sanctions, they should do something much harder: deal with inner pain and guilt with extra floor time and problem-solving time—you can't give your child too much of these.

Each child is different. For some, a dirty look is motivating; for others, a week of no TV may begin to get their attention. To be effective, make the punishment meaningful to the child.

Temper Tantrums

One of the most difficult challenges for parents is a temper tantrum. One dad told me, "When he seems so mad, it feels like he hates me and I can't stand that." A mother exclaimed, "I can't stand that loud screech. It drives me crazy. I would give him anything just to make him stop." On the other side a little four-and-a-half-year-old told me, "Yelling and having tantrums is my best weapon against my parents. They don't know what to do. I really get even."

As you can see, tantrums can have different meanings and serve different purposes. There is a big difference between a child who, overtired or ill, cries at every little thing; a child who has a fit because of the frustrations of doing something like tying his shoe; and a child who is uncontrollably angry at you because you won't let her have a chocolate bar before dinner. Knowing the kind of tantrum you are dealing with will help you handle it.

The overtired child needs you to help him calm down—holding, reading, talking, or getting him interested in the nice flowers in the garden. The goal is to teach him that even when he is really upset, he can settle down using certain tools. His favorite sights, sounds, and movement patterns help, as well as particular activities such as a favorite story or videotape while you are hugging him. Try not to get caught up in "I'm being manipulated," and so on, while your child is overtired and fussy.

For the child who is frustrated because he can't do something he is trying hard to do, like tie his shoes, the tantrum may be similar to an adult's anger at hitting his thumb while trying to build a bookcase. There are occasions when one is entitled to express frustration. Remember that even if your angry three-year-old throws his shoe down, it is still an advanced communication, involving "gestures"—and words come after gestures.

Limits are only necessary if your child becomes destructive and tries to hurt someone or break something. The child, out of frustration, might discard a toy to indicate his disgust. That's okay, but if he throws it down too hard, a limit is necessary.

If we sympathize with our fellow adults' moans and groans when they can't do something, why not extend the same sentiments to our toddler or preschooler? In this situation, empathize with their frustration and outrage at the ornery shoelaces or toy. Then, after they calm down, see if they want your assistance. If not, cheer them on from the sidelines as they try again. If they want your help, don't take over—be a consultant. Ask them how you might help and then follow their directions. If more help is needed, offer some constructive suggestions, such as breaking the task into small parts. For example, just crossing the laces may suffice for day one.

Children with motor-planning difficulties (that is, planning out complex movements such as tying a shoe or getting dressed) especially need your patient admiration and consultation in the "step-by-step" approach. With the frustrated fit-thrower who is communicating his disgust, the goal is empathy and eventual resumption of the task.

Now, to address the real temper tantrum: the child who throws a fit because you won't give her what she wants or won't let her do what she wants requires strict limit setting. Most parents find this situation the most difficult of all, especially if the child is strong-willed and the parents are sensitive to loud noise or angry feelings. To help the child, first to make sure that there is (1) ample warmth, closeness, nurturance, and respect in your relationship; (2) ample opportunity for her to communicate her feelings to you without the tantrum; and (3) limit setting for infractions, such as hitting a sibling or not putting away toys.

The best way to make sure these ingredients are present is through half an hour per day of floor time for goal 1; 20 minutes per day of problem-solving chitchat for goal 2; and constructive limit setting as a learning opportunity for goal 3. By implementing these steps, you are dealing with intimacy, trust, security, and the expression of feelings.

Now you are ready to deal with the tantrum itself. Your attitude is: "I understand you are mad. You didn't get what you wanted." Then wait out the tantrum until the child is able to communicate in words or gestures, not just by crying, why she feels you have been unfair to her. It is not helpful to further hype her up by yelling back at her nor necessary to defend your position after you have made it clear; to bribe her with compromises; to woo her or comfort her out of her angry expressions; or to banish her to her room because you can't stand to listen to her. If she chooses to let you know how mad she is by using sounds or gestures, you are ready to listen.

Many parents report that as they combine limit setting with extra floor time and problem-solving time, their discipline-problem preschooler becomes warmer, more secure, and more cooperative. But they also report that for a while the tantrums get sharper and more intense. Any child worth his salt will resist giving up his means of protest.

If the tantrum brings out a tendency for self-injury (biting or banging), for breaking things, or hurting you, immediate and firm limits are necessary. Firm holding will often do the trick—in such instances, be prepared for a workout.

Only if your child's tantrum seems so out of control that it is building on itself and he cannot calm himself down should you move in and try to help him calm down. Often, parents feel guilty because of tantrums. Extra floor time at other times will help your child feel loved and understood and help you feel less guilty.

Limits as Opportunities to Teach
New Coping Strategies

Setting limits can also be an opportunity to teach your child to use higher developmental capacities, find new ways to get his needs met, and feel a sense of self-respect rather than humiliation.

FACILITATING DEVELOPMENT

Let's go back to eighteen-month-old Molly, who wanted to touch Mom's lamp. She not only had a lesson in limits but also one in a more advanced form of communication—the use of complex gestures and words.

With your two-year-old, an exchange of words will teach him to use ideas in the heat of battle. Emotional ideas are a big advance over simply yelling, crying, or pouting—all of which are characteristic of the stage preceding ideas, the stage having to do with complex behaviors.

Similarly, when you and your three-and-one-half-year-old have a twenty-minute discussion on bedtime with his contending that extra TV is better, you are teaching (through the process of negotiation) complex emotional reasoning. By listening to his argument you are not being a pushover; if he does not persuade you, you can still insist that he go to sleep.

FINDING NEW WAYS TO MEET NEEDS

It is relatively easy to discipline a preschooler when he covets someone's toy. But it is harder to try to figure out what needs the child is trying to meet. Perhaps behind the child's greediness is a hectic home life where he is given lots of toys but little pride, respect, or floor time. The greed in this case may be an attempt to feel important. The question then becomes "How can I help him feel respected and important in other ways? If I want him to equate importance with something other than the biggest and best toys, then how can I help him realize that his interests, skills, silly jokes, feelings of frustration, and loss are important and worthy of respect?"

While limiting an inappropriate way of meeting his needs, his parents can direct him more appropriately by coming to an understanding of his motives. It takes a lot of work, especially floor time and problem-solving time, to discover what these needs and motives are. But whenever there are serious challenges to limits, you can bet the child has basic needs that should be addressed. These needs may concern family issues, such as the parents' relationship, problems with another sibling, or problems with his own physical development (including delays in gross or fine motor skills, receptive language, or other motives discussed in chapter VIII).

RESPECT RATHER THAN HUMILIATION

Power struggles with your child can be so infuriating that you become too preoccupied about not losing face. You may get so angry that you, not surprisingly, want your child not only to do what you want but to say "uncle" as well. But intimidating and humiliating your child only teaches her that your "guidance" denigrates her self-esteem. On the other hand, helping a child save face and feel self-respect when following your guidance lets him associate cooperation with feelings of positive self-esteem and success at overcoming a "fussy or stubborn" feeling. Johnny, as usual, doesn't want to go to sleep. After a long argument, Dad insists and is so furious that when Johnny finally walks into the bedroom with his head down, Dad yells, "And next time you better not give me a fight, you selfish, ungrateful kid!" Dad then proceeds to angrily lecture Johnny—"You better obey me or else!" Dad can't understand why Johnny never apologizes for his transgressions.

Consider another scenario. As before, Johnny argues about bed but goes upstairs. Angry Dad, realizing that Johnny is conceding, goes up with him, commenting on how good Johnny will feel tomorrow after a good night's sleep and asks about school and tomorrow's activities. Dad intuitively helps Johnny talk about something he likes and elicits such responses as, "I get to go on the outdoor climber at recess tomorrow," and Dad responds with "How exciting climbing higher and higher must be." The participants in the battle are now comrades-in-arms, each one feeling respected. Of course, an angry Johnny may still say, "Out of my room! No goodnight kiss!" which is his way of trying to salvage some dignity. Respect his need, and say, "I hope you will let me kiss you goodnight tomorrow." After all, he *is* going to sleep.

As your child builds his psychological structure, he is using several building blocks: his experiences with being loved, understood, and accepted for all his feelings (floor time); a sense of logical connection to the world of reality (problem solving); and an ability to feel secure in his own internal limits (limit setting). With these tools he can feel your love and empathy for his special wishes and fears; in turn, he will learn to think and be aware of the feelings, interests, and rights of others.

IV

Mood and Self-Esteem

All parents want their children to feel good about themselves—
to be generally optimistic and stable. Self-esteem, a feeling of your
own worth, lends a buoyancy to personality, a feeling that, even
in times of challenge and stress, one can manage—even prevail.
We naturally gravitate toward, and admire, the person who seems
to meet life with a smile of anticipation and a ready embrace.
Where does this feeling come from? How does it grow? How can
you help your child gain and sustain the feeling that he or she is
a strong, competent, caring, and altogether wonderful person?

Self-esteem is one of those emotional functions that for many
appears at a very young age. But it is a delicate business. For the
seed of self-esteem to take root and grow, it must be nourished
carefully and regularly, and it must be grounded in a predominantly joyful and positive emotional tone in spite of shifting physical or emotional states. Parents need to provide a mixture of
timely admiration, understanding responses, and firm limit setting, all the while being respectful of their child's special needs
and preferences. From that first light of satisfaction in your baby's
eyes to her ability to congratulate herself for a job well done to
her permanent feeling of security in her own being—*you* are essential. Your love, constancy, admiration, and respect are all nec-

essary nutrients for the growth of this all-important emotion in your child's life.

The Growth of Self-Worth

Like other emotions, pride in oneself unfolds gradually, in predictable stages. And, as has been said, your role in this development is crucial.

You can see self-confidence in your healthy four-month-old who greets the world with a wide and toothless grin or your eight-month-old who dives in to explore your hair. This healthy, optimistic interest in the world develops further in the second year of life as your toddler and you—joint adventurers—explore the corners of your home confident in your search for toys. Look at your three-year-old who congratulates herself with a satisfied smile after putting a puzzle together as though she's saying, "Aren't I terrific!" Your lucky girl's self-esteem is built on internal, loving images. Even when there's no one else around, she can imagine a loved one saying to her, "What a terrific job you did with that puzzle!" The transition from external pride and admiration to internal pride and admiration has been accomplished. Pride and admiration have become part of how your little girl sees herself.

Low self-esteem also has a developmental pattern. Let's take a specific example.

Eight-month-old Harold looks away when Mommy first comes home from work. He may be saying, "You're going to have to woo me a little if you want me to be involved with you." But if Mommy or Daddy, feeling miffed at the apparent rejection, goes about making dinner and reading the newspaper, then Harold's non-expectancy has been justified. For an eight-month-old to look away from his parents after a separation is perfectly normal. We see many babies making "look away" into a game, but a pattern of ignoring a baby's gestures of unhappiness may incite the beginnings of low self-esteem.

These beginnings can be seen in a fifteen-month-old who habitually looks sad and fears being assertive at a time when the toddler's norm is "Do it my way!"; in an eighteen-month-old who seems unable to stop doing what she is forbidden; or in a two-and-a half-year-old who expects to fail at everything he attempts, like knocking the blocks down before the tower is built or scattering the puzzle before it is put together.

Let's now look at a self-esteem as it develops, as well as some of the difficulties that can confront it, from infancy up through forty-eight months of age.

Stage One:
Regulation and Interest in the World
(0 to 3 Months)

A budding interest in the world is the foundation for growth toward self-confidence. At this early age, your child learns to sustain an emotional tone that will override fluctuations of his physical state (e.g., hunger) or mood state (e.g., annoyance). Whether hungry, tired, or wet, he will gradually be less distracted from his interests. He is learning to superimpose a stable mood onto his fluctuating internal physical and emotional states.

His sense of himself and his emotional pleasure in himself will be closely related to your admiration of his interest in the world. This is no time to stand on the sidelines. Your child senses emotional contact and can already feel differences in the way he is being held, the quality of your voice, and the difference in facial expression between an admiring caregiver who is tuned in and a distracted or uninterested one who is not. Forget your worries when you are with your infant. Enjoy these precious first moments of contact, however fleeting they may be in the first weeks and even months of life.

FLOOR TIME

Your smile and gaze into the eyes of your newborn are not necessarily one-way trips. Though you may not receive a response you can interpret for a few weeks, *something* is happening, and as early as two weeks you may even begin to see a return smile. Your voice as well—its tone, pitch, and rhythm—helps provide interesting experiences which include sound, vision, touch, or movement. Remember that even if your baby can't formulate a wholly understandable response, he will soon be capable of longer periods of attention.

So, show him how great you think he is by looking into his eyes and show him respect by letting him look away for a moment when he needs to. Smile, talk, and gesture your love and admiration to him. Find out which senses he favors, what type of movement he enjoys best, how he likes to be held, what sustains his attention. Even if you are not sure of your baby's special pleasures, your own mood and joyous feeling toward your infant will communicate the message he or she needs to hear.

DIFFICULTIES

Even when all else is going well, it is not easy for a household to be run by a newborn's sleeping pattern. How can you share pleasurable experiences with a sleeping infant?

It seemed Roxanne wasn't going to give anyone much satisfaction. At two and a half months she was still sleeping away the majority of the day and waking up every two hours during the night to feed. Neither parent was much interested in playing or trying to stay up with her in the wee hours; so life continued, with both Roxanne and her parents missing each other as though they worked different shifts. Although her parents felt helpless, they figured that once she was a little older she would naturally begin to wake more during the day and they could play with her then.

Early infancy involves so many shifts and adjustments in lives, schedules, and responsibilities that sometimes whatever pattern the new arrival seems to prefer is the one her parents tolerate. In Roxanne's case, her daytime sleeping allowed Mother to get some of the rest she knew she wouldn't get at night. It also allowed her to keep her household at least jogging along, if not running smoothly. Though she felt guilty about letting Roxanne sleep so much, Mother was relieved in a way, too. But gradually she realized her need for a relationship with her new baby and worked out a plan. She began talking and gesturing to Roxanne more while changing diapers during the day and gently waking her earlier and earlier for her last feeding, engaging her in gazes, making faces at her. Now that Roxanne was getting more interest from her mother, she slowly became more and more interested in staying up. Father did his share as well, telling his new daughter how wonderful she was and holding her upright so she was less likely to drowse off. Soon enough Roxanne's parents were rewarded with their first smile and gurgle, which was all the confirmation they needed that they were indeed launched on a grand adventure. Much like a traveler returning from abroad, they gradually helped Roxanne shift her main sleep time to the evenings rather than the day—which enabled them to get a reasonable night's sleep as well!

Stage Two:
Falling in Love (3 to 7 Months)

As your baby begins to interact with the human world at around four months, it is *essential* to respond to her rhythm for involvement. At this age, babies generally show enormous, joyful smiles, vocalize happily, and move their arms and legs to the rhythm of Mommy's or Daddy's voice. But sometimes they prefer to suck their fists and stare off into space for a few minutes. Your child will vary these moments with periods of intense involvement lasting for a good 30 to 60 seconds each. These periods of involvement also have their own quality and rhythm, usually building up to a peak of pleasure then relaxing, building to another peak and relaxing again. Your baby may disengage for a few moments, then reengage again. You can experiment with various senses, change your speed, or throw in a few surprises. Now you can really begin to find out what kinds of play your baby loves and how many variations you can come up with.

FLOOR TIME

Just as a plant stretches toward the sun as it grows, your child will naturally gravitate toward new challenges and experiences as he grows—and you can help if you learn how to make the most of your baby's own special rhythms and the unique way he is falling in love with the world.

Some babies build up to a peak of excitement quickly, then drop off quickly. Try to match your baby's quick sense of excitement and, at the same time, help him elongate the peak so that the curve downward is more gradual. Don't let him be like the person who shakes your hand, pats you on the back, and then runs off. Meet and greet your baby, then, as he's "turning out," say something like "Hey, how about a little longer smile this time?" Presto! You are learning to woo your baby in a way that tunes into his natural patterns and rhythms.

While you are engaging your baby at her level of readiness, always respect her emotional tone as well. If she doesn't seem to want to climb the mountain one more time, don't force it; see if you can read the signal she is sending—perhaps for a quieter period of interaction, perhaps to be left to herself for a moment or two. The important thing is to tune into your baby so that she feels her individuality being respected, even when you are encouraging her to sustain contact just a bit more.

DIFFICULTIES

Some babies become disorganized easily—their arms and legs may move so frantically that they get frightened and upset by stimulating contact. This behavior can be a challenge. Holding your baby tightly and securely will provide a base; her disorganized motor patterns will be limited as she is held, and she will appreciate this. Learning to read your child's signals will help you to differentiate between a baby who—for example—wants to be moved through the air a bit, or who revels in doing deep knee bends on your stomach, and a child who feels disorganized and frantic. In the latter case, you will see that she enjoys being held snugly and even likes having her arms and legs limited a bit—though at other times she may ask for a workout. Respecting and appreciating your baby's needs tells her that her feelings and preferences count and establishes a good basis for her own self-respect.

The infant who is *not* very interested in the world and seems to be almost overly calm may appreciate extra efforts at "wooing." Supporting your baby's head so he can look at you and cherishing each second he looks or listens can make all the difference. Remember, one second leads to two, and two to three. Don't become discouraged. It is natural for a parent to just stop trying with an infant who is not responding; it is so painful for parents to have their overtures ignored that they may decide, "My baby is a thinker." But even "thinkers" need to be engaged, if only for a second at a time. Take pride in each second. It may help your baby feel important.

Stage Three: Purposeful Communication (4 to 10 Months)

By eight months, parents and babies are well into the stage of purposeful communication, or interaction. Now you have your first clear opportunities to really respect and respond to your baby's expression of different emotional needs. Through different facial gestures, arm and leg movements, and perhaps even crawling, your eight-month-old is able to communicate a wide variety of emotional states, from reaching out to be held (closeness), to poking a finger into your nose (curiosity), biting, banging, even glaring (aggression and anger). The window of opportunity has opened wide. Your response of "Oh, aren't you proud!" as he beams at his latest accomplishment sows the seed of identification and recognition of the emotions he is feeling.

FLOOR TIME

You will notice now, too, that your baby has a real span of attention. A healthy eight-month-old can focus his attention on an interactive game for a number of minutes. So, as he is bouncing on your lap, or crawling away, or examining his blocks, you can now show your respect and admiration for his fine or gross motor interests, vocalizations, or emotions. You can join in his interests and at the same time encourage longer periods of emotional contact.

Most important to your baby at this stage is your responsiveness to his intentional signaling. For example, as his gestures become more defined, the question for the parent is, "How well am I able to read each of his signals and respond differently to his displays of closeness, anxiety, or even anger? Is my understanding of him keeping up with his emerging communication skills?"

DIFFICULTIES

The child who intereacts with you fleetingly can leave you feeling you are the world's most boring person or lead you to the conclusion that yours is a child who simply doesn't need your emotional involvement. Don't let yourself be convinced of either. Your child needs to interact with you, to play, to experiment, to explore and develop the dimensions of his personality, to build his self-esteem. You must make the extra effort to be innovative and original in attracting and keeping his attention. You needn't dress up like a circus clown (although you certainly can if you want to); but you should provide little twists, small surprises to keep his interest alive. Take the example of the parent below.

Taylor would focus on his red ball and ignore his mother, glancing at her only occasionally. Taking advantage of this small window (a porthole?) of opportunity, Mommy would pick the red ball up and put it in front of her face. Taylor would then flash a mischievous grin and try to take the ball away from his mommy's face. When Mommy hid the ball partially from view, Taylor would search for it, and they would both laugh as he found it. Mommy had to make sure that she did not inadvertently frustrate him too much so that he would continue to find the game interesting. She also had to use this interest to generate some interaction between them. She helped Taylor sustain his emotional tone (curious and playful) in spite of Taylor's desire to disengage, by staying playful and relaxed and by not interfering when Taylor wanted to play with the red ball all by himself for a while.

In every case, parents who have the most success in communicating their nurturing messages to their babies do the following three things. They:

1. *Tune in* to what their baby is feeling at the moment.

2. *Respect and admire* (in words, gestures, and with their own feelings) what is being uniquely expressed—the special-ness of their infant.

3. *Try to sustain* the emotional connection between them.

At this stage your baby's emerging individuality is already the cornerstone of his self-esteem. Respecting his special needs, while helping him sustain his emotional tone in spite of his desire to be moody, is a trick you might wish on a magician. However, the more time you spend with your baby and the more "in sync" you become with each other, the easier it becomes to know what to do, when to do it, and how to set limits when necessary.

LIMIT SETTING

Pride and admiration for your baby's ability to communicate his range of emotional states does not imply the absence of limits. Although it is hard to think of imposing limits on an eight-month-old, at times it is helpful in connection with mood regulation and its effect on self-esteem.

An eight-month-old can sometimes overstimulate himself. He may get involved with so many things at once that he becomes frenetic and needs to be calmed down and focused. Should you see your baby begin throwing toys around or looking over-whelmed, pick him up, talk to him soothingly, and play together with one of the toys he was playing with before. This will give him the focus he is lacking and limit the overstimulation and disorganization he is experiencing. Another tactic to reestablish his sustained interest and positive emotional tone is by involving him in a vocal game. You can make certain sounds and then encourage him to imitate you.

Much to the point for this age also is limit setting for the eight-month-old who begins to behave in perfectly normal but unacceptable ways. She can now begin to understand the meaning and relationship between your shaking head and the tone of the words, "No, no! Don't do that!" Even though she may not pay attention too often, getting her used to the gesture "No" (shaking your head) and the vocal tone "No," together with all your "Yes's" and "That's terrific's," provides her with the basis for learning about limits through communication. You always have the option of picking your baby up and pulling her away from something you don't want her to do. But teaching her through words and gestures gives her a unique opportunity to learn the self-restraint that contributes to future self-esteem.

Stage Four:
The Complex Sense of Self
(9 to 18 Months)

Between the ages of nine and eighteen months, your child will discover what we call the "complex sense of self," a stage at which he learns to put the bits and pieces of his behavior together. Accordingly, if you show him the food you want him to eat in the morning, he may very well protest and point to another food he would rather eat. As he begins to make known his desires and preferences, encourage his creativity and pride in these newly emerging independent and imaginative endeavors.

Your toddler will begin to do things that will surprise you—things you haven't taught him. He now knows his own preference for either rough-and-tumble play or fine motor activities such as puzzles. He can present himself as an assertive child or a shy child. He also begins to identify roles. Your sixteen- to seventeen-month-old may put your shoes on and giggle—he knows he's imitating Mommy or Daddy. He may take a pretzel and fly it through the air like a butterfly or an airplane. And, like an airplane, your toddler is really "taking off" during this stage of development, learning about the unique little being he is.

FLOOR TIME

One of your goals during this stage is to build on your child's pleasure in being original. Try not only to respect his originality and creativity and the way he chooses to show it to you, but also to take him one step or even one-half step further. For example, you and your toddler are playing chase. After a while you can take it one step further by doubling back and surprising him. He will giggle and laugh and maybe double back on you. In a little pat-a-cake game, you can try a novelty like going from pat-a-cake on the hands to a little squeeze of the nose. The next time he may squeeze your nose and you can say, "Toot-toot" or "Boop-boop" and pretty soon he's got a human toy that he can make say, "Toot-toot" and "Boop-boop." Build on your toddler's original pattern by making it a little more complex and adding one more degree of spontaneous creativity.

At this stage, too, your toddler's motor development has reached new levels of sophistication. Her crawl or walk gets her where she wants to go. She can take a pencil or crayon and perhaps make some lines or circular markings. Her vocalizations encompass many different sounds, including some words. And, since your toddler now has control of all of her facial muscles and movement of her hands and arms, as well as the ability to crawl or walk, she is able to employ a whole array of gestures that tell you when she wants to be close—and how close—or when she's angry—and just how angry. You can now read her feelings of joy, assertiveness, curiosity, or adventurousness with much more certainty. Whether she is more interested in doing things with her fingers or in walking, more interested in vocalizing or in toys or in you, by building on her interests and respecting her initiative you'll be constructing a solid and satisfying relationship between you.

As your toddler progresses through this exciting stage, you may notice that your baby all of a sudden seems quite grown up. In part, it may be because he is beginning to rely on communicating across space. Let's say that he is playing with his blocks one day while you read the newspaper. When he looks at you and you say, "Hey, that's terrific!" he will continue to play with blocks, feeling enriched by your proud, admiring interest in him. You have just sent him a big symbolic hug and a kiss across the distance of a room and he's understood it, even if he doesn't yet understand the actual words. This is a big day in your toddler's emotional life. Now he doesn't have to be in actual physical contact with you in order to know you feel love, pride, and admiration for him. This ability to feel your joy even when not in your arms is an important step toward having a sense of worth and pride that comes from inside, like a little voice saying, "Good job." First he had to be in your arms, now he can feel you even from afar, and soon your pride will be inside him.

During this stage, it is important to provide your toddler with many opportunities to decipher your communications across space. Tell him and show him frequently, through gestures, how proud and interested you are in what he is doing. To reinforce a major source of self-esteem, show respect for his ingenuity, initiative, and individuality. He will be one big and important step closer to having a permanent internal sense of worth.

At the same time, understanding communication across space helps your child and you sustain emotional tone in a new way. You may recall that we talked about the importance of sustaining positive emotional tone over time. Now that tone can be sustained over space. This is how it might work.

Jamie, sixteen months, is playing with her colored plastic rings, stacking them and unstacking them on their pole, sometimes in order, sometimes not. Initially, Mother is in a chair a few feet away.

MOTHER: "Oh, Jamie. I like the way you're stacking those rings!"

JAMIE: (Makes an unintelligible comment, continues to stack)

MOTHER: "Yes, you can even talk and stack at the same time! Do you know that's a ring?"

JAMIE: (Says something sounding vaguely like "ring," holds one up and smiles at Mother)

MOTHER: "Jamie, that's super! That's a ring all right!"

JAMIE: (Bangs one ring on the floor for a bit, then picks another up and does the same)

MOTHER: (Stays silent for a moment, watching Jamie with a smile), . . . "Bang Bang!"

JAMIE: (Says her word for "ring" again)

MOTHER: "That's great! That's a ring. You're learning to say 'ring.' Isn't that wonderful?"

JAMIE: (Gives Mother a beatific smile, then begins to stack again)

Jamie's mother continued watching and tried to keep their little conversation going for a few seconds more each time. As Jamie returned to her toys, she was well aware of her mother's interest in observing her. Mother changed position every so often so that Jamie had the freedom to involve her in different ways. Sometimes she got right down on the floor next to her, other times she was 10 feet away on a chair, but Jamie now had a way of sustaining Mother's interest in her that did not require her running to Mother's side. Even when Jamie was not actively looking at Mother, she was still actively involved with her, knowing that Mother was interested and took pride in her and what she was doing.

These are golden moments, when you feel the "electricity" of communication between you and your toddler. He will not only respond to your involvement when he is playing with his toys, but he will delight in performing for you, imitating you, singing you a lullaby, feeding you with his spoon, and so forth. Your sustained, joyful involvement with each other is as necessary to your toddler's growing feeling of self-esteem as it is precious to both of you at that very moment.

DIFFICULTIES

Often parents like to shy away from the challenging aspects of their child's development, hoping these will "take care of themselves." True self-esteem and pride, however, don't come only from focusing on the things one does well naturally, they also come from meeting a challenge and developing new abilities, even when it requires hard work.

In the previous stage we talked about the minimal-contact child— one who may only give you a little look once in a while, seemingly content to do what he's doing. Frequently, parents don't become aware of the child's lack of pleasure in connecting with you until now. You will need to get down on the floor and let him involve you in his play. (For those children who are both active and in-attentive, look in the previous chapter at the little boy who had not learned to respond to his parents across space.) Show him how much you appreciate the way he likes to bang the blocks together or take the crayon in hand or the way he likes to crawl all over you. Any of these will give him the message that you are interested in him. Playing together will also give you opportunities to sustain vocal, eye-to-eye, and emotional contact.

Getting to this point may take you a few weeks of concentrated effort and much floor time. But once you can get some reliable contact and communication going between you, you can begin to help your child maintain this across space. Use your voice and gestures from short distances at first, then gradually increase the distance. When you lose contact, get closer again and reestablish; woo him, get him involved with you, then slowly try to sustain this interest as you move away again. Your baby needs this contact. In order for your child to develop self-esteem he must first feel involvement, pride, and admiration from you. Don't mistake his attitude for one of independence or rejection of you. Remember that his premature independence really can be a type of rejection; but it is a rejection of himself and his sense of self-worth rather than a rejection of you. True independence at this age can be attained with lots of joyful communication and pride from afar.

The child who is at your knee, pulling and clinging constantly, may also lack the self-esteem to survive a separation of 10 feet of space. She can only feel good when she is in your arms. Stifling as this may be for a parent, think of what it must be like for your toddler. As with the minimal-contact child, the clinging child needs patience and extra floor time in order to address her needs.

You'll probably need to begin with your toddler in your lap. Play together for a while. Then, let's say you have to cook a meal. Put a few of your pots on the floor beside you for your toddler to play with while you are cooking. At first, help him get going, then look down every five seconds and make comments like "Hey! That's terrific! We're cooking together!" Your baby can grab your leg whenever he wants to, but he can also copy you, cooking with you and enjoying your attention every five to ten seconds. Gradually, he'll work up to being able to tolerate being 10 feet away with attention every 20 to 30 seconds. Then, one day he will be cooking quite on his own and you will say, "Well, how's it going?" and he will mumble something which probably indicates he's cooking a better meal than you are. Teaching self-esteem across space may take some time, but the rewards are sweet.

Another type of difficulty which can present itself again at this stage has to do with the baby who operates at a normal, but slightly lower or higher muscle tone than others (see chapter VIII for more on this topic). The former may be slow to walk and seem loose in his muscles; the latter, overly tight in his muscles and somewhat clumsy. When something as fundamental as controlling your own body doesn't work well, it is a source of profound frustration. No amount of superficial praise will change a child's awareness that he can't make his arms and legs do what he wants to do. To him, just climbing stairs can feel like your walking a tightrope every day.

It is important to help your child improve his skills as early as possible. Parents who gloss over a difficulty to help their child save face are unintentionally contributing to the child's fundamental lack of self-esteem and frustration with his own sense of internal mastery.

A fifteen- or sixteen-month-old of this type, given extra practice using his large muscles, will soon enough be playing chase games. If this same toddler has to stop and start and change directions every time he chases you, his muscle tone will soon improve. As you work on these lesser abilities, however, you must also emphasize and build on your baby's strengths—perhaps fine motor coordination or speech is his forte. It's important for your child's self-esteem, as well as for other kinds of development, to be able to make his body do his bidding. By letting him know you admire what he does well while giving him extra practice in the areas that are slower, you are helping him master a developmental task that will make him more self-confident. Ignoring the areas that need extra practice does no good—it only creates a false sense of momentary worth. A baby knows what he can and cannot do and he appreciates help and extra practice as long as it's done with respect and pride.

Similarly, some children need extra support in the areas of focusing and concentrating. At the toddler stage, your child should be able to play with you or favorite toys for a few minutes at a time. Some toddlers, however, tend to be fleeting in their interest—a few seconds here, a few there. Mommy and Daddy feel grateful for five consecutive seconds of their child's attention. If this is the case in your home, recognize that "attending" is also an emerging ability that may require extra practice.

Like the child who finds emotional commitment difficult, the inattentive child needs to find activities that will help him learn to pay attention and concentrate his efforts. Sometimes you will have to combine attending activities with large muscle activities, such as jumping on your tummy while you make interesting gestures and vocalizations. (If you notice that he attends more to either your facial expressions or to gestures or words, use this movement to attract his attention the next time.) At other times you might give him a big hug or nice firm back rub while chitchatting with him. "Reading" a book together, encouraging his digressions about the pictures, such as pointing to the red ball, will get him involved. Remember, attention will not develop magically; it develops from pleasure in interacting, and is often manifested first in small steps as you and your toddler interact and "close circles." Each time you respond to each other there are a few seconds of shared attention strung together—first one, then two, then three of these sequences. Patience and a step-by-step approach works best.

All of the above difficulties have a cognitive component. Further examples of these difficulties are discussed in chapter VIII with more emphasis on the cognitive element.

LIMIT SETTING

Part of fostering self-esteem is to teach your toddler, by your use of words and gestures, how to deal with his feelings and actions appropriately. When your baby pushes his food off the table, sometimes you might catch the food and show him you are willing to play a game as you substitute a ball for the food. He will see that you respect his interest in learning about throwing things on the floor. At other times, however, you can tell him, "No, now is not the time to throw, but to eat." He will learn that on rare occasions food can lead to play, but at other times it's down to the serious business or special pleasures of eating.

You may be a bit leery about mixing responses, but children can abstract rules out of different contexts. Your child *can* learn it's okay to run and jump in the playroom, but to be more careful in the living room. Your baby can now begin to understand "Yes" and "No," as part of setting limits with voice and gesture through space. Feeling the security of your limits helps your toddler take pride in her own self-control and expansiveness.

By the end of this stage you and your baby will be able to practice—across space—three abilities crucial to the development of high self-esteem: sustaining positive and joyful emotional tone in spite of changing mood states (e.g., the block tower can fall without ruining the next hour's play); receiving special interest in his unique abilities (and perhaps some that aren't unique, but are his); and accepting limits.

Stage Five:
Emotional Ideas (18 to 30 Months)

We now come to what we call the level of emotional ideas. Your little child (for you are beginning to call her a child, not a toddler) is now able to picture herself and you in various interactions in her mind's eye. Her pretend play gives you some evidence of this: the doll for hugging now becomes the doll who fights, has a tea party, or goes on a trip. You can almost see the wheels turning as you watch the emotional ideas that guide her play. And, if you are really fine-tuned to your child's abilities, you'll notice that she is actually communicating not only across space, but across time as well. That is, you can be away and she can picture you (whom she hasn't seen in five minutes) in her mind's eye as though you were there, similar to an adult fantasy or daydream. She can even play out her daydream with her toys if she desires.

Her new ability to formulate ideas allows her the luxury and flexibility of replaying experiences for herself that have occurred in the past or in another setting. She can also create new experiences, original ones that are made up of pieces of what she has experienced before. The scary monsters or witches that she dreams are under the bed could be based on books or on television programs or movies, but they may also simply be your child's budding imagination. Now your pride and admiration become her inner image of an approving, loving, prideful Mom or Dad, which she can learn to create inside her when she wishes.

FLOOR TIME

In using floor time to help your child construct a positive self-image, your first challenge will be getting into your child's rhythm during pretend play and seeing how long you can be a play partner to her. Can you both last five minutes? Can you go for half an hour? On a good day can you play together for as much as an hour? How long can you thoroughly enjoy being part of the tea party, or being the assistant cook as your child fills her pots and pans with water? How are you at playing the monster the policeman must put into jail?

If you are like many parents, chances are you may tire of these activities before your child does, especially when she wants to repeat the same scene over and over again—sometimes without variation. Rote repetition will put anyone to sleep, but connecting emotionally with your child, sustaining the connection, and jointly adding to it is an enlivening and inspiring activity. Remember to focus on the relationship between the two of you as you act your roles.

An equally important and inspiring task for you at this stage is to discover your child's strengths. Keep asking yourself where your child's special or unique talents lie, what distinguishes her from other children. Any individual characteristic is a special talent in these early stages and needs your encouragement. For example, is your Sally great at playing tricks on people? Then it might be "Sally the Terrific Trickster." Is your Warren excellent at figuring out directions (he tells you where to turn the car to get to Aunt Sarah's even though he is behind in language)? He might be "Warren the Navigator." Or is your Margaret a great eater of candy? How about "Margaret the Best Eater in the Whole World"? Because you praise her doesn't mean you will give Margaret candy. She, being the great eater, may need to learn to eat broccoli. Don't think only along conventional lines—"Is my son big, coordinated, speaking, reading?" Instead, be original and find out what is original about your child.

Remember the rules for success change. In grade school, reading counts. In high school, there's more emphasis on math and science. In college, it's knowing how to develop ideas. And in one's career and family life, it's knowing how to solve problems and think on your feet. People don't change so much; it is the rules for success that change at different ages. One trait, however, is necessary at any age: a sense of your own uniqueness and originality. Therefore, parents need to enhance self-esteem by appreciating originality in their children.

DIFFICULTIES

Parents sometimes assume that children who are slow to talk can't engage in pretend play. For some children, slowness in talking is simply related to their difficulty in making certain sounds, getting their tongues into the right position. Your child may have a firm grasp on your words and may be excellent at manipulating dolls and at complex babbling. So, just as she communicates with you over the course of a day in her own special way, she will do the same with you in play. The best thing is to get down on the floor and help her communicate her "words." You can grasp her meaning through her play, sounds, and intonations. When possible, verbalize some of the ideas she has tried to say: "Oh, you want to put the *red* block on top?" or, "Oh, the dog is hiding in the house." Engage in two-way chitchat with her, trying to understand as best you can. This will give her extra practice in making herself understandable, in addition to showing her that you respect her creative ability and want to join in her play. On top of all that, it gives you the opportunity to tune into all the emotions she lays out during her various games: closeness, anger and competition, pleasure and excitement.

Another challenge is the child who has difficulty on the uptake. Children whose comprehension is a little slow have a receptive language problem, as we discussed in the previous chapter. Your request, "Please go get a fork and bring it to the table," may only bring partial results: he heads toward the fork but seems lost once he has reached it. You may impatiently say, "I said come back to the table," thinking he's being deliberately disobedient. In fact, he needs extra practice in figuring out what you have said.

Here, too, floor time and pretend play are excellent vehicles for learning to decipher complex instructions, questions, or comments. When your child is pushing her trucks along, you can wonder aloud whether the truck wants to go this way or that way. If she seems to ignore you, say something simpler like "I wonder if you want to pick the truck up and put it on my head?" She may giggle at the thought of the truck on your head, but through her reaction, you know that she has processed your remark. Besides making your head into a mountain for her truck, you can also make your hand into a tunnel, saying, "Do you want the tunnel here or there?" Your playful query may get a playful response (or sometimes an impatient one) that incorporates *your* comments. Make sure she answers your questions, even if you have to ask them six times, because every answer means she is taking in your words or gestures and getting practice in receptive language.

Often, the child who is a little slower on the uptake may have an enormous imagination. Not deciphering so much of what the world is saying to him, he may, as he is learning to create ideas, find it easier to communicate with himself; so he develops a rich imagination. We don't want to see his imagination develop only in relation to his own mind, however, like the person who says, "I have the most interesting conversations with my best friend— myself." We want him to develop his imagination in relation to you and to other people. Your practicing receptive language with him helps him to balance his considerable inner world with the outside world. Build on his special creative imagination, but always tie it to demands that he figure out what you are saying to him.

Besides doing this in play, you can do it in your normal conversations at dinnertime or bedtime. It will require lots of patience—finding different ways to repeat the same instructions, making your comments simpler and simpler until she gets it. For example, Dad asks Sally if she wants to sit next to him. She ignores him. He repeats his request gently in different words, adding on hand gestures until she either says, "No way!" or, "Okay." While he does not permit her to tune him out, he also lets her know that being close to him can be fun. Only patient, kind interaction of this sort will enable her to feel that her unique abilities are being respected and lead her to take pride in the fact that she can understand. If, for some reason she decides she can't understand, she will tune out and not only lose self-esteem at the moment, but low self-esteem will become engrained and prompt her to tune others out as well.

Some children, by the time they are two to three years old, let their parents know that "It won't be easy helping me feel positive about myself." Their own physical make-up may make it hard. They may be sensitive to either touch, sound, movement in space, or loud noises. They may process information slowly or have a hard time planning their movement patterns. For others, interactions with their parents may have been challenging earlier in life and now they already feel unsure of themselves. For still others, it is a combination of both these factors. But this time of life when ideas are first forming presents us with a wonderful "window of opportunity" vis-à-vis our most challenging young children.

The very cautious, sensitive child requires a patient, supportive environment where, during floor time, themes of assertiveness (good guys looking for bad guys or cars going from one place to another) are especially encouraged as they arise, and where overprotective or overly demanding family styles are replaced by warm, supportive "you can do it with extra practice" ones. Control over bathing, eating, dressing, and even picking out foods in the supermarket may need to be encouraged, so that the sensitive child can "take charge" rather than feel overwhelmed.

The angry, negative child will have often discouraged his parents from playful interaction because of his obstinacy—"Put the doll here!" "You did it wrong!"—and temper tantrums—"I don't want that cookie. It has a crack in it!" Here, the challenge is to balance firm limits with extra floor time and problem-solving time. (When demands become completely unrealistic, tolerate the inevitable crying without overreacting to it; after all, a child is entitled to cry if he is mad.) During the half hour of floor time, don't be put off by the child. You not only don't mind being told that "you are holding the teacup wrong," you welcome it. You play out the slave/master relationship as much as your child wants you to. That's what floor time is all about. During your chitchats, in addition to reviewing the day, you try to focus in on why everything is always "no" or "wrong." Perhaps months later your child will tell you of his emotional aches and pains.

Some excessively negative children have heightened sensitivities and therefore experience things with greater harshness than other children. Others are rebelling against overly controlling parents. In either case, broad limit setting and more involvement through floor time or chitchats often proves helpful.

The rejecting pseudo-independent child may require an approach which persuades him that his parents, and adults in general, can be joyful and esteem-enhancing, not overly controlling, undermining, competitive, or rejecting. Too much independence early in life, in terms of a lack of real joy with parents, is often a sign of a child's attempt to minimize his discomfort. Needless to say, this child may appear supercompetent. Teachers and friends may rave about him. But unless the joy of closeness is there, the glow of warm internal self-esteem may not be.

Here, it is very important to look at our family patterns. How do we nurture closeness and dependency? What is the family's attitude toward people's needs and neediness in general? Children require enormous acceptance of their needs while we teach them eventually to meet them themselves. Floor time with the very independent child often lets us see how the child deals with closeness: what happens when the baby doll is lonely, hungry, or unhappy? Extra floor time and wooing combined with an understanding of our own family dynamics lets us help the excessively independent young child.

At this age, the very anxious, clinging child who won't let Mom out of his sight presents yet another challenge to self-esteem as well as to his mother. Mother is struggling for some breathing room and little Johnny is spending all his energy keeping her suffocated. This need for closeness eclipses any opportunities Johnny has to master new experiences as a basis for positive self-esteem. To deal with this situation, parents need to be aware that some children require more practice in dealing with space. Because they find it hard to learn how to be close from afar, they are unable to gesture across space or picture a warm, smiling Mom inside their minds. Not surprisingly, they want to keep Mom in their sights.

First, parents need to take charge. Stop running or escaping. Each day have floor times of half an hour each to offer plenty of one-on-one pretend play. In the play, pay special attention to themes concerning closeness and distance, love and rejection. Help put these themes into words.

For example, Emily put all her dolls in one room. She never spread them out over the dollhouse. "One room only," Mother empathized. "Yes!" said Emily. "How come?" Emily didn't answer. "Oh," suggested Mom, "so they could always see each other and be close." Emily broke out into a broad grin. The next day, for the first time she began having the "big sister sleep in her own room." But as the play developed, it became clear that children could get "lost" also. Verbalization and empathy alone helped Emily *start* to become independent, but more was needed. Mother, realizing that Emily liked physical proximity, used floor time to experiment with "distance." Mother built on Emily's interest in talking (she was a terrific talker) by talking up close *and* far away. Sometimes Mother "made a trip" to get food for the pretend family and called Emily from across the room because she forgot what Emily wanted. In all talks during pretend time or in regular conversation, Mother made good eye contact, verbalized clearly, and made sure to use her hands and facial expressions to gesture carefully. Instead of trying to disappear so Emily wouldn't bother her, Mother gave Emily extra practice with being close from afar by talking and gesturing to her across space.

Emily was not only demanding about closeness with Mom; she was also demanding about staying up late, not picking up her toys, and more. Mother helped Emily learn to deal with these frustration by setting limits. No cartoons and other sanctions led Emily first to cry—which her mother tolerated—and then to begin cooperating. Emily's dad noticed that she was a great artist and he worked with her each evening (in addition to his floor time) over her drawings. She took great pride in what "Dad and me did."

Emily was still reluctant to take pride in going to school or playing at a friend's house, but the foundation was laid. She was experiencing more self-esteem and now seemed to want to master the next challenge, so Mother and Emily worked out a program where Emily let Mom leave her for increasing periods of time—first for 15 minutes, then for half an hour, one hour, and so forth. Pretty soon, Emily was beaming with "I want to play at Barbara's house."

By this stage, children are usually playing with each other. At first, they may play in parallel, just sitting next to each other. Frequently, however (and this can begin as early as nine or ten months), we see children playing interactively: sometimes they will giggle at one another or crash their cars together or take turns with a doll. Sometimes one child is more lively and the other seems to be victimized by his aggressor, or there are difficulties in getting a nice rhythm going between the two. If a parent stays on the floor, not too close but not too far, then when the going gets rough, or the children seem to ignore each other, the parent can help them cooperate more successfully.

There is nothing wrong with a parent/referee who rolls the ball to one child and then to the other, or who enters the game to make sure the cups in the tea party don't get thrown, or who plays the policeman who tells the trucks to go left or right. The key here is to notice patterns and encourage the more aggressive child to be more respectful of others, while encouraging the more cautious child to reach out a little and to jump into the game when needed. Be aware that in the play groups during this time of life, parents can't be off in a corner, chit-chatting. Your children need you to be a buffer and to teach them how to relate to one another. The best way to do this is by entering into the fun.

LIMIT SETTING

By the stage of emotional ideas, most parents are facing some tough questions as to the whens, wheres, and hows of limit setting. You may wonder, however, where limit setting and self-esteem intersect. During this stage you will see your child begin the struggle to internalize limits. How she begins to handle her natural aggression is a good example.

For healthy self-esteem, your child needs to know that when she gets angry and frustrated she won't go out of control and hurt anyone. If your child doesn't feel that you can help her control her anger and aggression, she will become frightened. If she is afraid that she can make the sun fall out of the sky, or a hurricane destroy the house, or can even hurt Mommy and Daddy whom she needs for security, she is going to start worrying. If she worries, she will begin to feel that she is a bad person because she might do these terrible things. If, instead of ignoring the problem or being overly punitive, Mommy and Daddy help her realize that she can control her angry feelings, she won't in fact do terrible things, even if she sometimes may feel like doing them. Little by little she learns the difference between a feeling, a desire, and actual behavior.

We all get angry—the angry feeling is fine. But its manifestation in pinching, biting, and hitting, for example, is not permitted. Your child can learn to feel pride in her ability to control anger. It is important for you to take advantage of learning opportunities which clearly present themselves as unacceptable behavior. When your child does something you want her to do, take advantage of it. Go eyeball-to-eyeball, use words and "No's." Explain to her why she can't do what she wants. As her vocabulary allows, engage in conversations. When this doesn't work, there are other methods.

Take twenty-eight-month-old Max, for example. He is a little older than Molly, who wanted to get Mother's lamp in an earlier discussion, but he's still got a lot to learn. Max is in his car seat. He spits at his four-year-old sister and won't stop even when told to with an emphatic "No" from Mommy in the driver's seat. He shouts "No" back at Mommy and continues to spit. Sister begins to cry. Mommy pulls the car over, ready for a "learning opportunity."

Mommy looks Max right in the eye. Max has now realized that Mommy has stopped the car and he isn't quite as much in control as he was while she was driving. As she looks him in the eye, she asks sternly, "What did I say?" Max, now looking a little pensive, pays attention. At this point, some of the defiance should evaporate because of the seriousness Mother is conveying to Max. Once the message has gotten across, she may try to empathize with what is making Max mad. Perhaps his car seat is too tight, perhaps he is feeling tired, the car ride may be boring, or perhaps he simply thinks this is a good time to get even with his sister whom he has been jealous of for a long time. Mother can show that she understands a little bit of how he feels by touching on some of the possibilities—big sister, the car, and so on. Max, if Mother happens to hit it right, will appreciate her empathy. He may nod his head "Yes." At the same time she is looking at him clearly and letting him know that what he is doing is not appropriate. She should be patient and try to get Max to acknowledge through a word, look, or head nod what she is saying.

Max has had a good learning opportunity because (1) he has seen that Mother takes it seriously, and he can't get the best of her just because she is driving the car; and (2) he sees that in spite of her annoyance at him she is concerned that perhaps he has reasons for his misbehavior. But even if Max has good reasons, it doesn't mean he can misbehave. There are other ways to communicate that the car seat is too tight or that he is mad at his sister.

Later that evening, Mother should have another talk with Max about spitting in the car. In susbsequent floor time, she can keep an eye out for play about sibling rivalry and help Max with this issue.

Of course, one can ask, "What if Max keeps spitting in the car?" In that case, Mother will have to make the best of the situation and use whatever limit-setting devices she can, including cartoon-watching restrictions or loss of a favorite toy, to control Max's behavior. But once at home, extra floor time, combined with the extra limit setting, should boost Max's learning experience.

In another example, two-year-old Bonnie struggles and cries until Mother lets her out of her stroller at the mall. Before unstrapping her, Mother tells Bonnie firmly that she must stay near. As soon as Bonnie's feet touch the ground, however, she's off and running, ignoring her mother's voice as she calls her back.

In the short run, Bonnie needs to be caught and put back in her stroller or held. In the long run, the agenda is teaching Bonnie to listen to and respect parental guidance. Often, children who lack this sort of respect show it in many ways, but their parents don't see it. For whatever reason, Bonnie's parents overlooked her impulsive and aggressive destruction of her toys at home. They only saw the crisis when their eyes were forced open.

Parents need to see the overall pattern and to begin moving in on non-crisis situations. Waiting until the crisis occurs, when the child who won't listen must be restrained for safety's sake, will never cure the problem. Bonnie will learn as long as Mom and Dad have resolved that they are willing to put in the time each day for however long it takes. If they don't assert their will, Bonnie knows that if she persists she will win. (There are times to give in or negotiate, to let up on your resolve, but this isn't one of them.)

The best learning occurs when parents are on their own turf. Your child will usually choose situations where she thinks she can win—supermarkets, shopping malls, or the car—to pick fights. Sometimes, parents can pull the car over and turn the child's turf into their own turf. But it is better yet to provide opportunities at home on your own turf for learning these lessons.

Here, as the mothers of Max and Molly did before, Mother can use a combination of words, strong gestures, and physical restraint to show her resolve. She has to make certain that the child really understands the issue and, therefore, pretend play and practice situations will carry the day.

Even when you feel strongly about setting certain limits, always encourage your child to voice his opinions. After you have heard him out, show respect and understanding for what he says, but stick to your guns and be extraordinarily firm if you must. Don't be fearful or intimidated by your child's temper.

A child who doesn't get his way may resort to a tantrum: yelling, screaming, thrashing around, kicking, and banging hands and head. There are many opinions as to how parents should deal with temper tantrums (see chapter III). As long as you protect your child from hurting himself, you, or the furniture, a temper tantrum is pretty good emotional and physical exercise. In the face of a tantrum, your resolve, firmness, and lack of intimidation are the tools that will teach your child to feel secure in his own ability to set limits.

When parents habitually use either brute force or isolation as a way of stopping their child's emotions, they rob her of the opportunity to learn to deal with her feelings in the heat of battle, face to face with another human being (see chapter III for a discussion of time-outs). The child who gets so out of control that she needs to be calmed down can be soothed by being held, or by being talked to in a calm voice, or simply sitting quietly in the same room as Mom or Dad. Proximity to other people allows her to see that her strong emotions don't scare and intimidate them and that her intense feelings are not so scary that she must be banished.

After the tantrum, try to reestablish normal relations, but give your child (and yourself, if need be) time. Make some gestures and wait for her to make gestures also. In terms of self-esteem, by staying "connected" before, during, and after the tantrum, your child can feel worthwhile even when she feels she has misbehaved or been out of control. In a way, you are showing her that self-worth and self-control can both increase together. This does not mean that there are no limits or sanctions for disruptive behavior. Maintaining connectedness and limits can go hand in hand. Wait awhile after a heated eyeball-to-eyeball confrontation, and then give it some floor time. This may give you and your child a chance to express the natural, but often upsetting, emotional struggle between you.

Again, the three components necessary for building a positive mood and self-esteem are in operation—this time at the level of emotional ideas. We've seen how to help your child sustain her emotional tone by becoming an involved play partner, how an admiring interest in your child's special abilities can help build self-esteem, and how limit setting can help your child feel proud of her growing ability to set limits for herself.

Now, you will see how your child can achieve the full bloom of self-esteem as he or she draws on your resources and their own during the next stage of emotional development.

Stage Six:
Emotional Thinking
(30 to 48 Months)

By internalizing your high regard for her, your child can learn to approach the world with optimism, curiosity, attentiveness, and a positive expectation of herself as well as others.

How can you help your child expand that sense of self-worth? Self-worth seems to be very closely related to whether your youngster feels that she is being valued for her uniqueness as opposed to your expectations for her. So our ability as parents to value, admire, and empathize with our children for what they are is critical. But at this stage, your child's ability to deal with frustration and loss are new skills that bring the quality of self-esteem into a more mature realm.

FLOOR TIME

As your child grows from two-and-one-half to three-and-one-half to four, you will see that many of his make-believe dramas have to do with predictable themes: closeness and dependency, assertiveness, anger and competition, and curiosity about everything, including sexual matters. And, although on one level he is struggling to reconcile himself, his feelings, and his behavior, it is still an exciting, joyous time in the life of your child—the perfect moment for you to rediscover the child in yourself.

Floor time or pretend play with your child doesn't mean that he should be looking and smiling at you all the time, but it does require a partnership that helps sustain the emotional tone of your relationship. Staying connected with your child during play, even through mood changes, enables him to feel the constancy of your involvement and your acceptance of a whole range of feeling.

Let's take an example. Sam, two and a half, and his daddy have been playing with his farm for the past ten minutes or so. The tone is playful and happy, with each taking an equal part. When Daddy begins putting some cows into the barn, however, Sam becomes upset.

SAM: (Raising voice) "No! Cows not in barn!"

DADDY: "I thought it was time to milk the cows."

SAM: "No, no." (Begins to cry) "No cows in the barn. You're bad!" (Yelling at Daddy)

This sort of interaction goes on for a few more minutes. Daddy, to his credit, remains calm and involved.

DADDY: (Picks up farmer doll, pretends to talk through him) "Oh, I'm sorry. I made a mistake. I guess I'll take those cows out of the barn."

SAM: (Slowly, but obviously feeling better, picks up another doll) "Okay, I'll help."

By maintaining calm and constant contact with your child over a period of time in which you encounter different (and sometimes difficult) emotions in pretend play, you are tuning into his rhythm and helping him realize that emotional tones can be sustained for lengths of time. In this way, you minimize emotional chaos. For example, a child who is angry for three seconds, happy for three, aggressive for three, then back and forth again until she is overwhelmed by her own inner turmoil often has a parent who either overreacts, doesn't get engaged in the first place, or withdraws easily.

For the three-second child, who has the tendency to shift from mood to mood in a chaotic way, it's important first to slow her down. "Hey," you can say. "You were just telling me what a nice Mommy I was. Now you are irritated with me already." "Well, you didn't do what I wanted," she may reply. Your simple acknowledgment that a shift in mood has taken place can help her realize that a change *has* occurred and also help her see what triggered it. You can then reestablish the first mood and try to sustain it for a longer period of time. By doing this, you can help the child who has difficulty maintaining any one emotion for a length of time sustain engagement and contact.

While you are making many judgments, you are never controlling—it is important to let your child be the boss. You have plenty of opportunity to be the boss when it comes to mealtimes, bedtime, and most other aspects of your child's daily schedule. During floor time, let your child be the director. To be sure, a few little wishes of yours may sneak in, but once you have tuned into whether your child likes best to play out themes of assertion and exploration (soldiers of fortune, searching games), socialization (school), nurturing (feeding dolly), or curiosity (doctor)—go along and enjoy it. Whatever the theme, your acceptance of your child's lead will give her the sense that her unique abilities are being respected and that she is a capable and trustworthy person.

If, after the twenty-third tea party in a row, you think you want to find an opportunity to broaden your child's interests and range, you will need to collaborate with her. You can begin by helping her to expand her dramas. At the twenty-fourth tea party you can suggest that one of the guests can invite the others to go for a trip down the Amazon, or as the monsters are fighting their endless war, you might suggest bringing some of the wounded to the hospital, or as the cars race around the track and crash into the wall during the 4,000th lap at the Indianapolis 500, you might wonder aloud if a car or two might need a pit stop to refuel or for some fine mechanical work. Making similar suggestions during play gives you a way to introduce a balance of activities that will satisfy gross and fine motor interests, pure competitive aggression, nurturing care, and so forth.

Some children play silently, expressing everything with action. You can add to the richness of your child's play by introducing vocalization: "Gee, I wonder what the policeman says when he's chasing the bad guy?" This gives your child practice in putting thoughts into words, an important step in helping him conceptualize emotions.

Common also is the child who is all words and no action. You might interject: "Seems like the policeman talks a lot. I wonder what he wants to do?" This is neither interfering nor taking away your child's prerogative to be the boss. You are starting from where your child is and, at the same time, broadening his base and range of interest. If you follow his emotional lead while adding your admiration for his individuality, he will show you a loving self, comfortable with an active role in the world.

Special themes on the ascendancy at this time have to do with power, curiosity, independence, and sensitivity to humiliation. Empathize with David's desire to be stronger than He-Man or Susan's desire to be more beautiful than She-Ra, and be careful how you tease.

DIFFICULTIES

Even at this young age we often see two types of children who are already experiencing problems with self-esteem: the child who is overly active, and the one who is despondent.

The overly active child is the one who shows the tendency to "rev" herself up. She exists in a state called "I'm terrific," through perpetual motion and agitation. By "stroking" herself, this child tries to supply her own self-esteem. She's trying to feel good inside by convincing herself that she's the srongest, best, most wonderful, and intelligent person in the world. She generally tends to show some volatility of mood—seeming alternately elated and deflated. Her job is a difficult one—she's like a tire with a hole in it that needs constant pumping up. Of course, your pediatrician should be consulted to make certain there are no physical reasons for her overactivity.

This pattern may become evident as early as the second year of life in a home where, for a variety of reasons, the child doesn't experience warmth from her loved ones, or, if the warmth is there, maybe Mommy's or Daddy's beaming admiration is missing. She may initially try to create a sense (a false sense) of well-being through sheer activity. At a later stage, she may turn boastful, or even provocative and nasty, which is her way of saying, "I'm queen here, and I can do whatever I want." She may also withdraw into herself, focusing only on what she wants. This type of child is likely to be labeled "selfish" when in fact she is trying vainly to provide herself with the self-esteem that she missed getting from her loved ones.

Picture someone who is frantically trying to deal with a terrible loss and trying, at the same time, to deny the loss. The child who feels empty inside tries to fill herself up in any way she can so that she can deny the terrifying absence of empathy from her loved ones at a time when love and caring are most essential to her. This does not necessarily mean that empathy has not been present in her parents. For some reason it may just not have reached her.

Helping such a child requires parents to do two things at once: First, slow the child down. Soothing, reassuring limits are important and sometimes stone hard—but never stone cold—limits are important. Second, establish the rapport and empathy that has been missing.

Here is how one family coped with their overly active three-year-old daughter. Michele was a very active, almost frenetic little girl who liked to play with her dolls. Her mother was a woman who was always very methodical, very controlled, and liked to do things very slowly. Father worked all day and often on weekends. His fantasy of an adoring and adorable little daughter was easier to maintain when he was out of the house. Michele reminded Mother of her sister, who was just like Michele in emotional tone. Her unresolved competition with her sister, coupled with Michele's tendency to overwhelm her, led Mother to prefer to be away from Michele. So when Michele was fourteen months old and playing frantically with her blocks to try to catch Mother's attention, Mother would read her newspaper and tune out.

This didn't lead Michele to become more independent; it led her to play with her toys at greater and greater speed, hoping to get from her dolls what she couldn't get from Mommy. She became more agitated, belligerent, and provocative with her mother. Her mother, needless to say, only felt more overwhelmed and withdrew from her even more. While Michele's mother loved her and was conscientious in terms of providing her with responsible daily care, they didn't experience much spontaneous emotional pleasure and joy together. Nor was her mother very comfortable setting limits. She would either leave the role of disciplinarian to

Michele's baffled father or sometimes, out of sheer frustration, punish Michele severely for minor infractions that were "the final straw."

Once the family decided to seek help, it was agreed that Mother needed to learn to soothe Michele and establish a mutually pleasurable relationship with her. She also needed to become comfortable with setting limits over small transgressions. Father would need to work on assuming a more active role in family life. Let's see how the first of these goals was accomplished.

First of all, mother and daughter needed activities that would connect them in pleasurable ways. It didn't take long to discover that Michele enjoyed having back rubs, loved playing chase, and delighted especially in Mother being her "horsy" and giving her rides around the living room. Mother decided she would do the latter (horsy rides) for a minute here and there as a special treat for Michele when she had been especially "good." At the same time, Michele and Mommy needed to find some common emotional ground where they could begin relating to each other. During initial floor times, Mother's main goal was simply to observe Michele and try to spot opportunities to play with her and admire what she did. Initially, she took the role of Michele's assistant, helping her do what she wanted. Pretty soon, Michele was directing complicated and fast-paced dramas. Mother was ordered to dress one doll, wash another, put yet another to sleep, and feed still another her Cheerios. Mother, a little overwhelmed by having to carry out all the instructions at once, reasoned it was better to do it in make-believe play than in real life.

As Mother tuned into Michele's intense and frenetic style, she began suggesting, "This doll is a little tired and wants to do things a little more slowly." At first Michele would say, "No, hurry up." After a few tries, they started to negotiate and eventually, over a period of weeks, they found the middle ground—Michele let Mother slow down a bit. By talking about letting the doll slow down, Michele was symbolically agreeing to let Mother slow down. Michele was now motivated toward agreement because Mother and daughter were in emotional contact, enjoying their play activities. And so, both Michele and Mother were willing to compromise enough to find a rhythm somewhere between the two of theirs that allowed both of them joy and pleasure.

Soon afterward, Michele was able to experience positive self-esteem in a new way. She was able to internalize an experience that she had had with her mother and connect it with her sense of self-worth. She no longer had to create pseudo-self-esteem, since now she knew the feeling of emotional connectedness and admiration in her relationship with a loved one. Her life was enriched in a new and most profound way by the type of experience we all too frequently take for granted.

There are many children who, almost from birth, walk to the beat of a different drum than their parents. Whether faster, slower, or just different, parents must realize that adults are the ones with more emotional flexibility and must look at their child's rhythm and pattern and say, "How do we tune in? How do we connect?" It's important to make the effort as soon as you spot potential difficulty. It's a lot easier at the three-year-old level than it will be when your child is seventeen or eighteen. Remember to do these things: help the child slow down; set limits, but also tune in and find those moments of pleasure and connectedness; then try to sustain these at an even level over increasing periods of time. Self-esteem is initially the esteem you feel from your closeness with another. The importance of pleasurable emotional interaction cannot be overestimated.

Another example of the child who lacks self-esteem is one who seems sad and despondent a good deal of the time. This child is a different challenge from the overly active child we've described. The sad and despondent child may be one whose troubles began as far back as Stage Two, between three and seven months. Most babies begin to show a vital interest in and preference for the human world. However, occasionally one pulls away from the world of feelings in relation to some challenge he felt he couldn't meet and is left with emptiness. The despondent child needs to go back to what he missed at that all-important stage. He may need to be convinced of the benefits of having a relationship with other human beings.

Parents will now need to find the right way to woo their child in order to get him to see the enjoyment of other people. Once this has been achieved, the child will still need to be helped through the other stages of the development of self-esteem that he has missed. Chances are that his hunger for this emotional knowledge and the positive feelings it brings will make his forward journey a rapid one.

One very bright three-and-one-half-year-old looked very sad, always focusing his eyes downward. He seemed tired, and was never interested in doing anything except watching TV. Mother was concerned that he might be "depressed." Father was busy with his work and avoided his son as well as his wife. It was a sad family. Trying to help Mom and Dad woo Brad into a state of pleasurable engagement would be no easy task. After an evaluation, however, it emerged that Dad was as scared of his competent little boy as he had been of a "competitive" younger brother. Interestingly, now involved in floor time, the father saw he had good reason to be concerned with his son's anger. Brad played out shooting scenes where he killed his dad, the "bad crook," in at least two different ways. And when not being killed, Dad was a "dark horse." Also during this floor time (at least half an hour per day), Brad and his father enjoyed islands of joyful electricity that over time co-alesced into a bright, happier Brad.

Simultaneously, Father saw that he had withdrawn from Mom, feeling "she has a son now and doesn't need me." But she desperately did need him. And when he became more involved with Mom, she had more energy for Brad, so she, too, engaged in floor time. Brad treated Mom more kindly, having her play the part of a "messy kid" who needed to be controlled.

As such a little boy begins to feel understanding from his parents, he will begin to show the angry side of his sadness and despondency. He may, for example, start to tear his dolls' arms and legs off or behave provocatively with Mommy and Daddy. It is as though he's making up for lost time. Parents need to be aware that some of the anger may be over the previous absence of close-ness and contact. He's finally protesting something that would have been easier to deal with when he was much younger—but better late than never.

Now that he had his parents' interest, Brad would take his

aggression one step further and yell into their ears, punch, and hit. His parents needed to set firm limits on this behavior, but not without empathizing and understanding that Brad had reasons for his anger.

Helping Brad called for two measures. First, empathize: the empathy lets the child see that his feelings are accepted and can prompt him to articulate them further. As an example, if you say, "Boy, are these dolls angry! They must have good reasons," perhaps a story will evolve. One doll may leave another doll or make fun of one.

At the same time, provide security and structure for him in the form of rules: things can't be broken or hurt beyond repair (assuming the dolls' arms and legs can be put back) and people can't be hurt.

Once you see more aggression in the story, your child may become more demanding and more provocative in his interactions with you. While limiting any hitting or biting, try to empathize with the child's wish for you to carry out commands quickly and efficiently. Setting limits helps the child to feel in control so he doesn't become frightened of his aggression.

When the passive and compliant child beings to argue and be feisty, he needs admiration for his debating ability, for his new assertiveness. Take pride and listen to why he feels that things are unfair. You can still maintain fair standards if sometimes you let him get his way, while at others you rule. Expect a temper tantrum or two—don't be shocked by the changing nature of your child, appreciate it. Be firm with broad limits, but within those limits respect the increased resistance. In time, your child will find a happier balance between his former, more passive style and the new, more active one that's emerging. By holding the ship on its course in spite of storms that might brew and blow, you will reach your proper destination.

Another type of sad child is exemplified by Robert. Robert was sad-looking, wearing a big frown on his face. And he was also very negative. "No" was his favorite word and he did not like to do anything except eat sweets (which his parents limited) or watch cartoons on TV. Even when his dad offered to throw a ball or play a game, the answer was, "Don't feel like it." Robert always avoided new things as well. He would play with a new child or try a new puzzle, but certainly not a new food. He often also seemed inattentive. Mother had to ask him to do things three or four times before he even shook his head, "No."

Mom was a tense person who worried a lot and, sensing Robert's difficulties, tried to do things for him. Dad quickly became impatient with Robert and ordered him around, but when Robert would cry and then avoid the task by going back to what he was doing, Dad often didn't follow through.

In an evaluation, it was discovered that Robert had a slight difficulty with receptive language. He could follow simple instructions, but had a hard time holding in mind two or three things he had just heard. He also had a slight lag in his ability to plan complex movement patterns like tying his shoes or drawing squares and triangles. Caught between Mother's desire to overprotect and Dad's tendency to order but not follow through, Robert exaggerated the natural tendency of children with lags—avoid at all costs the tasks that are difficult. Unfortunately for Robert that meant avoiding a lot of the fun and joy of life, including talking and finding new friends and games. Down deep, when a child avoids, he invariably feels badly about himself.

Robert needed attention to each of his needs: extra practice with closing circles, and "conversations" to help him with taking in information. For example, if Robert's preschool teacher said, "Hello," and Robert ignored her, she would follow up (for as long as needed) with "Robert, don't you want to say hello? Oh, I guess you don't feel like it, huh," and so forth. Robert could respond in any manner, even, "I won't say good morning," or, "Don't talk to me," as long as he acknowledged what was said to him. In this way he closed his circles and practiced taking in information. Because it was easier for him just to listen to his own thoughts, we had to make it fun for him to concentrate on others.

Extra practice with games that involved motor patterns, such as "Simon Says," playing the drums, and drawing games, were also helpful. Robert had a great sense of humor and liked to "trick people." This became a source of family pride—"Robert the Trickster."

SELF-ESTEEM IS INTERNAL

Many parents feel, with some cause, that self-esteem is best enhanced when their children are like other children and are valued by their peers. By not being different, they reason, children will feel accepted and feel good about themselves. The same holds for whether their children are well groomed or are involved in the same activities as other children, such as dancing or singing. For many parents, the desire to have their children be and feel like other children is at the heart of their confidence-building goals for their child. This is a natural desire for parents to have and, for the most part, one that works out quite well.

Occasionally, however, in focusing on this external aspect of self-esteem, parents may miss what can be a more significant aspect of the child's self-esteem, which is how the child feels about herself in a deeper way, inside. A child certainly feels good about being accepted and involved in activities with peers. But this won't make up for a child who, inside, feels that she is a bad person because she feels angry at Mommy or Daddy. It won't make up for the child who feels unsure of herself because she can't control her movements.

Unfortunately, focusing on the outside sources of self-esteem too often takes our attention away from the inside sources—the harmony within ourselves. When harmony with the self is achieved, the external aspects serve to heighten our internal world of self-esteem. But it won't work the other way around.

Take the example of James. James was desperately upset. He was gloomy and often angry with himself. At the age of four-and-one-half, he would hit his head with his hand when he made a mistake. He often got into accidents that were clearly within his control to avoid. Sometimes he would say, "I am a bad person." This little child, who had the admiration of his teachers and was popular among his friends, was a bafflement to his parents. Why didn't he have a better self-image?

When a friend suggested that James might need to talk about his feelings, however, his parents were reluctant. They feared that seeing a therapist might make him feel different from his peers and would create a stigma that would further cripple his self-esteem. For the outward appearance of conformity, they were willing to sacrifice their son's internal harmony and the opportunity to understand why his self-esteem was so low. When eventually they began to understand the importance of James's feeling, they agreed to a few consultations.

James's main problem was a heightened case of jealousy of his new little brother. He extended this envy to his classmates who could do things only half as well as he could. He saw all his successes at school as meaningless and negative—"I was the leader, but only because Justin wasn't there." He was convinced he was really a bad person inside. Once his feeling were out, he soon became more relaxed about the jealous side of his nature, and he learned he could allow conflicting feelings to co-exist. When his feelings got to know each other, he felt better about himself.

An older child said to me recently, "When I feel jealous it makes me feel weird inside." She felt she was supposed to admire the accomplishments of her peers. Feeling jealous or envious was "weird" because it wasn't supposed to be a part of her. Another child identified his feelings toward peers as "fiendish." He had a side of him that was like an "angel" and another side of him that was like a "fiend." He felt terrible about himself, which led him to act provocatively when he couldn't work out a way for the two sides of his nature to operate together. His problem was, in part, that when he was "angelic" he didn't want to acknowledge the "fiend" inside; and when he was feeling "fiendish" he couldn't acknowledge the "angelic" part of him.

Internal harmony and outside relationships and events are both critical sources of self-esteem, but if a child's internal feelings are discordant, she can misinterpret even good outside experiences. A sensitive balance must be struck to allow a child's inner harmony to permeate and strengthen her role in the outside world.

LIMIT SETTING

With children between three and a half and four and a half, the importance of limits cannot be underestimated. Invoking limits concerning stubbornness, negativism, or outright aggression toward a peer are obvious. A more subtle set of limits may become necessary, however, particularly with the youngster who is being sneaky and, at the same time, may feel negative about herself inside. Sometimes a child may be secretly taking money from Daddy's wallet, or deliberately hiding his younger brother's toys or, when no one is looking, even stealing things. This more secret kind of aggression is often hard to discover and not readily acknowledged in the family. When parents become aware of it, they wish to look the other way because they're scared by the sneakiness and because they don't know what to do with it. Since their child is good at school, they feel that maybe they can ignore the little transgressions at home. But the child who is acting out his anger doesn't feel good about his behavior—he's living in two worlds. He may feel relieved momentarily after discharging his anger, but at the same time the mischievous deed itself contributes to his low self-esteem later.

It is very important to tease these transgressions out into the open at home through some long and serious conversations, conversations in which you allow him to explain his point of view with empathy and respect from you, coupled with your conviction that he has to find other ways to deal with his problem.

First, during these conversations tell your child that you know what he's been up to. As he looks embarrassed or tries to change the subject, focus in on the issues, ferreting out from him the basis for his behavior—his jealousy of his brother, for example—and giving him firm limits including sanctions (no TV, loss of a favorite toy, earlier bedtime, or other punishments that will have meaning for him). Try not to weigh in on one or another side of this equation. Empathy alone won't do the trick if he feels there are no external limits on his behavior. Impressing external limits alone (the long lecture without letting him talk, without trying to understand the reasons for his behavior) will not suffice either. Don't drop the issue until it's resolved, even though it may take weeks to discuss in bits and pieces.

In the meantime, if, say, jealousy is the basic problem, mount a sincere effort to make things more equal around the house by giving the child more floor time or play time. Simultaneously, limits will help him realize that he must find a different way to deal with his angry feelings. Your willingness to listen during your extra time together gives him a way to do this.

Gentle but firm limits will increase your child's security and help him internalize a sense of appropriate behavior. Such limit setting is important during this stage for maintaining self-esteem.

Early in infancy, babies act as though they have an endless capacity to be filled up. "Give me more and more," they seem to say. And to some extent, our ability to read our infants' needs and help them play, eat, or sleep has a major role in their state of bliss. But as our infants and toddlers become highly intentional, gesturing powers to be reckoned with, their self-worth is very much related to what they can do for themselves. Now their pride is not only in their first steps, but in figuring out games or being the boss in floor time. And by the preschool years, self-esteem is enhanced by the expansion of what they can do for themselves—dressing, grooming, toilet training, and the like. Self-esteem now centers on a new ability to think about an increasing range of feelings (closeness, assertion, excitement) and about the needs of others. Bouts of empathy enhance self-esteem even in preschoolers.

The sad child who feels bad about himself is easy to recognize. Less obvious is the tyrant who holds on to the "fill me up notion" or the self-absorbed person who never progresses to concerns for others. They may not seem to lack self-esteem but, in fact, are quite limited in this development. In many respects, they reflect problems of the early developmental stages of self-esteem.

Parents can help enormously by recognizing that self-esteem, like other abilities, develops in stages and requires helping every child to use his or her unique characteristics to enjoy and master each of their developmental opportunities.

V

Sexuality, Pleasure, and Excitement

Freud astonished the world at the turn of the century—not all that long ago—when he announced his discovery that children experience sexual feelings and fantasies. The Victorian era, ill-equipped to deal with such a revelation, reacted immediately with suspicion and disbelief. Unfortunately, the fundamental misunderstanding that greeted Freud's assertions has taken many years to dissipate.

Freud did not believe that children experience sexual feelings in the same way adults do. What he understood was that children are interested in bodies, find different kinds of excitement in exploring them, and that the unfolding of a child's bodily interests becomes incorporated later into adult forms of sexual pleasure and excitement.

Once this premise was accepted and supported by direct observation of infants and children, the questions began—and may never stop. When do babies become interested in their bodies? What parts of their bodies? What's normal in terms of children touching their bodies? When do they get too excited? When do children learn about sex differences? Anatomical differences? When is the sense of gender well established? When is it appropriate for parents to begin educating children about sex and reproduction?

These are just a handful of the questions that are of enormous interest to parents, educators, and clinicians.

Then there is, most importantly, the question that parents ask themselves continually: "How will I ever deal with all of this?" Observations of infants and young children have provided a vital new understanding of the sequence of sexual development, as well as the development of a child's sense of his own interest in and excitement about his body. And along with this new information come potential guidelines for parents on a variety of issues that have confused, concerned, and bewildered in the past.

Life's sexual journey is no longer an uneasy trip through uncharted waters. We're not promising you a Caribbean cruise either, but with patience, interest, and humor, you'll see your child develop a healthy, appreciative, and pleasurable enjoyment of his body that will form the basis for curiosity and interest in the world and satisfying relationships.

Stage One:
Regulation and Interest in the World
(0 to 3 Months)

There have been pictures taken inside the womb showing infants sucking away on fingers and thumbs. So, right from birth, your newborn is ready to develop a sense of pleasure. Early on, the infant will show you that she takes in the world of sensation through her body, by touching and being touched, and particularly through her mouth.

From the first days and weeks of life, your infant's control over her mouth, as seen in her sucking ability, is one of the most developed. This ability is important for survival. Because the nerve endings around her lips are very dense and are a source of special pleasure, your baby sucks, and enjoys the rhythmic movements of the mouth. A special pleasure and comfort may even be found in thumb sucking. So, by using her innate ability, her accomplishment is fourfold: contact with the world, pleasure, comfort, and survival. Her mouth becomes a natural and delicious focus for her very first pleasures.

As with all special capacities, there is also enormous variation in how infants suck. Some want to suck almost continually, either for the sheer joy of it or because it helps relax them or eases the discomfort of a gas bubble. Some infants will suck intensely, while others are more delicate. There are also infants who have difficulty learning to suck. Sometimes this is part of a pattern of difficulties in regulating the motor (muscle) system. Extra practice, patience, and, when appropriate, asking your pediatrician for a referral for guidance, may make a difference.

Although the comfort, pleasure, and nourishment your infant gets orally may be of prime interest to her, her other senses begin to participate in the development of her pleasure as well. Enjoying touch is not only an important source of pleasure, it also seems to play a role in helping infants grow. Similarly, the availability of different visual patterns is important for proper development, as are sounds, smells, and movements. Early on, you will be able to see your baby experience different kinds of pleasure in all the senses. You will soon find the activities that bring out the coos, warm gurgles, and smiles, as well as the types of touch, sound, movement, or visual experience that are more difficult for your baby to enjoy. So, perhaps the best way to think about pleasure is in terms of your baby's entire sensory system.

Stage Two: *Falling in Love (3 to 7 Months)*

As your baby moves into the second stage of developing pleasure, he will be able to experience distinctly human pleasures associated with Mommy, Daddy, or another caregiver. He now recognizes that Mommy and Daddy are much more interesting than toys. Baby will know the differences in skin texture as he feels another against him. He will learn to smell the differences between people, as well as hear the differences in their voices and see the differences as his visual capacities emerge. He is learning rapidly to distinguish between what is human and what is not.

All these new abilities and sensitivities taken together create a second stage in pleasure which may be called the "Pleasurable

Other." Once baby recognizes the existence of a separate person, pleasurable experiences can be created in tandem. Your baby probably cannot yet distinguish how these experiences occur, but he clearly senses the union of himself and Mommy, or himself and Daddy, or himself and Grandma, and experiences pleasurable sensations of touch, soothing rhythmic sucking, familiar sounds and smells, and exciting motion. And if the baby is often in the company of a loving and involved caregiver, he will more easily distinguish this level of experience from the simple sensory pleasures derived from playing with rattles.

FLOOR TIME

It is unlikely that the baby can distinguish between the parts of his body yet, meaning that he cannot tell whether he is experiencing pleasure with his hands, nose, or mouth. It is more likely that he experiences global sensations of pleasure having to do, broadly, with human contact. So, contact with the human world—or what has been labeled "bonding and attachment"—is pleasurable. Thus the basic belief that human contact is pleasurable becomes instilled in the baby—and this essential belief will germinate with proper care.

During this stage, it is particularly important for you to explore different kinds of pleasure with your infant. Are the soles of his feet more sensitive to pleasurable touch than his arms? Does tickling the backs of his knees make him giggle? Does he enjoy being touched firmly more than lightly? What is the best water temperature for his bath? Does he like to get into the water quickly or slowly? All of these activities help him explore a variety of life's pleasures. Now that your baby relates much of these pleasures to human contact with you, you can help him enhance his "falling in love" by ensuring the depth, range, and security of the pleasure he experiences.

DIFFICULTIES

Chances are excellent that your baby will be more than ready to be your partner in the exploration of pleasure. But, strange as it may seem, it is often parents who begin to back off when the safari is about to begin. Worries creep in. "Will I hurt my baby? Will he reject me? Will I overstimulate him?" Sometimes a parent's own anxiety about experiencing "too much" pleasure may interfere. In these and other cases, a little self-exploration will help you to guide your baby on his pleasure journey.

However, sometimes it's the baby, rather than the parents, who hesitates to explore pleasure. Indeed, some babies seem to *reject* sensory pleasure. When you pick them up, they squirm; when you coo, they grimace. Often, they are sensitive in only one way that dominates their reactions to all pleasurable experiences. When this happens, the fundamental basis of the human relationship, pleasure in others, may be difficult to establish.

For such a baby, parents must be acutely sensitive to the frequency and type of stimulation their young one can tolerate. He will have to be brought slowly and patiently along until he is convinced that the river of human emotion, relationships, and pleasure is worth wading into.

Stage Three:
Purposeful Communication
(4 to 10 Months)

During this next stage of emotional development, your baby learns that she is an active little being who can make things happen. You will see this as she explores her own body, getting to know the difference between her mouth, her toes, and her tummy. She will also begin to realize that she is separate from Mommy and Daddy and will use this discovery to elicit certain behaviors from you. And once she is able to reach out and hold onto things, she will have even more control over the different kinds of pleasurable interactions you share. Go right along. Your young offspring will become quite a purposeful pleasure seeker, a development that will give you great pleasure as well.

FLOOR TIME

Young Helen, for example, loved to be held firmly. To accomplish this, she learned how to nuzzle into the right position and vocalize loudly until Mother got it just right. Mother soon realized exactly what Helen was after when she signaled in that particular way. And Helen was not only pleased, but satisfied to know that she could use both her body and her voice to get what she wanted.

Stevie liked to have his legs pumped in a bicycling motion while he lay on his back; he also liked to have the soles of his feet rubbed a little bit. He guided his parents to these pleasures by holding onto their fingers and smiling brightly. He frowned and withdrew his feet when they tried to play "This Little Piggy Went to Market." But when they stroked the bottoms of his feet, he giggled, gurgled, and cooed. His parents couldn't help but feel pleasure in Stevie's obvious excitement.

Martha used her mouth for both pleasure and exploration. She wanted to put everything into her mouth, including the parts of her parents she explored—noses, cheeks, foreheads. In fact, whenever her parents picked her up, she would assertively explore their different parts with her mouth. There was no question that she was experiencing a major source of pleasure, as well as satisfying her curiosity.

As your baby gets to know her body, you will probably notice her using it to bring pleasure to herself. This is the beginning of self-stimulation. Some call it the beginning of masturbation, using the term broadly to refer to any kind of self-stimulation. (The narrow definition of "masturbation" would involve playing only with the genital areas.)

Although some babies begin earlier, you will probably see your eight- or nine-month-old fingering her hair (or rubbing her "fuzz"), trying to get her feet into her mouth to suck her toes, or beginning to play with her clitoris. You will also see that there is a certain intentionality and focus to her exploration of her favorite body parts. As you watch your baby take an interest in her own body, be aware that it is a perfectly natural part of this latest developmental milestone—intentional communication.

DIFFICULTIES

Intentional communication, of course, occurs not only between your child and her own body. There is a whole world out there to take pleasure in and communicate with. With so many options, a baby need not become fixated on just one pleasure. If self-stimulation becomes highly repetitive and seems to interfere with intentional communication with others (the baby who twirls her hair and refuses to share a glance), it is time to offer "better" alternatives. Let the baby play with *your* hair, or find games, such as "Peek-a-Boo," that are more fun than self-stimulation.

Witness James. James's mother would take his hand away from his penis all the time, but James would put it right back. When she tried to tighten his diaper, he seemed to be able to get his hand inside anyway. Mother was perplexed and didn't know what to do.

All kinds of curiosity about the body are natural, and babies have preferences for different body parts at different times. However, if your baby's preoccupation with himself seems consistently greater than his interest in others—particularly Mommy or Daddy—the most effective remedy is to give him something that is better. A baby will almost always prefer to interact with someone than to be alone, although most like a balance. So, when the balance seems to tip too much toward solitude, introduce yourself as a better play object. Your nose, your fingers, or your toes will probably be far more interesting to your baby than even his own genitals at this age. Give him the opportunity to find out. You can also use such time to start your baby's verbal education (even though he can't yet speak). A "name the parts of the body" game will satisfy both objectives.

Sometimes, a baby becomes preoccupied with her own body because she doesn't have enough access to her mommy, daddy, or other loved ones in a truly intimate way. Or maybe play activities lack the emotional freedom, range, and pleasure that she seeks. Self-stimulation may represent her attempt to bring a certain needed level of excitement to her own body. For such a baby, games which imitate the self-stimulatory activity are an effective means of initiating interaction: for example, a baby who seems to rock and move herself a lot may crave movement; accordingly, she may enjoy games in which Mom or Dad moves her in space or becomes a human trampoline.

Parents who are confused about what is appropriate and what is not sometimes ask for hard and fast rules. There are none. There is no perfect answer to the question of "appropriateness." What there is, however, is a broad range of normal patterns (depending to a large extent on how a particular baby experiences her own sensations) with one important principle to remember: Babies need to have a *balance* between interest in themselves and interest in others. This balance should be expressed in terms of pleasure and excitation as well as curiosity, assertiveness, and anger. Even at this tender age, all of the emotions exist in your baby. So, if her predominant pleasures are self-directed, it becomes your task to sell her on the human world—on you.

Let's return to little James. As he lay on his back, intent on getting his hand into his diaper, Mother realized that just pulling his hand away wasn't working. So she decided to try another tactic; leaning over James, she offered her finger for examination. "How about playing with my finger a little, too?" Mother wiggled her finger, pointed out the polished nail, and gave James a tickle. James was soon grabbing for her finger and smiling as Mother tried to wiggle it out of his grasp. From there, it was easy to pick him up and continue body-part exploration, with the focus on Mother this time.

Frequent floor-time sessions like this, with the gradual introduction of textured toys to feel, music to move to, and safe objects to touch and smell, broadened James's pleasurable interests to include a wide range of experiences. Mother's presence and her active involvement, including plenty of hugs and nuzzles, helped him experience his pleasure and excitement in the context of a relationship with another human being. He didn't have to rely solely upon himself any more. James still loved to play with his penis, but now he loved to do many other things too.

It's probably worth a reminder here that different parts of the body are endowed with different types and densities of nerve endings, and therefore babies experience more pleasure in certain parts of their bodies than others. Your infant experiences mouth sensations differently than she does tummy stroking, for example. Similarly, the genital areas are different from the legs.

But biology alone does not explain your baby's tendency to prefer certain bodily sensations to others. Your baby is now an interactive being and, as such, is sensitive to what is jointly pleasurable to herself and to her caregivers. By eight or nine months, your child's definition of pleasure and excitement will include what you find pleasurable and exciting together. Thus, the baby's own tendencies are coupled with Mommy's or Daddy's interests.

For example, Mother enjoyed playing with feet. She had had her feet played with since she was a little baby and she thoroughly loved doing the same for little Teddy. She took such delight in his toes and feet that this became his favorite area, too.

In another family, Harry had wonderful long hands which reminded his mother of her uncle who was a famous artist. Mother played with his fingers and told him how beautiful they were and that he too would become a great artist. Pretty soon, Harry began looking at his fingers, playing little games with them, and sucking each of them separately, rather than his whole fist, as most babies do.

Stage Four:
The Complex Sense of Self
(9 to 18 Months)

As he comes to understand the interrelationship of his emotions during this stage, your baby will also begin to know how his arms and legs and tummy and belly button and genitals and mouth all work together as parts of a whole under his control. And as his self-knowledge becomes more sophisticated, your baby will begin to realize that *your* body is a whole entity.

When he was younger, if his mouth experienced pleasure, it was his mouth alone, or his mouth as part of a global body that did not differentiate other parts. There was no sense of his mouth as one of many parts of a whole "me." Now he relates his sensations to a conception of himself as an entity that experiences sensation.

Thus sucking is no longer an isolated act committed by the mouth, but something that contributes to the pleasure of "me." Similarly, if your child experiences pleasure by stroking his genitals, it's also "me" sensing that pleasure. Should your child bang his head on the floor, he is experiencing that banging as "me." What were separate or global experiences of pleasure before, now become organized into a pleasurable "me." This pleasurable "me," however, is still the "me" of sensation and behavior ("I am what I do"). Later on it will become a "me" at the level of symbols or ideas ("I am what I think").

Stage Four may be called "The Stage of the Pleasurable Me and the Pleasurable You," because your baby also experiences Mommy, Daddy, Grandma, and Grandpa as whole people. All the separate pleasures—talking, playing "Pat-a-Cake," being bathed, rubbed, massaged, and hugged—are now experienced as parts of being, and being with, a whole person.

FLOOR TIME

His new ability to "put the pieces together" allows your baby to pursue his pleasures in a much more organized way. Now, he creates larger patterns of behavior by combining his newfound sense of self with interaction. He will soon be able to enter into more complex configurations, like those of the two babies below.

Sixteen-month-old Robert developed an impressive bedtime ritual. Mommy had to rub each toe, massage each leg, give a tummy rub, a back rub, and then a face massage followed by a hug and back rub until Robert fell asleep. If Mommy missed any bit of the sequence, Robert would be quick to point to the missed part of his body and squawk, his way of saying "More." In order to do this, Robert had to have a clear and specific picture of how his whole body worked as a unit and a knowledge of each specific part.

Jessica's bedtime pattern was different, but just as complex. She would have the same story about a horse read to her each night (even though she only understood a few of the words), followed by a horsy game on Daddy's knees, a jump on his tummy, a pull of his nose, then a big hug and kiss. She, too, would point out anything that was missed in the sequence, and would insist that each activity be done in order. If she were tired and wanted to go to bed she would, at seventeen-and-one-half months old, jump on Daddy's lap to start the routine.

During this stage, the ability to "put the pieces together" also helps your baby formulate a sense of his gender. He is learning the difference between boys and girls in terms of body parts and, chances are, if you watch his way of joking around and his imitative play, you will see a pattern—a boylike pattern—emerge. So, at eighteen months your boy is likely to dress up in a cowboy outfit with a gun and cowboy hat more often than he dresses in Mommy's clothing, though he will do that, too. Children naturally experiment with opposites, but when all is said and done, boys seem to have a sense of those behaviors and attitudes that are more boylike, and girls seem to have a sense of those attitudes and behaviors that are more girl-like. Precociously verbal children will be able to label their body parts, with special interest in their sexual parts. Less verbal children give the impression that they have some understanding of gender by the way they react to each parent, by their gestures, and by the sense they have of themselves, as well as by the kinds of games they choose to play.

How your child will develop his sense of gender is a complex matter having to do with his biological endowment, physical development, and experiences. Perhaps most important is how you and other caregivers interact with your child. *Vive la différence* has never had a stronger meaning than it does now. While begun earlier, it is during the toddler stage that Mommies and Daddies react to their boys and girls in a more distinctly boy- and girl-like fashion. This hardly requires special effort, as you may already know. Parents tend to reactivate their own early learning of gender in a natural, spontaneous way to help their little boys and girls find their own sense of gender.

DIFFICULTIES

Occasionally, parents feel concern, anxiety, and conflict regarding the gender identification of their child. Parents may not feel natural in the role of "gender teacher," and may be uncomfortable with how things are progressing. Should you feel yourself harboring such feelings, don't underestimate the importance of understanding and trying to resolve them. Self-understanding as well as understanding your baby's relationship patterns often proves helpful.

Parents may become confused because their little boy seems to be acting more like a little girl, or vice versa. Sometimes parents aren't sure of their own feelings, expectations, and desires for their children. Perhaps they wished for one sex and got the other. Sexuality is not a simple issue. Biological, social, and individual factors play important roles in its development. Nevertheless, when difficulties arise, it's always better to cope with them sooner rather than later.

For example, Josh tended to be very shy and cautious. He also liked to put on Mommy's hat and giggle, drawing his parents' attention to himself in a delightful way. When his fascination with his mother's clothes and his general shyness continued, his parents began to worry that he was developing in more of a feminine direction than a masculine one.

Father, a high school and college athlete, had always had a macho style and had looked forward to roughhousing with his son, Josh. But Josh's muscle tone was on the low side, making it hard for him to move about as robustly as other children his age. He shied away from the rough-and-tumble activities his father expected him to like. His father, always uncomfortable with Josh's lack of physical prowess, had from early in Josh's life gradually withdrawn from him.

Through counseling, it became clear that Father was not comfortable with the holding and caressing that Josh enjoyed. Father's style was more aggressively physical. As Father came to understand the basis of their problems, he was able to become reengaged. Instead of giving Josh his routine quick-lift upon returning from work, which always left Josh upset and Father feeling rejected, Father sat down on the floor next to Josh and let Josh crawl to him. Father would follow with a big hug and kiss. Through such activities, their relationships became more pleasurable and less strained. Josh began to take Dad's hat from his head on his return in the evenings, heralding an end to the general discomfort that had previously precluded such interaction. And as his motor control improved, he also began to participate in the rough-and-tumble activity that Dad introduced very gradually. Josh became a Daddy's boy as the relationship flourished.

As gender identity is formed, it is especially important in two-parent families for the baby to have a close relationship with both parents. Put as a general principle, babies need to explore their own biological potential in relationship to different patterns, different experiences, and different reactions.

Your child needs to have a sense of himself as a physically pleasurable being in order to successfully consolidate all the pieces of his young life. An anxiousness or preoccupation with one particular body part, be it genitals, feet, or nose, may represent your child's worry over not forming this sense of a pleasurable self. Family tensions, maturational unevenness, or a combination of both might be responsible. The solution lies in your baby's behavior which, in turn, can present an opportunity to understanding the relationship between your child and your family. At this early age, you can do much to help your child align his view of himself as an enjoyable, pleasurable boy or girl. To this end, it is important to understand the numerous factors that contribute to your baby's interest and pleasure in his own body; yet it is also important to realize that certain babies require special guidance.

Little Colette, for example, had a preoccupation with "bottoms," both her own and other people's. She would run into the bathroom and touch Mom's or Dad's bottom. Although she was verbally precocious, she would only yell "Bottom!" and then grab their leg and giggle. When Mom or Dad tried to disengage her, a temper tantrum usually ensued.

In all other ways she was doing fine. She was bright, well coordinated, eating and sleeping well. But, over a period of time, Colette's mother became very worried. The "bottom" preoccupation was one concern, but paradoxically, at a deeper level, she worried about Colette's strength, competence, and intensity. Her summary of Colette was: "She always goes after what she wants."

After seeking help, Mother became aware that she had been hoping for a passive, coy, and gentle baby girl. Consequently, without even realizing it, she had tried to avoid Colette more and more. Bath and bathroom times were the only periods that Colette could enjoy some intimacy with her mother. As Mother finally said, "She corners me. She's getting even with me for avoiding her all day long."

A plan of action was developed as Mother and Father both became more aware of their feelings toward Colette. They put special effort into being in close physical and emotional contact with her whenever they could, at times and places other than the bath. Mother took the initiative by engaging Colette in playing with dolls, holding Colette on her lap, hugging whenever possible, stroking her neck, holding hands. Father, too, made an extra effort toward Colette: particularly satisfying were their horsy rides, which drew upon Colette's tremendous physical coordination. Thus, over time, Colette was given a much wider variety of opportunity for physical contact and closeness with her parents. As a result, her desire to grab onto their "bottoms" receded. At the same time, they firmly but gently restricted Colette's access to them in the bathroom.

It was important that Colette's parents provided a "better" way for her to be close to them outside the bathroom before letting her know that some bathroom activities were "private." Initially, when one parent was in the bathroom, the other would stay with Colette so that she would not feel compelled to get into the bathroom. It was also important for her parents—in this case especially her mother—to understand how their own underlying attitudes contributed to Colette's focused, angry interest.

Usually when your child requires limits for excessive activity, that child is trying to satisfy an underlying need. Thus, your guidance and limits must always be tied to a better way for the child to get what he or she wants. You need to figure out what the need is and help the child meet it. Coupling a better solution to the need with guidance and limits on the excessive activity will lead your child to be more content and to progress in a more balanced way.

Stage Five:
Emotional Ideas (18 to 30 Months)

As your child enters the wonderful world of emotional ideas, she attains the key that will unlock the door to her mind and her imagination. Her sense of self becomes elevated. She can actually picture her whole body in her mind. If her motor ability were equal to her imagination, she would even be able to draw a picture of herself and include all the body parts. The old notion that youngsters have a distorted body image based on the way they draw is, I believe, probably incorrect. Here is how I've come to this conclusion.

I have asked children of two and a half to point to where they would have me draw the various parts of the human figure—face, neck, tummy, arms, genitals, legs, feet, toes, and so on. The great majority do it perfectly. But if I give even a sophisticated three-year-old the chore of actually doing the drawing, he's likely to draw a circle for the face and have the arms and legs come out of the circle, often without hands or feet. If I say, "Can we put in a tummy? Where should it go?," he'll point to a spot just below where the neck would be, and so on. The distortion seems more a function of motor or perceptual motor maturation than a lack of awareness of where body parts are, or of the ability to form a mental picture of an entire body.

FLOOR TIME

In any event, by this stage your child has some mental image of her body. We can see this in the way she plays pretend, as well as in the way she guides you in drawing a person. In pretend play, your child's dressing, diapering, or feeding dolly acknowledges the dolly's different body parts. Exploring dolly, looking under the skirt or pulling down a boy doll's pants to look for a penis is another acknowledgment.

Near the end of this stage, your three-year-old may express great curiosity as to what's in the "bottom." Although her imaginative play shows that she understands the functions of the body, she still will want to know exactly what comes out of where and maybe even why.

Just as she is learning to translate her other emotions into ideas for fantasy play, she needs to practice a variety of ways of elevating her feelings toward sexuality, pleasure, and excitement into ideas that can be played out imaginatively. Floor time offers her this opportunity. She has less need to undress and show herself off to her friends if she can have her dolly undress and show herself off to another dolly. She can ask Mommy questions about the parts of the body and what they do. As your child gets older, you may even explore where babies come from through play with dolls, as well as through discussion.

DIFFICULTIES

Many parents become anxious when their's child's make-believe play begins to explore sexuality. In their anxiety, they try to steer the play to another topic. But, as with all emotions, ignoring or discouraging these ideas will not decrease the child's interest. Rather, her earlier mode of expression—direct exploration of her own or other people's bodies—may be intensified or her interest in sexuality may be distorted by anxiety and inhibitions. In her emotional confusion, she may substitute her feelings of aggression, for example, for her feelings of sexuality and pleasure, leading her to mistakenly label sexuality and excitement as aggression and frustration. "Which parts are for pleasure? Which parts are for aggression?" she may wonder.

Children don't seem to lose their interest in looking at each other or themselves, nor the excitement of peeking at Mommy and Daddy to see what big people look like. With your encouragement and guidance, your child's efforts at understanding through exploration become balanced with his interest in using words and make-believe play.

Sally loved to undress her dolls and examine them without their clothes on. An active three-year-old, she often took the doll, put it in her mother's face, and said, "See?" Mother was a very active woman who liked to be in charge, as in "There's only one boss in this house." Mother was also very cautious and anxious when it came to issues of the human body. When Sally pushed the naked doll toward her, she would feel "intruded on and annoyed." Her reaction was usually a moderate admonishment to Sally to "behave" and an insistence that she leave her alone.

Mother did not enjoy flights of fancy or imaginative play, preferring to do puzzles with Sally and occasionally some letter-naming games. Sally, however, was highly imaginative and would frequently play out little dramas involving elephants or her stuffed bears. In addition, dressing and undressing her dolls was becoming a favorite pastime. But when she tried this imaginative play out on her mother, her mother became more and more annoyed with her, particularly when it involved the body. And since Sally was just as strong-willed as her mother, a royal power struggle emerged. During these power struggles, Sally would throw a temper tantrum, sometimes taking her clothes off and running around. Mother would catch her, give her a spanking, and get her clothes back on. Frustrated and anxious over Sally's persistence, Mother finally sought consultation.

Sally very much wanted Mother involved in the full range of her imaginative play. To do this, Mother needed to become more comfortable playing with Sally. Gradually, Mother learned to tolerate her uneasiness with Sally's doll play. She even learned to be patient and supportive, helping her daughter to name the body parts. With this engagement, the aggressive tone of her daughter's play diminished and, after a time, shifted to one of power—airplanes and rocketships—and then finally to nurturing activities. While Mother was more comfortable with these, she recognized that her daughter had to engage in the full range of emotional themes, including bodily curiosity.

By offering Sally the important opportunity to relate to her, Mother was creating the basis for a warm, intimate relationship. Providing guidance for Sally's tremendous energy and setting limits with explanations and only occasional punishments all became easier for Mother and easier for Sally to accept. Over time, their relationship broadened and deepened and both became more happy and relaxed with each other.

This example expands on the important principle discussed in the previous stage, that of satisfying a child's underlying need. When a child is excitedly pursuing one of her developmental interests and cannot elicit her parents' support and participation, she may well become frustrated and angry. These feelings can become mixed with her healthy and normal curiosity. A parent often cannot tell which set of feelings is more prominent, and the ensuing power struggles obscure the real issues even further. It is important for parents to determine the age-appropriate needs of their child and to try to meet those needs, providing structure and discipline so the child can learn to formulate the full range of emotional ideas.

You need to respect your child's new and healthy ability to create emotional ideas which have to do with body pleasure and emerging sexuality. Chances are, if you are a parent who feels anxious about this issue, you would rather that this not be the case. By overcoming your own awkwardness you can contribute to your child's growth in all areas, not just his or her sexuality.

Stage Six:
Emotional Thinking
(30 to 48 Months)

During the phase of emotional ideas, your child has simply elaborated the theme of pleasure and sexuality as he elaborates other themes—curiosity, assertiveness, aggression, relationships, and dependency. As he gets into the stage of emotional thinking, however, your child will learn to organize his emotional ideas into more logical patterns. Just as he earlier conceptualized a physical "me," now he's putting together an emotional "me" and an emotional "you," and learning to separate a whole "me" from a whole "you" at the level of ideas.

The new ability to aggregate also works in reverse. Sometime during this stage (three to four and a half years of age), you will begin to see his general interest in the "bottom" become much more focused. His curiosity begins to seem more adult. The penis and vagina become of much greater interest than other body parts. Early in this stage, any reference to elimination or its products will elicit great laughter from almost all children of this age. As they mature, the differences between boys and girls and interest in exploring the genital areas take the center ring. This is due to their greater sense of how the body parts relate to each other and fit together at the level of ideas.

FLOOR TIME

Some girls take special interest in their nipples and take pride in their future ability to have babies. Others want to know why their brother has a penis and they don't. They may share fantasies of the kind one child did—wanting to "bite off Daddy's penis and swallow it so I will have one for myself," and giggle and say, "Ha, ha, but that's silly." Boys also may have many worries that their penis will not grow "big," perhaps amazed at the size of Daddy's, or that their bodies will be hurt—or feel jealous that only Mommies can have a baby or breasts.

Your child's sense of, and interest in, his own body, in particular his sense of himself as a sexual being, becomes coupled during this stage with curiosity about what happens in Mom and Dad's bedroom, how babies are born, and about why Mommies and Daddies are different. Your youngster's logic and new ability to connect many ideas allows him to explore the questions of why and how, not only to have a sense of differences. And—be prepared—you will also see your child use his emerging debating capabilities in discussing these questions.

In the absence, and often in the presence, of realistic explanations, your child is capable of creating his own fantasies about how babies are born, where penises and vaginas come from, and why boys and girls are different. Many four-year-olds have their favorite theories about the way the world works.

Samantha told of her notion that babies come from seeds in Mommy's tummy. She said she had heard a reference to this in a book Mommy had shown her. She figured that the seeds got there by being swallowed and that Daddy's penis did something. Perhaps it was swallowed and turned into seeds. After this explanation, she giggled and said, "That's silly, isn't it? I just made all that up." Here was a wonderful example of Samantha's appreciation of fantasy, which she readily distinguished from reality, although she didn't yet have a sense of what the reality actually was. She had a few facts that she pieced together in fantasy, and she thoroughly enjoyed it.

Michael had a different idea. He thought babies came out together with what he called "doodies." He thought Mommies gave birth this way and that was why all babies were "smelly and stinky." In fact, he had a little sister who he thought fit right into this model! When asked how the babies got there in the first place, he said, "God put them there." And when asked why God would want a smelly, stinky baby, his face lit up joyously and he said with great delight, "Because God likes to play jokes on people!"

DIFFICULTIES

Some children keep their thoughts to themselves, others express them easily to their parents. The less expressive child can be supportively helped to share his thoughts with extra floor time. One need not ask specific questions. In time, if you help your cautious child become a "chatterbox," his special thoughts will eventually emerge. Focus on the process of chatting. Let the content happen naturally.

Parents have reason to be perplexed about how much and what to tell their child about sex. We neither want to overwhelm, overstimulate, nor hide the facts. Generally, you should realize that your child's curiosity is much more limited than his questions indicate. He enjoys creating his own explanations. Often he will want only general information from you. When he sees a pregnant woman, he wants to know that there's a baby inside and that the baby grew from a special kind of egg. Initially, your child will probably not even be interested in how the egg got there or how it got fertilized. Having probably never heard of concepts such as fertilization, he won't have questions about it. Questions about the details of reproductive anatomy and physiology don't usually arise until eight to ten years of age. You need to provide just enough information to keep your child curious and interested, while at the same time maximizing the freedom he has to explore his own ideas before he is overloaded with too much information. Your child won't have the capacity to understand all the facts until he is at least seven or eight, and he may not want to hear them until he's closer to nine or ten. You will need to search for the right level of explanation and continue to add to it as your child becomes receptive.

Some children can become overstimulated with their own curiosity. They may be so interested in the body, its parts, and how it works that it becomes a little "scary" to them.

Hal started having nightmares in which he was hurt. His fears about robbers and being hurt, although talked about, really related to his curiosity about what went on behind closed doors—about noises he heard in his mommy and daddy's bedroom—and about the workings of his own body.

In a consultation, Hal confided that his curiosity wasn't limited to what he was asking his parents, but was also being played out with one of his friends. He played "doctor" with a little girl a year older than he was. She would answer all his questions with her "advanced knowledge" and they would undress and examine each other. As he talked in therapy about this, he would immediately go from interest and curiosity to the fear that someone wanted to steal his "doctor" bag. In his mind, he was punishing himself for his overexcitement by fearing he would lose "things." The kind of play he was having with his little girl friend was not just exciting, it was scary. Mother was able to help by simply keeping a slightly closer watch over him and his friend, and by letting him know that he needed to keep his clothes on when he played. It was okay for him to ask a lot of questions, and Mother made it clear she wanted to answer them all, but playing "doctor" had to be with clothes on.

Important in this situation was Hal's parents' empathy with his curiosity and wish not to overload him with facts. They helped him set limits on his curiosity when he got carried away with his peers.

In another family, little Martin had a thousand questions. In response, his parents, who did not want to mislead him, showed him pictures in books on adult anatomy and explained how babies came to be, complete with how the daddy planted the seed in the mommy. Martin did not like this. He worried that Mommy could be hurt by the way Daddy planted the seed. He went around describing this as "gross." Martin then gave his parents a way out. He suggested that the seed did not get in as they said. Instead, "Mommy must have eaten the seed, which you get from the doctor." Realizing that he had been overwhelmed with information, his parents went back a few steps and reassured him that everything was okay. They encouraged him to talk about how the baby grows from the seed, which he was comfortable with. Interestingly, he stuck to his own explanation until he was about nine, when he could comprehend the adult explanation without being too frightened by it.

Once Martin's parents realized what he was ready to know, they helped him address his questions on his own level with his own ideas. Sometimes the best sign of overstimulation in a child is the presence of such things as fears, difficulty with controlling behavior, and increased restlessness. One very verbal seven-year-old boy said, in response to his parents' too-detailed explanation, "That's disgusting. . . . I didn't need to know everything. Just how the seed grew." He felt at age ten he would have been ready for the "whole story."

Another frequent challenge is the child who overexcites himself, making his parents feel too uncertain or anxious to set limits. Frank liked to get into bed with Mom and Dad and nuzzle against Mom's breasts. After a few minutes of this, he would become overly active and aggressive, often jumping on and breaking furniture. Over time, Mom saw how she encouraged this pattern with the secret thought, "At least one man in the house finds me interesting." Dad also saw how he avoided setting limits on Frank in many situations because he was "tired." As both parents guided Frank out of their bed and offered other forms of family fun, Frank's overexcitement abated.

SEXUALITY AND SELF-ESTEEM

As your child becomes more logical and differentiates more clearly between fantasy and reality, he is learning how to stabilize his self-esteem. Self-esteem relates to the issue of sexual identity quite strongly. It goes beyond, "I'm a boy," or, "I'm a girl." It is more like "I'm a boy (or girl) with a penis (or vagina) and I'm curious about how babies come about, and I know there's something in all this—and I feel good about my interests." The sense of "me" as a sexual being helps foster your child's emerging overall sense of a "self" (now at the level of ideas). After all, his sexual sense of self is an important part of his identity as a person. His sense of self-worth, competence, and reality all are enhanced by his ability to distinguish, consolidate, define, and refine himself as a sexual being, as well as an assertive, curious, pleasurable being. A sense of sexual identity serves to strengthen your child's hold on reality and his ability to build positive self-esteem. This comes as no surprise when we consider the importance of an adult's sense of sexual identity to self-esteem and the importance of the understanding of one's own body to his or her overall comprehension of reality.

BEGINNING THE TRIANGLE

During this stage, your comfort with your child's sexuality, along with his other inclinations (assertiveness, curiosity, aggression, etc.), is not the only issue you will face as parents. There is also the issue of your comfort with your own sexuality. Since parents operate as a team, the patterns in their relationship become important—who's in control, who's undermining, how much respect exists between them, and the presence of sexual tensions all become significant. The unseen, but nevertheless present, sexual patterns between parents may emerge in power struggles during dinnertime or in the tenderness they show each other. These interactions will be astutely observed and interpreted by the fascinated young child. Very little is missed by the curious three-and-a-half to five-year-old wanting to discover himself through understanding his parents' relationship.

It's difficult to hide parental tensions. You should work out whatever difficulties you have as a couple rather than think you can keep them locked away from your child. The child may be confused or worried about your tensions, but will find the situation easier to accept if you are working to improve the harmony of your relationship.

During this stage, your child is also progressing from understanding the world in terms of the two-person system—"How do I get my needs met?"—to the more complex three-person system with its attendant rivalries and intrigues. In terms of sexual matters, it may mean "Who likes me best?" or "Whom do I prefer?" Your son may begin to prefer Mommy to Daddy because of his emerging interest in a new range of pleasures. He may behave more competitively and be feistier with Daddy. He still loves Daddy and wants Daddy's affection and attention, but he also wants to show that he can do some things better than Daddy can in order to endear himself more to Mommy. Your daughter may have the opposite pattern, trying to impress Daddy at the expense of Mommy. But, as children become anxious about their interest in the parent of the opposite sex, they sometimes show an expressed desire for the parent of the same sex.

When possible, your child will take an interest in the subtleties and intrigues of any relationship. After all, when there's a triangle, two can gang up on one. Earlier in your child's development, he was more concerned with having his basic needs met. Even though jealousies may have existed at an earlier age, Mommy and Daddy, while different, could more or less substitute for each other. Now, Mommy and Daddy don't substitute for each other as easily as they did before. To be sure, both still provide a sense of security when one or the other is away or when the child has a scraped knee. But when his environment is calm and uneventful, he might strive to impress Mommy at Daddy's expense. He may even say, "Daddy—out!" as he shows Mommy how he has learned to imitate the latest Samurai warrior with his big, new pretend sword.

Sally may have a similar idea as she reads a book and cuddles near Daddy. When Mommy asks, "Is it time for me to read, too?" Sally may offer a dismissive, "No, I'll call you when I'm ready."

Parents should be aware that such behavior, although it may be momentarily disconcerting, is part of a larger pattern of figuring out triangular relationships—that is, how to have a special relationship with one parent at the expense of the other. These are times also when your child is "flexing his muscles," experimenting with being the boss and controlling the triangle to suit his own ends.

Your attitude should be one of support for your child's new ability. You can help him experiment so that he gains a sense of security in this newfound world of triangles, having an alliance with one parent "against" the other. At the same time, it is *not* helpful for your child to get the sense that he can go too far. If Johnny insists that Daddy not come in the door at night because Johnny is king of the house, he may have taken his "experiment" too far. Daddy's good-natured response may be to come in the door and wonder aloud if he's permitted to sit down and eat, to which Johnny says, "Yes" or "No." But if Johnny takes the whole thing too seriously and throws a temper tantrum, it is time for Daddy to work at improving his relationship with Johnny by providing comfort and security, and at the same time setting limits so that Johnny doesn't get too carried away.

Similarly, when Sally suggests that Mommy get out of bed in the morning, Mommy can heartily empathize with Sally's desire to be with Daddy in bed, but supportively suggest that Sally come cuddle with both of them. Should Sally get mean or become physically aggressive, discipline will be needed as well as floor-time exercises to determine why Sally got so upset.

The combination of extra discipline along with extra empathy and understanding helps your child balance his need for experimenting with the security that is so essential to him. At times what appears to be indulgence may actually be support for a child's need to experiment with a new pattern of emotional understanding and behavior. Parents must decide how to set limits without disturbing the basic security underlying their relationship with their child. Parents must rely on their instincts of the moment—when has their child gone too far, when does his behavior compromise basic family values, and how should they support his patterns to help him flex his muscles and experiment?

You will not lack for interest or challenge during your child's pleasurable and sexual development. Your family's patterns of relationship—how you experience your child, how he or she experiences you, how you as parents experience each other, and all the variations and complications your relationships entail—can help foster your baby's progression from birth to a healthy, pleasurable, and sexual life.

VI

Anger and
Aggression

"The only way to handle aggression is to establish law and order through firm punishment very early in life."

"The only way to teach children to handle aggression is to provide them with loving support and indulge their needs so they won't feel frustrated and angry."

"Discharging is good because it gets you in touch with your feelings."

"The best way to discourage aggression is to forbid play with war toys and the watching of violence on television or in movies."

"The best way to control aggression is to help children learn to understand their anger by exposing them to its various manifestations in the real world."

You have probably heard each of the opinions above at one time or another, from one expert or another. Who is right? Is *anyone* right?

Anger and aggression are probably the most perplexing and difficult emotions confronting parents. And it is clear from the statements made above that even "expert" understanding is far from complete.

From the infant's point of view, however, *all* emotions have equal value. Love, warmth, pleasure, excitement, frustration, and anger are all parts of the human condition and are what defines humanness in all of us. Healthy babies experience all emotions, but at this early stage they are unable to do anything other than simply react naturally to what they are feeling, making no judgment about it.

To be sure, parents can encourage some emotions and discourage others. But avoiding an emotion that is part of the definition of humanity is dehumanizing—even though it is an emotion that is difficult and sometimes frightening to deal with.

Take, for example, the seemingly lucky couple who have an "easy" baby. Baby doesn't cry much and seems contented to lie in his crib or carriage, looking around. At fifteen months, the same baby never seems to get angry or "experiment" with aggressive feelings. Still sounds pretty good, doesn't it? Well, let's look again at around twenty-two months, when he begins to relate to children his own age. Now he seems to withdraw and is incapable of defending himself. He won't assert himself to keep a toy that is being taken away. Even more important, his shyness prevents him from exploring new relationships or settings, such as new equipment in the park, or children at a birthday party whom he doesn't already know. His emotional range is limited. He is a child who very much wants to please his parents but, in the process, has sacrificed, rather than incorporated, an ability to assert himself.

Your acceptance of the range of human emotions in your child (and in yourself) will give him an understanding of each emotion and the nourishment needed for growth. As your child matures, he will be able to use these emotions to help fulfill not only his ideals and goals, but those of family and society as well.

THE LEVELS OF EMOTION

You may wonder how anger can be expressed without being destructive or hurtful to others. It sounds ideal, but how do we actually do it? Do you let your baby cry so she can "experience" her frustration? What do you do when your two-year-old is on his back in the supermarket, kicking and screaming for a treat? Should you encourage aggressive play? Do you cheer when the soldier doll hits the bad guy? Or, rather than actually *discouraging* aggression, do you *en*courage compatibility and harmony through tea parties, hugging and kissing, caring for the baby, and so on? What kinds of playthings encourage an appropriate level of aggression in a child once he is capable of using imagination and pretend? Will you successfully guide your child's aggressive imagination by getting down on the floor and playing a game of "crash the car"?

There are a number of experts who take the position that the best way to handle aggression, especially at the older stages, is to discourage it while encouraging imagination that has to do with non-aggressive themes. This attitude is tantamount to pretending that aggression and anger don't exist and that, once swept under the carpet, they will cease to be a concern. We would like to share a different perspective: We don't really have a choice as to whether the emotion is there or not. We can't discourage it out of existence. Our only choice is in the tools we can teach our children to use in order to *experience, communicate,* and *cope* with it.

Let's take the case of a three-and-one-half-year-old who uses her finger as a pretend gun. Let's assume that parental discouragement of and annoyance at this behavior results in her having nightmares and reverting back to sucking on her finger. By communicating their disapproval in purely negative terms, the parents in this case have fostered regression rather than maturation in their child. If, instead, her parents can draw the aggression into interaction and help raise the behavior to a higher emotional level, the result might look more like this:

CHILD: (Pointing finger and pretending to shoot) "Hah! I got you!"

PARENT: (Doing same) "I got you, too! Who's on your team?" (Begins to line action figures up)

CHILD: (Taking other action figures) "All these."

PARENT: "Whose are faster or stronger?" (Moves them around)

CHILD: "Mine."

With this line of thought, parents help channel the child's unfocused feeling into an interactive and symbolic drama, involving tangible targets for her anger, such as proving who's fastest, whose team is biggest, or who can talk the best. Rather than forcing the child to retreat to a safer level of behavior, like sucking fingers, this type of play encourages enactment of a whole drama that symbolizes aggression, as well as other emotions (when the battle is over, the losers can be taken care of), and draws upon a higher level of imagination and conceptualization. During the battle, anger can be tied to a story involving protection, good and bad, and so on, so that the child can learn to connect her anger to other emotions, and thus see it in context. In this way, the child can begin to understand that anger is not a disorganized discharge of emotion, but can be understood and expressed through reason and ideas.

Anger can be expressed at three levels: physical, behavioral, and ideational. While we cannot dictate whether or not an emotion exists, we can influence its level of activity. To do this, parents must identify their child's level of feeling and gradually try to help him elevate it to higher levels of expression. We may see an infant turn purple with what certainly looks like rage, a two-year-old biting and kicking, or an older child in distress with stomach problems or breathing difficulty. But, as with all feelings, the expression of anger goes beyond these physical and behavioral manifestations and can be elevated to the level of ideas, where it can take the form of make-believe play.

Let's now trace the development of these complex emotions, and see how we, as parents, can overcome our feelings about them and help our children learn to cope with anger and aggression constructively.

Stage One:
Regulation and Interest in the World
(0 to 3 Months)

At the very beginning of life, your infant's anger and aggression can be understood best in relationship to the "equipment" he was born with. The infant's principal way of communicating is, of course, crying, and most parents learn to recognize the subtle shades of difference between one type of crying and another.

First-time parents may be startled initially when they hear the unmistakable tinge of anger in their infant's voice, but few deny that it's there. This added dimension that we interpret as protest or anger occurs when a baby doesn't get what he wants right away. Like a car going into overdrive, we hear that extra kick of emotion joining the feelings that were there before.

As upsetting as it is to parents to hear their child cry in this way, it isn't all bad. With your help, the baby can learn, even at this tender age, that although he may be feeling overwhelmed, confused, and downright angry, there are ways to conquer these feelings and get himself back on even ground. At this stage in your baby's development, he can use his budding interest in you to calm himself down: with your help, he can focus his senses on the outside world in order to make his inside world feel better.

FLOOR TIME

During infancy, irritability and anger will generally surface as a reaction to some physical complaint. At this age, anger is usually a reaction to persistent discomfort: your child may be sensitive to light, loud noises, or sudden movement; he may like to be swaddled in diapers or light blankets, or he may not; he may be more comfortable on his side rather than his stomach; he may be hungry, tired, or have a gas bubble. A number of things that aren't to his preference may lead to discomfort, irritability, and crying.

The feeling of being overwhelmed and out of control is as upsetting to the baby as it is to the parents. What you can do is help him calm down. Just as you discover your baby's joys to enhance early self-esteem, learn your infant's preferences and sensitivities in order to soothe his upset feelings and begin to forge his emotional link to you as a source of comfort. From experimenting with all the senses to exploring different movement patterns (as described in the *Regulation and Interest in the World* section of chapter VIII), you will find he has very definite preferences. At times when your baby begins to show signs of irritation, experiment with each sense slowly and one at a time. Your own concentration and resolve not to panic in the face of your baby's discomfort will go a long way toward helping him learn that his feeling can be dealt with in a calm and supportive way.

•

DIFFICULTIES

We all know that the course of true parenthood never did run smooth. No parent, to my knowledge, has yet escaped difficulties, whether large or small, with their child's development at one stage or another. In order to be prepared, we must tap into resources that will enable us to turn these inevitable challenges into learning and growing opportunities.

Your baby may be one who has come into the world with her "equipment" especially fine-tuned. She is an infant who has a hard time calming down, who is extremely reactive to light, touch, high-pitched noises, or to movement. She may awaken frequently, startle easily, or feed with more difficulty than you would expect. This baby, through no fault of either yours or her own, is more likely, even in the first days and weeks of life, to feel not only uncomfortable but also irritated, and in this sense we might say is already beginning to experience annoyance, if not anger. At the same time, even at this early stage, you're presented with an opportunity.

To the degree that both parents and caregivers learn to be aware of their baby's special sensitivities and adjust their own reactions accordingly, almost any baby will come to appreciate the environment as a place that can be comforting. Though he may feel irritable one moment, he can begin to learn that the next moment may bring relief.

Parents of a child especially sensitive to touch can learn to use gentle but firm pressure on his back, arms, and legs, rather than light touch. A mini-massage or simply swaddling may help.

Parents of a child especially sensitive to sound can learn to speak in low vocal tones rather than the high pitch most of us instinctively use with infants.

Parents of a child especially sensitive to movement can use gentle and rhythmic rather than robust movements. For example, one baby was quasi-colicky at three and a half months old and needed gentle firm holding. One day a babysitter was holding him and he was crying. Her reaction was to jiggle him up and down, which only made him scream louder. Gentle, soothing movement was all he could tolerate.

LIMIT SETTING

Your baby's infancy may seem a little early to begin talking about limit setting, but it has a very different meaning here than it does for the older child: limit setting at this age means employing soothing support for your baby's emerging ability to calm himself.

We've mentioned how parents are able to develop an ear for their baby's different cries. Though we do not at all advocate letting any baby "cry it out," there are different levels of tolerance parents need to have for their baby's various cries. Some babies need to yell before they can begin to soothe themselves. Parents sensitive to this may wait a minute to see if the baby is indeed in control. Since each baby needs a different degree of comfort, parents must be sensitive enough to respect the ability he already has, and to offer help only after he passes that level. This means that you must be able to give your baby different levels of help as well. For the not-too-upset baby, talking or getting him to look at something interesting may be all that's needed. If more is required, go to the next level of holding and rocking. The trick is again to meet your baby where he is.

Parents and caregivers can do much to soothe the experiences of irritation, anger, and aggression that come early in life. This doesn't mean that you should try to protect your little one from experiencing any discomfort whatsoever—you can't. What you're aiming for at this stage is to help your baby regulate his *internal* life, including his experiences of irritation and anger, so he will begin to notice that there is an *external* life.

Stage Two:
Falling in Love (3 to 7 Months)

The stage of falling in love is critical in your baby's development of the ability to handle aggression. Without a balance of pleasurable feelings, the baby may come to view people as things: the wish to hurt or pull away will not be tempered by concern for others' feelings.

To be sure, the world is still frustrating—it doesn't feed her when she wants to be fed, doesn't always change her diapers as quickly as she would like (if she is a baby who cares—many don't seem to), doesn't always rock her or talk to her in just the right way. But, at the same time, if she can experience a warm, comforting, and loving smile and joyful interactions, if Mommy's and Daddy's face, touch, and voice bring pleasure, she falls more deeply in love with the human world and begins to experience love coming from another person to her. Such a balance of anger and love is necessary for coping with future feelings of anger and aggression.

FLOOR TIME

The following example might better be called "Changing-Table Time." Often, at some point during this stage of development, babies have an experience similar to Brett's. At six and a half months, Brett had her first major cold. Her alternately congested and runny nose made her miserable enough, but coupled with being put on her back on the changing table at diaper time and the inevitable nose cleaning that would ensue, it got so that she would scream with absolute fury. Mother tried a mobile to distract her; it didn't work. Knowing that Brett was a very tactile child, she tried small toys that Brett could finger while on the changing table. Better, but still not great. Finally, by making the ordeal into a game of interaction, she got results. She would not only give Brett the small toys to hold, but also bring her face very close to Brett's, puff her cheeks, and lightly blow on her face, which Brett found to be fun. On the next swoop, in came the tissue. Before Brett could work up to a scream, it would be back to the game. It was certainly not a low-energy task to get through changing time, but it was worth it not to have a screaming, red-faced, and angry baby to calm afterward. And, after the cold was gone, the association between diaper changing and fun and games was further strengthened, defusing a situation that often becomes a battleground between parent and child.

DIFFICULTIES

Brett's solution worked because she already felt a sense of closeness to her parents and the world around her. But what of the child who doesn't fall in love so easily? For the baby who is having trouble beginning her relationship with her parents, the world is experienced as things. The human face, like a colored ball, is sometimes interesting, sometimes not. It is easy to see how essential it becomes that pleasure be your baby's dominant response to the human world. There must be satisfaction and joy to counterbalance inevitable frustration, irritability, and even anger.

Let's say you are pushing the baby in the stroller, trying to get a few errands done, preoccupied and hoping for an easy trip. Naturally, baby starts to fuss. You give her a bottle. She's okay for a time, then starts up again. You give her a quick diaper change, which buys a little more time. Next, you might adjust her stroller to a different position, give her some toys—basically anything to keep her out of your hair while you're busy. You run out of stopgaps, but not errands. She gradually works herself up to a squall. You push her along, not exactly cheerful yourself, and wait until she cries herself out and falls asleep.

This happens to almost every parent at least once, which is okay. But it shouldn't become a pattern. The angry baby whose cries are ignored may become even more angry. With a baby who is not so sure at the outset that human contact is a great thing, you may be courting a problem when you should be courting your baby. When she has simply "had it" with being pushed around, literally and figuratively, whether in a stroller or anywhere else, get down to her level and do a little wooing. Get physical by holding and talking, making eye contact, smiling, and comforting. Take time for yourself and your baby to feel close and relaxed with each other. Her eventual ability to deal with the anger, irritation, and aggression she feels depends, to a large extent, on the conviction she must develop that people and the world around her provide enough love, comfort, and pleasure to balance life's frustrations.

Stage Three:
Purposeful Communication
(4 to 10 Months)

As a baby progresses between four and eight months, we see two interdependent and marvelous new developments. Just as he is learning how to make his needs and wants known, we also see that the baby is developing much better control over his large muscle groups. He is now beginning to crawl; he may be able to reach out and put a finger in Mommy's mouth. While exploring Daddy's nose, he may belt Daddy a good one on occasion, or Daddy may find an elbow in his eye. Parents sometimes have trouble knowing if their little angel is exploring or being aggressive.

Sometime around this age, you'll begin to find your baby easier to understand: he is beginning to understand causality—or how he can make things happen. If he wants to feel close, he can reach out to be picked up. In another mood, he can look Mommy or Daddy in the eye and push his food off the table as though to say, "What are you going to do about it?" You will also find that, by nine or ten months, he can pinch, push, and poke, especially when sitting next to a sibling. If you think you're already seeing a little limit testing, you're probably right.

We can't immediately give him credit, however, for all of these actions, since the state of his motor ability plays a large part in how he expresses his anger at this stage. Some of his actions may be intentional, but many are still random.

Important to recognize is that your baby can now experiment with physical expressions of aggression other than crying. He has *some* purposeful control over his large muscles so that he can often make things happen. So, consider your baby's new ability to give you a black eye or a bloody lip a breakthrough in terms of his emotional and physical development.

INDIVIDUAL DIFFERENCES

The physical development of your baby takes on importance during this phase, for his emotions will very likely be interpreted largely on the basis of his actions. Parents must be sensitive and observant in order to avoid miscasting their child in a role he doesn't mean to play.

Let's examine the relationship between the development of motor ability and the expression of anger at this age for two very different kinds of babies. (Chapter VIII explores these physical differences more fully.)

The baby with high muscle tone (tight muscles) may want to reach out and put a hand into Daddy's mouth, but because his control is incomplete, his aim is poor and Daddy winds up with a bop on the nose. A surprise bop on the nose can elicit a sharp reaction from Daddy, "Hey, what are you trying to do? Stop being such a little monster." Curiosity can easily be mistaken for aggression.

On the other hand, a baby with low muscle tone (she may be slow to walk or handle things) may be struggling to lift her arm and pinch Mommy. Because she hasn't the strength or control to accomplish her task, she winds up unexpectedly rolling onto her side, crying in rage and frustration. Mommy reacts by picking her up and giving her a cuddle.

So, our high-muscle-tone baby is curious, wants to reach out and explore, and is unfairly accused of aggression, while our low-muscle-tone baby is feeling aggressive, wants to pinch, and is treated as though she's helpless. It's easy to understand how differences in motor control may play a role quite early in how your baby communicates his feelings of aggression and anger and how his efforts are characterized.

The ability to plan movement is also important to healthy emotional development; and even if a child does not have full mastery over this physical function, it can often give us insight into a child's true intentions. For example, with an older child whose tone is a challenge, we can often read his intent even though he cannot make his body do his bidding. On close examination, we may see the beginnings of such a problem in an eight- to nine-month-old baby. If a baby at this age can't yet coordinate two movements in sequence in order to reach for something he wants (crawl and reach for a ball, for example), there is a chance that motor planning is lagging. A baby who has motor-planning problems is likely to find it difficult not only to communicate his intentions but also to differentiate between anger, curiosity, assertiveness, and even love; a child who lacks the physical ability to express curiosity may not understand what curiosity really *is,* in part because he doesn't receive your reactions to his intentions.

Practice here is essential. If you have a baby whose gestures are unclear to you, you may need to see a movement twenty times rather than five before you can sort out whether your child is playfully squeezing your nose or means to pinch with a vengeance.

STYLES OF COMMUNICATION

We begin to see many styles of communication emerge slightly later in this stage. Some babies tend to use their motor systems to discharge frustration and irritability more than others. When angry, they bang their hands on the table, or butt Mommy or Daddy with their heads. These babies are using the parts of their bodies that they have the most control over at this age—the head and trunk and, to a lesser extent, their arms and legs—to dispel anger.

Other babies may favor vocal means to express anger and aggression from an early age. They may use twenty different kinds of cries and a variety of other sounds to express discomfort or anger.

Then there's the diplomat, who may opt for the silent stare to communicate his annoyance.

There are babies who, at this age, may already be deciding that it's too dangerous to express anger at the world, and who bite themselves or refuse to eat when frustrated and angry. Their negative stand gets the message across.

As with your baby's reaction to sound, touch, smell, and movement, his sensitivity to the way information—and especially emotional information—comes in will also determine how irritable and angry he is. In turn, the sensitivity with which Mommy or Daddy reads his signals and understands his need to express dependency and assertiveness, curiosity, and even aggression, will play a role in how the baby eventually comprehends feelings such as anger.

FLOOR TIME

A typical focus of anger at this stage of development is related to the issue of control. At even seven or eight months of age babies would rather share leadership than submit to another's control. Try getting in your eight-month-old's path and substituting another toy for the one she is after and you'll probably get a show of temper from any crawler worth her salt. This doesn't mean that your baby doesn't need your control at all, but it does show that she has a clear sense of intent and is likely to become angry if her efforts are controlled or undermined.

Power struggles can begin as early as eight or nine months. According to recent research certain forms of refusal to eat may be a disguised power struggle. During this stage, babies want to exercise "being the boss." They want respect and admiration for their emerging assertiveness; if they don't get it, that healthy assertiveness is likely to turn into anger, frustration, and aggression. Remember, though, guidance and structure are also of great importance at this time.

Let's look at the example of a perfectly average ten-and-a-half-month-old playing with blocks on the floor. Mommy, meaning well but not in tune with her baby at the moment, tries to "help" him play by showing him how to do it her way. The first few times, her interference is tolerated, but soon he begins to push Mommy's hand away. As she continues, he hits at her. Annoyed now, she slaps his hand back. He screams and tries to bite her.

What we've just seen is interest and assertiveness deteriorate into disorganized anger. Initiative was thwarted by control which, though well intended, undermined the support, admiration, and respect that are critical to children at this age if they are to learn the difference between healthy assertiveness and more disorganized aggression.

This brings us to the next ingredient necessary to the development of healthy assertiveness. During this stage, what your baby learns about anger and aggression begins to depend on *your response to his feelings and behavior.*

Your baby has two ways of defining himself at this age. One is "When I feel this way, I do this." The other is "When I do this, they do that." Your baby gets to know what the world thinks of his actions by the response he gets. In fact, you will quickly see your baby refine his notions of how to get what he wants by the kinds of reactions he gets.

Let's take another look at our ten-and-a-half-month-old, this time in a supportive play situation. He sits happily on the floor, alternately squeezing the soft block he has in his hand and putting it into his mouth and biting down with an angry glee. Mother sits beside him, picks up another block, and squeezes. Baby offers his block to her and she says, "Ooh! I want to bite that block hard," and pretends to take a bite. Baby grins and giggles. Mother holds her block out to the baby, who keeps his own and just looks at it. Here is an opportunity for Mommy to draw attention to the pictures on the block, pointing to and naming the object pictured. Baby grabs for the block; Mommy lets him take it. More smiles and giggles.

In the fairly short interchange above, Mommy has let her baby express a healthy and natural assertiveness by allowing the baby to call the tune and the pace of this play exchange. Mommy, in turn, has introduced a new dimension to the play (looking at the pictures on the blocks) as well as offered an interactive way for the baby to express his feelings (mimicking baby's play and then letting him grab the block). If the baby is still feeling aggressive, he may throw the block next, or if his mood turns more contemplative, he may explore the pictures on the blocks.

Acknowledgment of the feeling, interaction, and a broadening of the baby's repertoire of expression have all taken place, producing a successful and satisfying experience for both parent and child.

DIFFICULTIES

If a baby's efforts to achieve closeness are continually met with a response appropriate to aggression, closeness and aggression may come to feel like the same thing. A person who believes that feelings of closeness are always met with reactions of anger or aggression can come to see closeness as dangerous, to be approached with great caution and perhaps avoided entirely. Or, when a baby confuses closeness with aggression, he may try to get "love by irritation" (a phrase originally suggested by a distinguished colleague, Dr. Reginald Lourie); that is, he'll try to use anger and aggression as a means of getting close to people. Again, it is easy to see the disastrous implications this would have for subsequent development. As early as eight months of age, such patterns begin to assert themselves. For example, at eight months Ellen's shriek for wanting to be picked up affected her mother like chalk on a blackboard. After only a minute or two of her irritating wail, Ellen would get a response, but not the one she desired. Ellen's mother would come sweeping into wherever Ellen was, yank her up by her arms, and say, "I can't stand this noise! Here, what do you want?" Ellen's mom might hold her, but it was with annoyance and irritation. Still, to Ellen, it was better than not being held at all; so her shrieking continued.

Let's replay this tape and do some editing. What Ellen's mother needs to do here is to learn to read her daughter's signals. When she has a few minutes, she might try to notice Ellen's preliminary signs of wanting to be picked up and catch her before she begins to shriek. Perhaps Ellen flails her arms or becomes physically agitated in other ways; perhaps her vocalization has to work itself up before the actual shrieking begins. Early on, Mother can go over to Ellen and say, with both gestures and words, "Would you like to cuddle now? Do you want to be picked up?," and follow this with holding and comforting and later perhaps by positioning her nearby while Mother does something else. In addition, special play times should focus on reading signals. There might be a "Come pick me up game" when Mother and Ellen each practice their gesturing for initiating closeness. For example, Mother might wave and gesture "Come here" and hold her arms out. If Ellen moves closer, Mom can reward her with a big hug. If Ellen waves her arms, Mom can say, "Here I come," and give another hug. In this way, signaling is practiced when the pressure is low. If Ellen's mother can learn to read her signals before they become annoying to her, there is a better chance she will respond lovingly and with closeness to her baby's reaching out.

The importance of relaxed play time cannot be overemphasized. The more intimately you know your baby and her signals, the better your relationship will be. Calm and caring involvement together for 15 or 20 minutes at a time is a good investment, and necessary for any parent who wants to be able to read his or her baby's signals. When your child has lots of experience having her signals read and responded to, she will not need to "train" you to read her signals at inappropriate times. Also, you become more proficient at reading her needs so that even on the run you will do a better job.

You may find that it is difficult to read signals because of your own emotional reactions. Parents sometimes find themselves overstimulating or overcontrolling or rejecting their child, any of which can increase the child's anger. Remember, honest self-observation is the first and most important step in empathizing with your baby.

LIMIT SETTING

We've been talking about respecting your baby's signals, feelings, and needs, and can hear you asking, "How do I keep from overindulging my child?" Indulgence is not the same as respect. In fact, one could argue that overindulgence is a form of disrespect—that it's a form of infantilizing a baby and encouraging regression rather than maturation. If you treat your eight-month-old like a four-month-old, it will be no less intensely felt than if you treat a fifteen-year-old like an eight-year-old. Respect implies helping your baby learn to understand limits. To this end, taking your baby's autonomy, assertiveness, and competence seriously will make it more likely that he will respond to limit setting—but it still won't be easy.

If your baby is about to put his finger into the electrical outlet, or feels like flinging his food on the floor, or doesn't want to have his diaper changed . . . what should you do?

Let's take your nine-month-old who looks you straight in the eye while he drops his food to the floor. You apply the same principles described for older children in previous chapters. Look him right back in the eye, shake your head, and say firmly, "No, no." He is at the age when he's beginning to understand the difference between "yes" and "no". Take advantage of this valuable opportunity. If he does it again, pick the food up and try again. If he continues (of course he will), calmly remove him from his seat, continue to say, "No," shake your head, or use other gestures to get your message across. If you have enough resolve, are firm and persistent, show clear facial expression of disapproval (you may be tempted to smile the first few times, but you'll get over that quickly), and use appropriate words and tone of voice, he'll get the message. This is the beginning of learning to recognize limits. Although one should always try to communicate first with words and gestures, physical restraint may become necessary as well.

Here's an example of an appropriate reaction to a baby who is about to crawl somewhere her parents don't want her to:

MOTHER: "Mimi, no! No, Mimi, no!"

MIMI: (Keeps crawling)

MOTHER: (Marches over to Mimi, gets directly in front of her) "No! Go back, Mimi!" (Mother follows up with hand movements, like a traffic policeman, redirecting Mimi back into the other room. Facial expression is stern. Tone of voice serious)

MIMI: (She is hearing Mother's voice, seeing animated facial expression, and also seeing waving arms, clearly telling her to turn around and exit. Even if she can't decode the tone of voice and doesn't understand the word "No," she certainly can see Mother's discouraging expression and arms pointing her away from where she is going. She hesitates, then makes a tentative move forward again)

MOTHER: (Down on hands and knees directly in front of Mimi, looking into her eyes, she repeats) "No, Mimi. Go back." (She gestures again strongly with her arm, pointing.)

MIMI: (Remember, this is her first time! Stops in her tracks. Sits up to see what will happen next.)

MOTHER: (Puts her gently back on her hands and knees, pointing in the opposite direction) "Good girl, Mimi. Let's go back."

MIMI: (Begins to crawl again, this time in the right direction)

Mother may have to do this ten times before she gets reliable results, but consider the learning opportunity Mimi has gained from Mother's patience. She has had a multisensory lesson involving vision, sound, lots of feelings, and many different opportunities to get the idea. Mimi's mother, by orchestrating language, emotion, and physical gestures, provided a beautifully coordinated experience in intentional communication. Certainly, if Mimi had been approaching her mother's most valued glass collection, Mother might have only turned her around and said, "Come on, Mimi, not in there." But even this is better than carrying her out of the room, an option to use only if Mimi persists.

The key is interacting with your child. Let her *experience* the clear relationship between cause and effect. When you do have to do something directly physical, do the minimum; help her to do the rest on her own. Of course, you can only do this when you have five or ten minutes of time, but every second of active learning is worth hours of passive learning. And each of these learning opportunities adds up later on to the difference between a sixteen- or seventeen-month-old who is able to follow instructions and one who is not. So welcome the opportunities when they arise.

Certainly, there will be many times when you are in a hurry and expediency will demand that you simply pick Mimi up, get her dressed, and put her into the car, or take her out of the living room and put her into the car, or take her out of the living room and put her into the playroom. This is fine, too. But recognize that these are *missed* learning opportunities.

Stage Four:
The Complex Sense of Self
(9 to 18 Months)

Your little one, in learning to put together the pieces of her personality, is experiencing herself as a complex person with a repertoire of feelings and associated actions. She can deliberately poke Dad in the head because she's angry. At age fifteen or sixteen months, she can assertively take Mommy's hand, walk her to the toy store window, and point to a toy. If Mom says, "No," she can deliberately fall on the floor and cry. She is also a joking and mischievous little person who at eighteen months will take Daddy's hat and pretend to be Daddy coming in the door.

She may also imitate the way you express anger. Even though she can say only a few words, you can be sure she has absorbed, at some level, how Mommy and Daddy express this feeling. Not only will she step into your shoes, but she may borrow the familiar finger-shaking gesture. If Daddy and Mommy tend to withdraw when angered, baby may also act aloof. If Daddy is a tantrum thrower, watch out! The ways and means of your child's expression of anger may be humorously (or embarrassingly) recognizable. At the same time, some babies may do the opposite of what they see—so don't look for simple patterns.

Your baby can also now show her anger in a more complicated way. Believe it or not, by eighteen months, your angel might put her car in your path to see if she can trip you. She can also feign innocence when she semi-deliberately knocks over all the glasses on the table while reaching for her favorite food. This is pretty sophisticated stuff. You now have a complex little self who can take a number of units of feeling and behavior and purposefully link them in a chain. This is not yet at the level of ideas or thoughts—that will come later—but at the level of feeling and behavior.

And, just as your baby is now able to connect her different behaviors to feelings, she is also able to connect the pieces of her caregiver's behaviors. She can see and appreciate in her own pre-verbal way that Mommy and Daddy have many different ways of showing that *they* are angry. They may yell at her; they may be silent and not look at her; they may get controlling—bossing her around, and the like.

If all is moving along well, you will shortly see a dramatic and rather momentous developmental step occur: your baby now learns to connect *loving* behaviors and feelings with *angry* behaviors and feelings.

But, under the pressure of strong emotions, she may still keep these feelings separate. When I get down on the floor to play with a thirteen- or fourteen-month-old who becomes frustrated, the anger I see in her eyes and the rage I feel from her seems pure and complete. I have no doubt that she would "pull the trigger" without a qualm. But by eighteen or nineteen months of age, when I play with the same youngster, her rage is not all that's felt, even when that rage is intense. Along with the anger, I sense she knows I'm the same person who at other times has been a source of kindness and warmth. At this stage, she may threaten and try to scare me, but I would trust her not to "pull the trigger."

When your baby is angry and shows it, you should take care not to withdraw, isolate the child, or counterattack. Babies can be angry at you and comforted by you at the same time—the perfect demonstration of the coming together of the "angry me" and the "loving me."

We may know adults who seem to split their world into black and white, good and bad, and can't live with life's shades of gray. Their emotional life is still divided between the angry "me" and the loving "me."

A toddler's play gives us yet another clue as to when this important development occurs. In the early part of the second year, play may focus on anger for a period of time and only later on nicer things. For example, the child may bite or hit a doll and then later in the day she might hug it. By twenty months or so, this process is accelerated so that she may bite the doll and then pat it soon afterward: here you see the themes of aggression and caring juxtaposed much more closely. Our impression is that in the latter part of the second year of life, children begin to resolve this problem at a feeling and behavioral level, but not yet on a conceptual level. To achieve the next phase of development, they must reconcile the many emotions—including love and anger—that they can now perceive and express. This resolution is critical as their sense of "me" and "you" becomes more and more complicated.

So now we see the love that began emerging so clearly at two to four months, and the anger that's been developing all along, come together and temper one another. In healthy development, love and aggression are no longer separated as an excuse for antisocial, violent acts. Now, your baby's sense of caring will permeate her sense of self and of others, even when she's frustrated and enormously angry. It won't mean that outbursts, competition, and aggression will cease to exist; but it will bring these feelings together as part of a larger context dominated by caring.

FLOOR TIME

Now let's visit eighteen-month-old Justin's home. Daddy has just reprimanded him for banging his toy car into the wall. Daddy goes into the hallway to find the day's paper and, as he walks back into the living room, he almost stumbles over the same toy car, which Justin has left in his path. Justin, meanwhile, is eyeing Daddy from a spot near his toybox where he is pretending to play with a ball. "Hey, Justin. Are you mad at me? Did you leave this car for me to fall over?" says Daddy. Justin just looks. "Even though I yelled at you, we're still buddies. Want to play together?" Justin comes over, understanding Dad's gestures and tones, not his words. Justin brightens immediately. "You didn't like my yelling at you, did you? What if we line pillows up against the wall and then the cars can crash without hurting it?"

This might be one solution to the problem. Another might be to either establish, or remind Justin, that there are certain rooms in which he can crash his car and others where he can't. At the same time, offer him extra engagement, more freedom, and your time. You don't want to restrict his ability to flex his muscles, but you do want to show him where, when, and how it's appropriate to do so. Think of it in terms of giving your child a better deal. As you increase limits, you must find ways to increase freedom at the same time. This is how limits are internalized and respected. So rather than simply reprimanding him and then leaving him to stew and plot his revenge, show him another way to accomplish his aim and give him a little of yourself as well. Also, letting him know you understand his anger, even if you don't agree with it, will help reengage the two of you.

Questions often arise concerning the appropriateness of parents expressing anger around their children. Children may learn from seeing that their parents can be angry and can recover from it as long as you do *not* overwhelm or frighten your child or treat him as though he were older than he is. Parents must also learn to apologize to their children (and mean it) after an unnecessary angry episode. You'll feel better about yourself, and your child will feel better about you and himself, in addition to which you'll be setting a sterling example. Parents sometimes feel that the use of clear gestures—a stern look, firm pointing, increasing the volume and serious tone of one's voice—is unduly harsh. But toddlers need clear gestures, and often I have noticed a correlation between a family's lack of gestural communication and a high incidence of misbehavior in its children.

DIFFICULTIES

Sleeping problems are not foreign to many eighteen-month-olds and their parents. Erica, at this age, was a bit timid, passive, even scared. Though both of her parents worked full time, her babysitter was a warm and loving person, and her parents tried very hard to spend "quality, fun" time with her when they could. Still, Erica would frequently awaken at night with nightmares and wouldn't stop crying until she was brought into bed with her parents.

In consultation, it was discovered that Erica—like many children who do not display a range of emotions—was frightened of her aggressive impulses. As a result, Erica's parents agreed to let her flex some of her aggressive muscles. Extra floor time with dolls, animals, cars, and her parents' participation became a way for Erica to "work out" the part of her personality that had not been getting any support during the day. Now the cars were crashing and the house falling down during the early evening, instead of in nightmares, with the security of her mom as her play partner. Instead of being alone and overwhelmed by her aggressive feelings at night, Erica, with the support of both her babysitter and her parents, was able to stop regressing and begin sleeping through the night.

During this phase, when babies need to feel they are somewhat in control of themselves, eating problems may also surface. Jonathan's diet at sixteen months consisted of pasta and chocolate— period. Aside from being extremely bright and able to name things he wanted, he was very negative. His mother and father, who disliked arguments, dealt with Jonathan either by forcing him to do what they wanted or by giving in. Clearly, Jonathan was not getting the practice he needed with the skill of negotiation. So he exercised his control by not eating.

At quite young ages, children become powerful players in the family drama, with needs that must be respected. Accordingly, Jonathan's parents must learn to offer him choices and be willing to negotiate with him in a way that is pleasant and warm, yet at the same time firm. Sometimes parents don't recognize when their child is ready for such "grown-up" treatment, and they often confuse "grown-up" treatment with indulgence. Respectful, "grown-up" behavior can only be encouraged by treating your child like-wise: engaged negotiation coupled with limits when necessary, extra floor time, persuasion, and the presentation of choices around mealtime can help Jonathan become more flexible.

LIMIT SETTING

Sometimes, as a baby is making her first forays into the world as an independent person, Mommy or Daddy gets concerned about the amount of freedom she should have. They worry that she will be too destructive or that she will hurt herself or a new baby brother or sister. Or perhaps they just like to be in control, so they hover about and show her the "right" way to play with the blocks or where or how to walk or crawl. Under these conditions, any young pioneer is likely to become more irritable, more re-bellious, and more negative than she normally would.

On the other hand, for those of you who believe "it will all happen anyway, with or without me," be aware that insufficient attention—the lack of your admiring eye and respect—is also likely to lead to frustration and a very lonely sense of anger. In either case, should you begin to see patterns of negativism, pro-vocativeness, overt expressions of aggression (such as biting and kicking, sleep problems, or eating problems) that you think might be related to anger, you can do a lot to help your baby.

When she's nine or ten months old, your baby's anger will be quite straightforward. A baby this age, however, will need re-peated exposure to the co-existence of limits and support in order to begin the long process of accepting and internalizing limits.

It's easy to know that when she grabs something dangerous, like scissors, you need to quickly take them away from her. But how can this be accomplished in a way that allows some learning to take place too? Actually, you can use the same limit-setting lessons even in a dangerous situation. Begin by holding her hand firmly, looking into her eyes, and saying, "No, no. This is dangerous." Then take it away carefully. Baby may make a furious noise and lunge to recapture her now precious object. "Aha!" you think. "Another learning opportunity." Maintain eye contact and let her know you respect her desire to get it back ("I know you want this. I'm sorry I can't give it to you, but . . ."). In a firm, resolved voice—not mean, not hysterical—repeat your "No," adding a short, emphatic explanation. Then, remembering the maxim of "Increased limits, increased freedom," offer an alternative object of activity, along with your engagement and attention. Don't make the mistake of offering the distraction too soon. First get the sense that she has some understanding of the "No," and *then* offer an attractive alternative.

Using limit setting to help a sixteen-month-old practice her ability to communicate from a distance can be a more sophisticated event, although the same principles always apply: empathize, engage, and elevate.

Rosa is playing on the floor with her blocks. Mother is reading the newspaper nearby. Rosa picks up a block, walks over to Mother, and heaves it at Mother and her paper. Mother isn't slow to get the message.

MOTHER: "Rosa, no throwing blocks!" (Mother puts her paper down)

ROSA: (Picks up the block again and aims it)

MOTHER: (Loudly) "No!" (Gestures with her arms) "Put it down."

ROSA: (Looks and aims again)

MOTHER: (Gestures) "Put it down. Not nice!" (Even louder)

ROSA: (Finally agrees. If Rosa had not agreed, physical restraint, such as holding Rosa's arm, would have followed.)

MOTHER: "Do you need me now?"

ROSA: (Looking satisfied, starts back to her blocks)

MOTHER: "Rosa, I know you want me to watch you. Next time you can call me first, like this." (Cups her hands around her mouth and calls "Mommy") "Here, you be the mommy." (Mother gives Rosa the newspaper and sits her down on the chair) "I'm the baby." (Mother sits near blocks)

ROSA: (Watches, fascinated)

MOTHER: "Oh, I want my mommy to watch me." (Turns toward Rosa, cups her hands around her mouth again, calls, "Mommy," grins and then says, "Okay?")

If Mother can now get Rosa to actually imitate her actions, they both get a gold star; but even if it doesn't happen now, there's always the next time. If Rosa persists in using blocks, toys, or other unacceptable means of gaining her mother's attention, sanctions should eventually be used, such as taking away the block or toy with an explanation of why it's being taken away.

Children at this stage are capable of testing limits in a planned fashion, such as older children do. Don't be surprised if you find such things as food in the playroom, crayons on the wall, older or younger siblings being pinched or bitten, raucous noise—you can probably add a few of your own.

Don't despair. If you act quickly and respect your child's basic desire (and need) to express aggression, you need only change the context in which these emotions are expressed and make the learning *active,* not just a lecture. For example:

MOTHER: "Johnny! Did you draw on the wall?"

JOHNNY: (Silence)

MOTHER: "I know I yelled at you and you were mad, but don't you know that's a no-no?"

JOHNNY: (Silence. He begins to walk away)

MOTHER: (Loudly) "Come back here!"

JOHNNY: (He returns)

MOTHER: "Okay. Let's practice with crayons and paper."

JOHNNY: (Scribbles on some paper)

MOTHER: "Good." (Then she points to wall) "Is that okay?"

JOHNNY: (Looks guilty, then shakes his head "No")

MOTHER: "Let's do some more drawing." (They draw together)

We talked elsewhere about setting limits on this behavior and using floor time to learn about the reasons for the aggression. (Firm limits are especially important if the behavior is repeated.) But, as this example points out, you should also show respect for your child's basic interests and help him shift context.

Stage Five:
Emotional Ideas (18 to 30 Months)

This is the stage of emotional development where children who are ready to form emotional ideas learn to construct and "play out" their own thoughts. You will see this in your child's pretend play when two dolls or stuffed animals fight, or when the doll who has been naughty gets hit. We see it expressed, as well, in language such as "Me mad!" or "I hate you!" Even children who are delayed in expressive language can use this kind of make-believe play to express their feelings and newly formed emotional ideas.

What your child will need the most during this stage is *practice* for her new ability, and the best workout she can have is pretend play. Think of pretend play as the gymnasium for the exercise of emotional ideas.

FLOOR TIME

The child whose own expression of anger is limited to yelling and hitting is not as advanced as one who can also have her dolls yell and hit. Though this may sound like obnoxious behavior to you—behavior that you wouldn't encourage in your child—recognize that, as with any of life's emotions, anger and aggression need to be *practiced* and integrated to a higher level of understanding. The child who can shift from hitting to having her dolls hit is setting the stage for more complex conceptualization.

Between eighteen and twenty-two months, it is not unusual to see a child vent emotion by banging on the floor and yelling. Mother or Father can take this opportunity to sit right down beside her, say, "You're angry!" and perhaps pick up a doll and say, "Mad." Baby may imitate and get the underlying idea that she can use stuffed animals or other objects to help express her feelings. She may also look at her parents as though they have lost their minds, but eventually, with encouragement, she will begin to make the transition from yelling and hitting to identifying, articulating, and reasoning. If the parents remain calm and attentive, and use simple pretend play, the baby can use her parents as a model for this transition.

Thirty-month-old Jason has been grumpy since his return from the playground. He won't let go of his sandbox toys, so Mommy puts him on the floor to spend a little time. She adds a couple of rubber ducks to see whether she can encourage him to "play out" whatever is bothering him. "Here are duckies. They want to play, too." Jason glowers under his brows, holding his pail and shovel even tighter. After another moment, he places them carefully behind him and picks up the ducks. Pretty soon one duck is bashing the other and Mommy says, "Those duckies are so mad at each other. I wonder what made them so mad." Jason, continuing to bash, says, "Duckie take toys away. Duckies fighting." Mommy now remembers a seemingly slight incident in the sandbox. "I guess I'd be pretty mad if someone tried to take my toys away." "Yeah, mad." Jason was now visibly more relaxed, and when floor time continued, he even let the duckies play in the pail.

Jason is learning a number of things: that he has an outlet other than glowering and holding on to his toys to express his anger; that what he is feeling has a name; and that he can talk about his feelings as well as act them out in pretend play. He is also learning that his "bad" feelings can be understood by his Mommy and that she can be trusted to react in a supportive way when he elevates and shares them.

Samantha, all of three and a half years old, is mad as the dickens at Daddy because he wouldn't buy her a new toy. She's been thinking off and on all day about how mad she is, how much she wants that new toy from Daddy, and how she is going to scream and yell at Daddy when he comes home. She has been testy and screaming at Mom in anticipation. If, with Mother's help (who says, "Why so mad today?" instead of just yelling back), she can be engaged in floor time, she will have an opportunity to feel warm, close, and understood and, hopefully, to communicate some of her feelings. Pretend play can give her a way of thinking about her anger. With this practice, Daddy's homecoming may find her saying, "Where's my toy?" Daddy says, "No, I told you I'm not getting it for you." She can then look Daddy in the eye, stomp her foot, and say, "I'm mad!" The child who can do this is unlikely to need to bite and kick her sibling, be provocative with Mother, or use other indirect ways of dealing with anger.

This child, who can elevate anger to the world of ideas and ultimately to the world of reason, will likely be more caring than the child who cannot; she will worry less that her angry feelings will intrude upon and become confused with her loving feelings. She can label them, understand them, and come to see that loving Mommy and Daddy does not necessarily preclude her from becoming angry with them on occasion. To be sure, we all struggle throughout the entire course of our lives with how to reconcile our loving and our angry feelings, but those children who begin the process early have a big head start on a lifelong endeavor.

If you are going to help your children learn to put all feelings, especially angry ones, into the world of ideas, it means you have to come to grips with your own conflicts and anxieties about anger and aggression. Once you do this—and it may not be easy—you can face your child's anger and aggression with some degree of equanimity, and can turn expressions of anger into learning experiences.

Consider the following example. If, as Jill excitedly and even joyfully shoots the bad guy, you say, "Boy, you're really giving it to him," she will experience your empathy and understanding. Should the rambunctious play lead her to become overexcited, then you can intervene with "Gee. Sometimes you get so angry you feel like it's hard to control it," or, "You're getting so excited it's hard to stop." These comments help your child recognize her feelings—both the anger and the loss of control. With this kind of empathy, your child will most likely be responsive to your introducing a doctor to care for the bad guy. (It often happens that with your empathy for the angry side of the equation, your child will add the nurturing spontaneously.)

If, on the other hand, you become upset every time the doll gets angry or wants to hit another doll, your child will think that putting anger into pretend play, and then into words, is frightening and unacceptable. If you say, "Oh, but won't he hurt the poor doll?" when you see your child hitting one doll with another, your child will probably feel misunderstood—this is not where she's coming from at the moment!

Parents sometimes equate feeling and thought with action—"If I think it, I will do it"—they avoid "pretend" or even verbalization of anger. If this is so, it may signify that they face the same challenge as their children: how to get from behavior to emotional ideas. The sense that an idea equals action often means that the stage of "ideas" has only partly been reached in terms of certain emotions. Anger is a frequent "lingerer." A true emotional idea is free from action, and feels safe when thought.

DIFFICULTIES

Parents frequently have very different attitudes toward anger and aggression in boys and the same emotions in girls. Boys are thought to "need" rough-and-tumble play while girls require only gentleness. To be sure, the cultural and biological differences between boys and girls often dictate the ways in which we play with them. Enjoy these differences as contributors to a child's sense of identity, but at the same time, give both boys and girls equal access to their assertive and aggressive feelings. The little girl who has a tea party may spank the doll who spoils the cake. This girl is showing aggression just as well as the boy whose monsters battle with one another.

Let's juxtapose two examples. In one, Michael has two racers competing in his favorite racing cars, each struggling to be the winner. The competition is fierce and wild, particularly with Father as one of the racers. In the other, Holly wishes to have a dance contest like Bert and Ernie's on television. Mother plays with one doll and Holly another.

Holly's enthusiasm for winning the dance contest is no less than Michael's enthusiasm for winning the car race. However, Holly's mother is less aware of, and sometimes ignores, Holly's interest in winning and competing. Instead, she emphasizes her daughter's interest in dancing and friendship. "Oh, how nice. The dolls are dancing together." Holly may say in frustration, "But I won!" and Mother may respond in a placating manner, "Oh, it doesn't make any difference." Back with Michael and Daddy racing their cars, Daddy says, "You beat me. You're the winner!," clapping loudly at Michael's great victory.

So, because assertiveness and competition are in part defined by the reactions they get, boys and girls can get very different ideas about the appropriateness of this kind of behavior. When Holly goes to school and has to deal with a peer rejecting her or has to try out for a part in the play, her parents might be surprised at her anxiety about assertiveness and competition. But if they take a close look at the attitudes they've communicated to her, they won't be.

Whatever the play, you can tease out the theme. Being the best Mommy is no different than being the best football player.

Remember that at this time in your child's life, the desire to be competitive or assertive is only one of several emerging emotions. Equally important are nurturing and caring—areas where we also see differences between boys and girls. Nurturing and sympathy (discussed in another section) are often more supported in girls than boys, for example. And when we talk about equality of the sexes, we're talking about equality in all emotional realms. This does not mean sameness; it means providing the opportunity for experiencing, organizing, and expressing the full range of human feelings with respect for physical and cultural differences.

Benjamin is an exuberant twenty-one-month-old. He chases the cat at every opportunity. He screams with joy on seeing his older sister come home from school. During play together, he frequently hits her, pulls her hair, pinches her, and bites, all the while maintaining his high good humor and toothy grin. A kiss for Mommy is just as likely to turn into a bite. Daddy's ears get twisted with regularity. His intensity is exhausting, disciplining him a real challenge.

As it turned out, Benjamin's aggressive behavior determined the tone of his interactions with his parents. They spent all their time trying to control his behavior, and none either simply being with him or finding ways to help him to better express his natural aggression. Yet, how were they to get out of this pattern of power struggles without someone getting hurt?

They tried a new strategy (which follows suggestions from the Limit-Setting section in chapter III). One of the first things they did was to *categorize* his behaviors. Rather than saying, "No hitting," "No biting," "No pushing," they set firm limits emphasizing "No hurting." In this way, the child learns a core concept that ultimately is much easier to remember than twenty-three separate "no-no" behaviors.

Mother and Father provided lots of physical contact which allowed Benjamin to use his force in positive ways—rough-and-tumble play, chase and catch games, all accompanied by verbal exchanges helpful to Benjamin's struggling speech. The next aim was to help him feel part of a warm relationship, become more organized and intentional, and to express his aggression with ideas in pretend play—a tall order. Soon, he was expressing himself both verbally and physically, as he used his stuffed animals to enact dramas like "doggies fighting." With increased outlets for his forceful feelings, and extra warmth and understanding from his parents, Benjamin no longer had to resort to unacceptable and hurtful behavior in order to express himself. Over time, through pretend play and talking, it became possible to understand why he felt so angry in the first place. But that is for another discussion.

LIMIT SETTING

At this age, limit setting is quite important—and quite a challenge. As we've said, ease with both words and ideas will help your child understand limits. Don't be afraid of the long, and imperfect, dialogue in which each of you presents a point of view. Be open to listening to your child, even if all he has to say is, "I need that toy now! I want it, I want it, I want it!" Negotiate when necessary, but be comfortable in remaining firm. Being open to persuasion is very different from allowing yourself to be intimidated—and children "smell" the difference. They know it in their bones.

Consider the following scene with two-and-a-half-year-old Sam:

SAM: (Crying miserably—he's been at this a while) "I want to go outside!"

PARENT: (For the tenth time) "No—it's raining outside! You can't play in the rain!"

The scenario above lends itself nicely to endless repetition. Read on, however, for an instructive alternative.

SAM: (Still at it) "I want to go outside!"

PARENT: "I wish you could go outside and play. What would you do if you could go out?"

SAM: (Sniffling)"I want to ride my car!" (A new piece of information. Patience has allowed another aspect of Sam's desire to be identified)

PARENT: "Could you pretend to ride your car in here?"

SAM: (Beginning to cry again) "No! I want to ride my car outside!"

PARENT: "I guess you really do want to ride your car. It's raining out now and your car is wet. Can we play something else until it stops raining?"

SAM: "You play with me."

PARENT: "Okay."

SAM: "Play pretend cars inside."

PARENT: "Okay."

This scene could have easily escalated into Sam's misbehaving and being punished. The intervening factor was Mother's discovery of Sam's motive and her willingness to work with that information. In this case, the most effective limit was Mother's detective work. Good limit setting sometimes means limits don't have to be used. Firm persistence is essential. Two minutes after you're about to give up, Sam or Sally compromises. If they do not you are still able to maintain your firm limit.

Between the ages of two and three, your child is capable of understanding punishments. The child who is mischievous in the morning can even be reminded of her misbehavior later in the day when she is not allowed to watch cartoons (provided, of course, you have warned her that this will happen). Let your child know the consequences of her bad behavior at the time of the behavior, and let her know again when she is about to have her punishment.

Discipline consists of a combination of firm limit setting (verbal explanations, gestures, and emotional communication), together with physical restraint (only when necessary and only when either you are tired, need to do something quickly, or don't have the time for a *teaching opportunity*), backed up with punishments, and all balanced by extra floor time. This approach gives your child the tools and motivation to behave differently next time. Punishment provides the motivation. Floor time and chitchats encourage empathy, understanding, and the ability to use reason.

Whenever you increase punishment, always increase floor time and chitchats, where you listen and empathize with the child's perspective. Remember, a lecture is not a dialogue and it may not be heard or understood. Two-way discussions let you know what your child understands, even if he disagrees.

Limit setting also gives the child the security to know that she can control her angry feelings. So, while you might feel that limit setting undermines spontaneity, it's actually just the reverse. Your child must feel secure—must not be scared that her anger will get out of control—in order to be able to experiment with the various dramas of life. Your child doesn't yet trust her own self-control. She does trust you. If she can't rely on you to help her restrain herself when she is very angry or demanding, she often feels she has only three choices: (1) become overly passive to avoid anger; (2) become inhibited and rigid to make sure she doesn't go out of control; or (3) behave very impulsively and in a disorganized way (the "daredevil") to pretend she isn't scared, even though she really is.

Stage Six:
Emotional Thinking
(30 to 48 Months)

As your child goes from ages three to four years, he will be able, more and more, to separate reality from fantasy and to separate his feelings from those of another person. He will come to know that one idea can cause another. His arguments will become more logical: "I don't want to eat this food because it's icky, it smells bad, and furthermore, I think it's been in the refrigerator for three days"; "I want that toy because I need it and because my friend Susie has it." Even though fantastic, the organization of his stories also becomes more complex and logical as the spaceman needs just the right rocket ship to get to the moon.

Your child is more interested in power and grandeur. He is the biggest and the strongest. This view of the world, alongside a private feeling of being vulnerable, makes negotiations all the more difficult. He is beginning to feel more competitive with family members. More and more he wants to be special.

FLOOR TIME

During this stage, encourage your child's logic, listen to his arguments, try to understand his point of view—and *debate with him*. You don't need to give in, but you should take advantage of this opportunity to allow your child to *exercise his emotional logic and his emotional reality testing*. Doing this will enhance his ability to deal with his anger, and increase his self-esteem as well as his logical abilities.

But before the debate occurs, his feelings have to be identified and engaged.

Let's look at Jeannie's introduction to nursery school. (Separation anxiety is one of the negative emotions covered in chapter VII.) Timid and shy at first, Jeannie seemed afraid of both children and teachers. She clung pathetically to her mother. For the first few days, Mother was sympathetic and understanding, then feeling pressured about getting to work late, she decided that Jeannie had better go it alone, and she left. When she picked

Jeannie up the next few days, she got the cold shoulder from her daughter. At home, Jeannie was irritable. Constantly spilling her drinks was one of the ways she showed this. Mother, feeling guilty about leaving Jeannie at school, would wipe the spills and not say anything, sending the undesirable message that it was okay to be aggressive in a passive way.

After reexamining her motives, Mother decided to try to woo Jeannie into a new level of communication.

MOTHER: "How did you feel when I left you at school this morning?"

JEANNIE: (No answer)

MOTHER: "Were you mostly sad, mad, or scared?"

JEANNIE: (No answer, and then she says, "Not talking.")

MOTHER: (Picks up a nearby doll) "Oh, I know why this doll won't talk to me. It's because I left her alone all day. Now she's going to leave me all alone and no one will take care of me."

JEANNIE: (Picking up another doll) "Oh no. Don't leave me all alone. Boo-hoo."

Jeannie finally goes over, mumbles to Mother's doll, and then walks away, repeating this again and again. Then her doll gives the other doll a spanking for "going away" and she says, "Never do that again!"

In this interaction, Jeannie is in the driver's seat. *She* is the one who is leaving and Mother relives Jeannie's feelings. Mother makes it clear that she can empathize with Jeannie's feelings, while giving Jeannie the opportunity to get some satisfaction and communicate her anger through fantasy. Three days of this sort of play were needed before Jeannie was able to really grin at Mother and forgive her. The next game Jeannie suggested was that the two dolls go away together for a trip, leaving Father behind! This solution let feelings be put into words and ideas and helped Mother woo Jeannie into a pattern of relatedness that—incidentally—relieved Mother's guilt.

Once Jeannie was able to express her feelings, she decided Mother should "work less and help in school." A great debate ensued when Mother explained why she had to work. Jeannie countered each argument with her point of view, "Let Daddy work more. I will give up my toys!" Jeannie got great practice and now at age eight still loves to debate with Mom. No long-run resolution occurred, but Jeannie and Mother stayed engaged and aware of each other's viewpoint—no small accomplishment.

When your slightly older, but still little, child comes home from nursery school looking frustrated and sad, it's problem-solving time. You can comment that he looks like he's had a rough day. Maybe not after the first minute, but after about ten minutes of non-pressured "hanging out," perhaps playing on the floor with a toy, he'll talk about how another child took away his favorite toy and wouldn't give it back. "How did you feel about that?" you'll ask. Your child may ignore you. "I remember when I was little, someone did that to me. I was pretty angry." Then he might come out with, "Yeah, she really made me mad." And you can respond with "I can see how mad you felt."

With encouragement, your child may go on to tell you that he felt like kicking and biting her, but was afraid the teacher would be mad at him, so he just let her take the toy away. Sympathetically, and without judgment on your part, you two can talk about what he can do in such circumstances—how he can protect his property better, either by holding on to the toy or calling the teacher over for help. You will want to explore with him why he's afraid that the teacher would be mad at him for protecting his property, as well as the limits of appropriate assertiveness at school.

These chitchats must not deteriorate into your lecturing at him. *He* must talk 50 percent of the time. Let him tell you why your suggestions are not so good—as one child told me, "Kids can't say that." Even if your suggestions are rejected, as long as your child is talking, something much more important is being accepted— the process of interactive reasoning. The talk will often be intermingled with other play and may take half an hour or more. Forget the quick five-minute chat. Would five minutes work for you if you were very upset? Remember, a few chapters back it took Drew's mother three days to get him to talk.

Such an instance can be a really wonderful opportunity to strengthen the bonds between you and your child. The emotional closeness that comes from the understanding and empathy on your part can enrich you both. Your child will see that he can come to you when he's troubled and you won't either denigrate his feelings or immediately tell him what he did wrong. Once he knows you're "on his side," you can next begin to help him define different elements of assertiveness, anger, and feelings about other people's anger.

DIFFICULTIES

Normally during this stage children begin to spend some time away from home, whether in a play group or in nursery school. This means that both parents and children are now coping with two (or more) environments, each having its own set of problems as well as rewards. Children typically face many difficulties during this transitional time. Here are some of what you can expect.

IN SCHOOL:

Possessions and territoriality. Mixing ten to fifteen little personalities for the first time can set off the need for some big adjustments. At one extreme are children who may hoard toys and possessions and threaten others who want to use them. They may feel the need to extend their ownership to certain chairs or other places in the room. At the other end of the spectrum is the child who allows toys and possessions to be taken away from him, who may cry but won't defend himself. Both types of children need to learn more balance. Extra floor time and chitchats are a good start.

Teasing and name calling. You've heard about the cruelty of small children—believe it. Believe also, however, that parents often take offense sooner than their offspring. If your child is on the receiving end, ascertain the degree of *his* hurt before you say what's on *your* mind. If yours is the perpetrator, examine your family's interactions to determine whether it's part of the family style.

Physical aggression. Some children are just more physically rough and tumble than others, but hurtful aggression and aggression designed to intimidate must be worked out in a way that teaches limits and lets the child find better alternatives for these feelings.

The old standards of floor time and chitchat, combined with limit setting, all apply here.

Fear of physical aggression. The timid child who encounters physical aggression in one or more of his classmates may withdraw in order to preserve his safety. Often a fearful child will not admit what is troubling him directly. It may take gentle probing and alertness on the part of parents to find the source of the problem and provide him with extra practice in the larger group at school. Inviting one and then two and even three kids from school to your home can create a sense of security in a small group. Then the child can use his new "friends" for security at school. Teacher can also be encouraged to bring him along one step at a time. In any case, it's important to recognize that there are many approaches to large groups, as will be discussed in the chapter on peer and group relationships.

AT HOME:

Power struggles. This is the name of the game for this age. Your little one is caught between complete dependence on you and wanting to be entirely free. From dressing in the morning to going to bed at night, the great majority of issues you will face have power as an underlying theme. You might alleviate some of these struggles by making sure that they are all worth fighting over. If your daughter really loves the red blouse with the orange pants, need you care? Or how about offering a range of choices on some sticky issues?

As your child's struggle for autonomy begins, provide rules and structure, but also make yourself an ally rather than an adversary. Power struggles and floor time can combine to provide both you and your child with a fresh and often funny change of perspective. Wouldn't you say that, one way or another, your child goes along with you about 90 percent of the time? We're not saying that this happens without a fight, but ultimately our young children are pretty much under our thumbs. So, how about changing places to even things out? During floor time, let your child get a taste of being the boss, while you feel what it's like to be bossed. There are innumerable family dramas you can concoct together that will permit your child to both flex his muscles a little and vent some of those frustrations in make-believe instead of at the dinner table or bedtime.

For example, he may cherish the idea of being the tyrant in a bedtime drama, with you the tyrannized, of course. Once the drama is set and he's enjoying ordering you around, you might say, "I know it's my bedtime, but please may I stay up with you for a few minutes more?" Here is what's likely to follow:

CHILD: "No, now you must go to sleep."

PARENT: "But what if I won't?"

CHILD: (With great delight) "You can't watch television for ten years," or perhaps, "Your favorite toy is gone for the rest of your life."

You'll be surprised to see that his punishments are far greater than any you've ever served and that he takes great delight in being the one who is dishing them out.

You may decide on a different drama. You may say you're going out to play in the rain. He'll take great delight in telling you not only to stay in but to go to your room and look at the wall. When you ask why, he might say, "Because I said so." Or you may ask for a new toy and threaten to cry until you get it. You'll soon see that he has no tolerance for your "spoiled behavior." He'll tell you quickly, "Cry and you'll get your feet squeezed," or your nose bopped. And if you say, "Please, please, please don't hurt me!" he will look at you angrily and say, "You'd better do what I say."

Through these dramas you will see how much your young child enjoys being the dictator. He can gain much pleasure and understanding by acting out his dictatorial tendencies. These times will also give you insights into the nature of this side of his personality. Many parents are surprised that their child may not only copy their disciplinary style, but go way beyond anything they have imagined. Some parents also see more of themselves than they wish to. It can make one reconsider one's approach.

Understanding your child's desire to be the boss and to be in charge helps you to empathize with the supreme compromise your child is making when he agrees to go to sleep, not to throw his food around, to stay inside when it's raining, or to wait until next weekend for a new toy. Children, in part, feel very, very powerful; at the same time they feel equally helpless and vulnerable. They need to be in touch with each side of this equation. Pretend play is the perfect arena for them to enact the need for power. And from time to time pretend play can also help your child experience themes of vulnerability: a doll who is sick, or the little kitty cat who has lost his mommy. Help create a wonderful balance in your child, so he can experience both sides of his emotional equation— and all the steps in between.

LIMIT SETTING

Punishments can now be removed from the scene of the crime, so to speak. Your child can behave badly in the supermarket and you can warn her by saying, "I'm not going to have a scene with you now, but tonight we will discuss this." Later that evening, remind her of her unacceptable behavior, discuss it with her, and arrive at a punishment if necessary. She'll remember her behavior quite clearly. You may have noticed your three-and-a-half- or four-year-old child has an excellent memory now; better than many adults. She also understands the logic of sanctions for "crimes committed in the past." Don't expect passive acceptance, however, of your judgments. Remember, your child is now experimenting with the power of logic and will probably exercise it to the utmost in justifying her actions and avoiding punishment. This is healthy and good. Try to retain your sense of humor. Try also to turn the occasion into an opportunity for problem solving rather than the accomplishment of punishment for punishment's sake alone.

As we have described, anger, like other important forces shaping your child's personality, has its own developmental progression. It begins as a purely physical expression (irritability) when your child's sense of himself and the world are not clearly separate. As he grows, his ability to gesture with arm or leg movements or facial expressions helps him conceive of himself as a behaving, intentional person who can have an effect on others; and finally, his ability to use ideas to symbolize or "picture" anger emerges, teaching him to anticipate the consequences of being angry, plan out different strategies to deal with his anger, and even figure out why he is angry. Toward the end of this latter stage, we even see how his conscience is being formed as he begins having opinions about good and bad ways of dealing with anger and tries to abide by his own rules.

As with any other emotion, your child needs to practice anger and aggression. But he also needs to have limits set on this behavior in order that it may evolve to a higher level of understanding and expression. Remember your floor-time ground rules: Acknowledge the feeling, engage your child in interaction, build on his level of response. Understand that circumstances may heighten your child's feelings in this area, that experimentation is natural, and that your child will certainly challenge whatever limits you set. Isn't that what children are for?

VII

Negative Emotions: Separation Anxiety, Fears, Sadness, and Competition

The emotions that give us the most trouble are the ones that are rarely talked about. It may take a while to get used to the idea that separation anxiety, fears, rivalry and competition, and even sadness—what we call "negative" emotions—are a normal part of the growth process, like life's positive emotions, such as love, sharing, or empathy.

If you can learn to see the adaptive side of negative emotions, it will help you appreciate your children more and enjoy their new talents, whether these be competing more effectively with siblings or finding a new way of being rivalrous with a friend— or with you. Even their fears and sadnesses can be feelings you can learn to appreciate in them, as well as help them through. Certainly any emotion that your child feels as painful requires your support, security, and guidance to help him over the emotional hurdles. If you are able to understand the hurdles from both sides—the frightening and the adaptive—you'll be able not only to cope with, but also to see the value in feelings and behaviors many think shouldn't exist.

Separation Anxiety

Separation anxiety is an emotion that most people would assume is negative; but in order to have this feeling in the first place, your baby has to feel she has something to lose. This means your baby has invested in the world—she has passed a major milestone in her emotional development. Let's take a closer look, and trace the development of separation anxiety from its beginning.

In the first couple of months of life, your new baby is not only awakening to the world but beginning to take a special interest in the *human* world. Shortly after this time you may also see that your baby reacts with some cautiousness around certain strangers, while with others she is quite outgoing. This could be viewed as friendliness or naivete depending on your perspective. Should Aunt Sally, who hasn't been around for a while, come for a visit and want to pick the baby up, baby may grab onto Mommy and turn away. Uncle Joe, who is a real flirt, may get a big smile. Often the first signs of separation anxiety will appear just as your baby is making an emotional investment in one or two key people. As you notice her wariness you'll also see the beginnings of her attachment to you consolidating, although if she has frequent contact with a variety of adults she may be less cautious and shy.

At eight months the intensity of your baby's awareness of others and discomfort with strangers increases since, by that time, she is becoming more intentional: now she can reach out when she wants to be held, and make her needs known. The ability to distinguish different internal states, including feelings, has arrived. Once she knows what it feels like to be close, she'll want to reach for those she trusts—like Mommy or Daddy—and will turn away from a stranger with purpose. Some parents feel their baby is becoming a little tyrant at this stage, since she can be very controlling and manipulative, but this is also because she knows who she does and doesn't want to be with.

So at eight or nine months you may have the following typical separation scenario: Mommy and Daddy want to go out on Saturday night. The babysitter (who is wonderful, of course) comes over and—guess what?—the baby has a temper tantrum. Aside from how Mommy and Daddy should deal with this, or whether they should or shouldn't leave (we'll get to that later), the anxiety, the protest, and, yes, even the temper tantrum, are products of your child's ability to reach out, know what she wants, and demand her rights. That's the positive side of the equation, which you can keep in mind.

At fourteen or fifteen months, your toddler will be even more intentional. She's beyond crawling and probably beginning to take her first steps. She understands herself as a person who is either mischievous or nice, and Mommy and Daddy as people who are either mean or loving, accepting or rejecting. She begins to see that these different parts of herself all belong to one person, and Mommy and Daddy's different inclinations are parts of them, too.

Your baby is also trying to integrate her need for independence, her new motor ability, and her navigational ability, which allows her much greater range than before. Her ability to see, hear, and comprehend your signals helps fulfill her need to be independent. A nineteen- or twenty-month-old may be able to talk to you from the playroom, even when you're out of sight in another room. (If she happens to have some difficulty with this, you may find your child clinging to you in order to deal with worries of separation and get the feelings of closeness she needs.)

It is often assumed that separation anxiety is only an emotional phenomenon. It is also in part dependent on how a child figures out where he is in physical relationship to his mother. Can he figure out where the room he is in connects to the room Mother is in? This visual, spatial, or navigational ability is in part related to the maturation of his nervous system, just as is learning to walk or talk. Interestingly, an advanced talker may lag as a navigator, and vice versa.

As part of all this, your baby may experience various degrees of separation anxiety, depending on how he's beginning to see the world. He can become more controlling and demanding, or more frightened, as his new ability to understand what a big place his world is also shows him how small and helpless he can be. These same abilities, however, can serve to make him feel more secure, and once they do, he will begin to ease up on you. The struggle for independence will have a lot to do with the interplay of his new abilities (feeling close from afar, for example) and his tendency to overstep them (for example, when he goes into another room and feels insecure about finding you). The emergence of these two factors makes it possible for him to experiment with separation in new ways.

TWO TO FOUR YEARS

Sometime between two and four, children are able to take a picture of their mommies and daddies with them wherever they go by using their new ability to create mental symbols. Your child can now carry her "security blanket" with her by picturing Mommy giving her a hug. But she can also use this to compare what she wants to what she has. She may look at the teacher and say, "Not my mommy!" She may picture Mommy and say, "I want her for real, not just in my imagination." Or, because her ability to picture Mom is new, she may lose it temporarily when she's tired, angry, or frightened. Your child, because she can now use a certain logic and intentionality to figure things out, will manipulate these skills to get what she wants, but—rest assured—you can also enlist these new logical capabilities to persuade her to consider your point of view.

As a parent, if you are able to understand problems of separation anxiety from both sides, you can often avoid a power struggle and lead your child to a solution that satisfies everyone involved. A good example recently took place at my house.

Four-year-old Abigail came over to play with our daughter while my wife and Abigail's mother went out for an afternoon by themselves. Everything depended, however, on the visiting four-year-old's willingness to stay. Mother brought Abigail in and introduced her to my daughter and me. The two girls stared at each other, and the moment of truth arrived as Mother prepared to leave. Abigail fastened herself to Mother's leg and started to cry. To help Abigail and her mother with their challenge, I called upon two principles.

Principle 1. Whenever a child is scared and panicky, create a sense of extra security.

I encouraged Mother to forget about leaving for the next 20 minutes. She took off her coat, relaxed, and conveyed the sense that she was in no hurry and that we would all have a good time together.

This is a good general principle to use when helping your child overcome a developmental anxiety such as separation. At the base of mastering any new task is feeling secure. Your child cannot achieve that if she feels the rug has been pulled out from under her.

On the other hand, any new accomplishment comes at the price of giving up something else. When a child learns to walk, he gives up being carried around. Eventually he will come to the conclusion that walking and independence are worth the loss of contact with Mommy or Daddy. But this is something your child has to decide for himself. Initially he will experiment; he'll walk a little, and then ask to be carried a little. A firmly established sense of security will help him decide whether or not his new achievement is worth what he's going to lose. Now, back to our story.

With Mother relaxed and all of us moved to a location good for running and game playing, Principles 1a and 2 were considered to further help Abigail and her mother master their anxieties.

Principle 1a. Try to enhance the sense of security with a concrete symbol: special toys, food, and the like.

I offered both girls some fruit which they ate together. So, with Mother offering the concrete security of her admiring and involved presence and with the food increasing Abigail's sense of security and forging a link to her new friends, we continued.

Principle 2. Promote activities the child associates with a sense of active competence and, therefore, internal security.

Abigail was a good runner and jumper, we learned from her mother. The two girls were soon, with our support, racing each other around the room, jumping hurdles, and doing all kinds of other physically active, muscle-flexing activities. Right then we were interested in supporting the active learning side of Abigail's personality that was trying to achieve mastery and take charge, rather than the passive learning side (reading or watching), which takes things on with a less pronounced sense of achievement.

Soon, Abigail and my daughter were completely caught up in each other. Mommy waved goodbye, Abigail waved back, and we had a wonderful day. Time from entrance to Mommy's exit—15 minutes.

The same principle can apply to a frightened child starting nursery school. Mother or Father should relax and remain in the classroom initially, thereby avoiding a power struggle at the door. This can continue through the first or second class, or for however long it takes. The teacher will gradually become the one who engenders a sense of security in your child by making her comfortable and involving her little by little in activities with the other children. If your child is very shy, perhaps she will play with one or two others at first until she is comfortable in the larger group— for example, the teacher or mother and just two children can play a game that is active and within the child's mastery. Then perhaps another can join the group, and then another . . . Once your child becomes comfortable with the whole group, Mother will be able to say goodbye: what your child is giving up—being with Mommy or Daddy—will be far outweighed by the pleasure of having new playmates, new games and activities, and a teacher who is sensitive. Your child may be one who enters one toe at a time, or perhaps she'll plunge in head first; but either way, this is a time to pay special attention to and respect individual differences.

Two other things that may contribute to the child's sense of security are her bringing along a favorite toy to bridge the unfamiliar, and inviting a new friend over after school, thus bringing the less familiar to secure turf.

An additional piece of the puzzle for many children in the two- to four-year-old range is the need to understand their own experience. You can help your child translate his or her behaviors and sensations into mental images, or ideas. The ability to symbolize the world is vital to comprehension. So, should your child still experience a great deal of separation anxiety after your careful attention to the principles discussed here, there is still hope. Sit with her in a quiet corner with a few dolls and see if she might be able to play out a situation in which people or animals leave each other. (For the very active, hide-and-seek could uncover some worries about being left.) Your child's ability to play out a troublesome situation in make-believe can help her feel more comfortable.

Reading and discussing nursery school stories also encourage the child to reveal her feelings. The verbal three- or four-year-old may be able to talk quite directly about how scary, exciting, lonely, or sad going off to school is. Daily chats about what happens at school and how it feels can help. Remember that her saying, "Nothing happened," or her ignoring your question only means that she wants you to be more patient and help her communicate. Simply putting her feelings into words in the presence of a comforting adult will make her predicament less frightening.

It's much the same as it is for an adult confronting his worst fear. When the listener is sympathetic, reassuring, and absorbs what is said, even without offering any deep insights or analysis, it enhances the speaker's ability to comprehend what he is experiencing. With your help, your child can also comprehend her experience through make-believe play. She can communicate, partially through words and partially through play, what's on her mind. And whenever she seems excessively preoccupied, extra pretend play provides a vehicle for mutual understanding.

At school, a child may be frightened of two things at once: leaving Mommy or Daddy as his base of security, and going into a situation that is scary. The activity level, the noise, the aggression of the other children, the personality of the teacher—just the strangeness of everything can be quite frightening to some children. In such a circumstance, extra floor time with you provides an opportunity for your child to let you know the nature of his scary feelings.

Little Molly may be worried that this new setting is far from safe. She experiences all the newness, strangeness, and activity as a major calamity. Hurricanes may knock the dolls and animals over, giving you a quick picture of how he probably feels in school. Or perhaps the dolls have power struggles—they fight over a toy. This gives you a sense of more intimate, one-on-one competition, perhaps with one aggressive child. Or there may be illness, with doctors taking care of the dolls, suggesting a concern for her physical health when she's separated from Mommy. You might see themes of possessiveness—she may be overwhelmed with her own greed over the new toys and all the beautiful clothes the other children are wearing.

The possibilities are endless—you shouldn't even try to guess them in advance. Nor do you need to play therapist to your child. You need only to be a good play partner, helping her to continually put the themes of her play into words, helping her to elaborate—both in play and in talk. Doing this in the context of a secure relationship with an empathic Mommy or Daddy will allow her to work out some of her fears and concerns.

Eddie was just such a youngster. He cried when Mommy left him, he cried when she came to pick him up. He had nightmares the first two weeks of school. Extra floor time revealed his feelings of greed. Eddie's doll wanted everything the other dolls had. In school the teacher reported that Eddie tried constantly to take the other children's toys. It became clear that he was trying to make up for his loss of security by making sure he had all the toys in the world. As Eddie began to play this out more and more, Mommy sympathized with how much Eddie wanted and how important it was for him to have everything. Eddie then began to talk more directly about wanting Tommy's new truck, new house, new spaceman doll. Eddie felt he needed lots of things at school, Mommy said. Were there things at home he wanted too? Eddie asked, "Where's Daddy?"

As it turned out, during this difficult transition to school Eddie's father had been traveling a lot; Mommy quickly picked up on Eddie's concern. "Oh, you know, Daddy's in Chicago, but he'll be calling in a few minutes. Tell Daddy how you feel when he gets on the phone." When Daddy called, Eddie, for the first time, said "I miss you."

Fortunately, Daddy's travels were almost over. Once home, he could act as another ally for Eddie, helping him master the new experience of going to school. He made a special effort to have floor time with Eddie, engage him in special activities, and go with him to school when possible. He'd stay a few moments in the morning or come early and participate with Eddie and his new friends at the end of the day. This seemed to do the trick. Eddie began playing more cooperatively with friends at school and seemed more secure. Mother's quick attention to the way Eddie went from talking about needing toys to asking "Where's Daddy?" had been critical: she had avoided saying, "It's naughty to take things from anyone" and picked up on the underlying problem. (Moralizing can always come later.) Eddie himself identified the link between the toys and Daddy, thus prompting his mother's insight. She could then urge Daddy to be sensitive to Eddie's new challenge.

With many children you will find that extra floor time reveals what the child needs that you can supply—and a strong foundation at home will give him the extra security he needs to master new challenges.

The principles for handling separation anxiety in the two- to four-year-old can be adjusted down developmentally to apply to children who are a little younger. The four-month-old, the eight-month-old, and the eighteen-month-old all need the same elements when confronted with new developmental challenge (like the eight-month-old who knows it's not Mommy but someone else who is trying to take care of him).

For example, twelve-month-old Susan protested vehemently when Mommy and Daddy wanted to go to the movies. They realized that her assertiveness was a sign of her awareness that they would be leaving. So, they decided to have Susan's babysitter come half an hour early so that they could all be with Susan together. In this way (1) Susan could get used to the babysitter, and (2) they could involve her, themselves, and the sitter in activities that were pleasurable and engaging. Susan experienced increased relaxation and security, since the babysitter became a comfortable person identified with fun. In addition, Mommy got Susan's favorite toy animal for her to hold and said that she wanted the animal to tell her how everything went when she returned.

Of course, Susan at twelve months didn't quite understand the chitchat that Mommy was making, but she did get the basic message: Mommy was concerned with her. Although she still protested when Mommy and Daddy left, the crying lasted only a few minutes because the sitter, after some comforting, was able to reengage her in games and eventually even in jumping on her tummy. While some children prefer more fine motor or contemplative activities, Susan had a fine time with various large muscle activities and fell asleep long before her parents returned. The next morning she greeted her parents with a big, warm smile. By the fifth time this occurred, Susan began to look forward to spending time with her sitter. The general principle here is: Extra security seems to pave the way for successful transitions.

Often parents sneak out to avoid the crying or become so anxious that they rush the transition between them and the sitter. The quick escape does not provide any security. While you may escape the initial crying, your child is more likely to be perplexed and confused and will show the signs of his distress, if not immediately, then later on. I've seen too many competent twelve-month-olds "get even" with their parents the next day for this kind of escape.

Some babies are especially reluctant to let their parents out of their sight. Eight-month-old Amy was always watching her mom and squawked even if Mom wanted to leave the room, let alone go out without her. Amy was only beginning to crawl and was sensitive to light touch and loud noises. Described by her mother as the "scared tyrant," Amy would sit in the middle of the room and control everyone with her yelling. Clearly, Amy needed to achieve an active sense of mastery. Floor games—where Amy reached, squeezed Dad's nose, banged and slithered across the room—helped her control her world in a new way that emphasized doing rather than squawking. In turn, Mother, who was quite anxious and overprotective, learned to tolerate Amy's anger (even crying anger). Mother had always picked Amy up before she had even finished her first squawk. Now she learned to give Amy a chance to "state her piece" and calm down on her own. If Amy was unable to calm down herself, Mother would help. Mother would also divide Amy's challenges into small steps. For example, after 20 minutes of floor time, Mom would take a break and talk to Amy from across the room and eventually from another room. With this firm foundation laid, the introduction of a babysitter confirmed—rather then undermined—Amy's newfound sense of independence and flexibility.

The message is: Be patient, provide extra security, and try to help your child achieve a sense of mastery with the new experience.

Fears

Fears in children are very common. Infants are sometimes scared by noises, strange machines like vacuum cleaners, or even people who look different, like clowns. This reaction is often related to special sensitivities (touch, sound, sight). One eighth-month-old, sensitive to sound, cried and stiffened up, looking scared, every time a fan went on. At first the mother panicked at her baby's distress. But as she relaxed, stroking the baby and saying in a soothing voice, "Just a fan," the baby relaxed too. Relaxing, showing your baby how to master his fearful reactions often helps soothe him through the experience. Extra security, in the form of soothing and active practice rather than passive acceptance, often helps an infant adjust to difficult sights and sounds. For example, a twelve-month-old who is scared of the vacuum cleaner may enjoy learning how to push around a play vacuum cleaner and imitate the "varuuum" noise herself. Of course, it is important to respect a baby's individual tolerances for new sights and sounds. Some will require more practice and smaller steps on their road to mastery. And some babies may just flatly refuse to tolerate certain experiences.

Early childhood is the most common time for fears. Early childhood fears can be expressed in either specific or non-specific nightmares, or they can be experienced during the day. And although no parents look forward to the night when their child wakes up crying from fright, there is an adaptative side to this behavior. In order to dream up those scary monsters, your child must have the ability to create mental pictures or images. In fact, nightmares don't usually appear until this capability emerges around eighteen months of age.

It's not by chance that most fears begin to occur at the same time your child is learning how to translate bodily sensations and behaviors into emotional ideas. Imagery and the power to create it can be frightening—even adults scare themselves with what they can imagine. What's more, the images your child is able to conjure aren't only the two dimensional movie-screen variety, they are multi-sensory images, images of sound and smell, of interaction and texture. Each sense becomes elevated to a higher plane as your child's brain matures, combining in a creative process that results in imagination. Taking images both from real life and from fantasy, your child makes a little three-dimensional movie for himself—and that movie can be scary sometimes. But, if you can recognize the creative element of your child's fears, it may suggest approaches you can use to help him overcome their negative aspects.

Your child's growing ability to play with his imagination is much more frightening than other developmental advances, so he needs extra practice using his imagination in a secure environment. Nighttime, when he is alone, is probably the worst time for experimentation. More engaged, interactive play during the daytime will help the child with a runaway imagination to keep his fears at bay during the night.

During the day, he can experiment and create in the context of a secure, loving relationship because you are there and interested. "Oh boy!", you say, "Look what that nasty, mean so-and-so did to that doll! Isn't that awful?" What was scary during the night is not so frightening in the presence of warmth and security. In addition, the opportunity you give him to talk about his feelings and experience adds one more piece to the puzzle—words. Putting an experience into words helps your child understand it a little bit better.

As your child approaches three-and-a-half to four years of age, he may express new and different fears often related to a new perception of himself and his body. First, you'll see an increased interest in rocket ships and dinosaurs or action figures such as He-Man and She-Ra; he's expressing his need for control. Then enters a new array of fears centered on sexual curiosity. He follows Mommy and Daddy into the bathroom, compares genitals with his peers, wants to know about babies—a scary set of experiences. As discussed in chapter V, children at this age can create their own fantasies about how babies are born. Some of these can be frightening to them.

Not only sexual curiosity, but new interest in and awareness of aggression, one's own vulnerability, separation and loss, physical injury, a sense of shame and humiliation (as when a child's friend calls him names), and competition create a basis for a vast array of new fears. With change and growth comes the opportunity for fears.

You may be asking yourself, "How can I identify the fear bothering my child?" Your main resource is noting the topics that come up repetitively or are avoided in play. Other behaviors will probably reinforce your hunch. The child who excitedly undresses dolls, keeps following you into the bathroom with anxious giggles, and then has nightmares, is probably having fears related to his curiosity about the body. The child who must win all the time, is always pretending to be the most powerful, and never evidences concern with loss, separation, or vulnerability may be having conflicts about vulnerability and/or competition.

The more inventive the child, the better his imagination, the more he can scare himself. At each stage (even in adolescence when your child will be able to project into the future), he can scare himself in a new way. Each time he begins to do this he will need the same remedy: extra security through warm engagement, and extra practice using his imagination during safe times.

SPECIFIC FEARS

When your youngster has a specific fear, whether it is a fear of elevators, heights, or anything else, it can either be an isolated fear or a fear that is symptomatic, that is, indicative of a more general problem.

The first helpful thing to do is to take inventory: examine how your child is doing at home, in relationships, in school, and the level of his self-confidence and self-esteem. If you decide that his fear is only related to a specific situation, use these three principles: (1) extra security; (2) floor time; (3) extra practice in the *real* situation.

Talk with him about his fear more rather than less. Don't only talk about it at the time he is fearful. You must create in your conversations or make-believe play enough opportunities so your child can talk about and understand what it is he fears.

Let's take an example.

Elevators scared Jesse. Crying and pulling away, he resisted going in them. Mommy and Daddy didn't fully understand. They tried to reassure him that elevators are safe but to no avail. Extra floor time was employed.

Jesse was initially quite cautious, putting each doll securely in a separate room of his dollhouse. No one was allowed from one room into another.

From this scene, his parents weren't sure of much but they figured making him feel more secure couldn't hurt. The "cuddle time" at night which had been rushed lately was again set at a more leisurely pace, accompanied by long back rubs. Dad tried to get home half an hour earlier and run around and play "throw the ball" with Jesse. Mom greeted Jesse when he came home from preschool and didn't get on the telephone. At the same time, when Jesse had a tantrum because Dad was sitting in his spot on the couch, Dad set some limits and didn't indulge him—on Mondays, Wednesdays, and Fridays the spot was Dad's; on Tuesdays, Thursdays, and Saturdays it was Jesse's. On Sundays, it belonged to "the first one to get there." With some protest, Jesse agreed to this compromise.

Security flourishing, Jesse's drama during floor time started to expand past the separate-room stage. Finally, when Dad remarked that "everyone seems to have to be in his own place. I wonder if each one likes that or not," Jesse started showing Dad how the dollhouse figures were "mad." Soon walls were being smashed, followed by the house falling down. For the next week the drama was filled with aggression and chaos, but finally all the figures came together in one big room.

Shortly thereafter Dad took Jesse to a restaurant on the top floor of his office building and let Jesse choose his favorite lunch. His parents ensured that he was well prepared for the trip by discussing it for a few days before. In these "problem-solving" discussions, Jesse shared his worries that either he or his parents could get hurt if the elevator went "out of control." Even so, he wasn't thrilled about the trip but he was willing. Over time Jesse became more relaxed in elevators.

Jesse's parents never quite understood the origin of his fear. But understanding wasn't necessary. Once given support, security, and his parents' attention to his play, Jesse did the rest. Expressing his concerns in play and conversations, followed by more frequent elevator rides, was all he needed.

Fears can also be a signal that there are more general problems. Chronic fearfulness may be produced by physical or sexual abuse.

It can be hard to recognize because it is sometimes hidden by a seemingly indifferent attitude. Any dramatic change in mood or behavior, including indifference or apathy, can be an indication of this type of fearfulness. Professional consultation is always indicated in these situations.

If your child seems excessively fearful, he may be worried about losing control. After all, he can now walk and run, punch and bite, and cause more damage to the world, to you, and to himself. So, he may be worried about his behavior getting out of control. And if his behavior can get out of control, what dangers can his new ability to create ideas bring? The basic fear of losing control may be related to fears of loss, separation, injury, death, and the like, and will often have roots in issues discussed in the chapters dealing with self-esteem, sexuality, aggression, and relationships.

This brings us to limit setting, which makes an important contribution to basic security. Ask yourself if you are making the world feel not only loving, warm, and secure but also safe in the sense of protecting your child from going out of control. Are you helping your child with his fears of hurting or being hurt by using effective limit setting? If you are intimidated, your child will be too. If you are frightened of his crying or tantrums, he will be even more frightened of himself. So you can increase security by looking for opportunities to set limits (most children give you at least two thousand a day—and the best situations don't always arise in the supermarket, they arise in your own home). Choose your battles, and then show that you're able to offer guidance and structure. In the long run your child will be grateful for the extra security.

Sadness

Sadness in a child causes much concern for parents. No one likes to see a sad four-year-old. Sometimes, even if a grandparent passes away or a pet dies, parents will try to distract a child from her sadness, or cut short her expression of feeling. Yet the ability to express sadness and to recognize and accept loss is a major developmental accomplishment for children, similar to the appearance of separation anxiety or fears.

Many adults are limited in their capacity to accept loss. To lose something or someone we care about, to accept the fact that we aren't as capable as we'd like to be (which is the loss of one's expectation of oneself), to mourn the loss of a love relationship, or even a temporary loss, creates difficulties for adults as well as for their children. Some may become enraged rather than deal with loss; others "externalize"—that is, blame others rather than accept a personal limitation or the loss of a relationship. We all have different ways of dealing with loss, and it's a high achievement to be able to accept loss as the painful, hollow, and lonely feeling it can be. None of us likes to feel it.

But, as with all other feelings and emotions in life, loss is a necessary and human ingredient. While children experience loss and disappointment from infancy on, the experience of sadness as a distinct feeling probably doesn't occur until the later preschool years. Toddlers, for example, may get irritable, protest, and finally look despondent if they lose their parents for a period of time, but it's not clear that they feel sadness at the level of ideas. Even two- and three-year-olds are more likely to become angry, negative, destructive, aloof, and withdrawn in response to loss—without a clear feeling of sadness.

It is surprising to many people that most children may be capable of feeling true sadness at around age four or five (it is often thought that such loss isn't felt until seven or eight). Typical but very different situations involving loss at this age would include a grandparent passing away, or a close friend preferring someone else. In dealing with the latter types of loss your child is angry at first, but finally accepts it, begins working it through, and eventually moves on to find another friend. This ability to face loss, feel it, accept it, and go on to other things is an important developmental milestone.

If, on the other hand, your child isn't able to accept loss, then she may begin to personalize the feeling into"I'm bad," or "You're bad," or her lack of acceptance may cause her to dwell on the loss. From there she may begin to develop other theories, everything other than accepting that sometimes she can't get what she wants.

For children who do not accept loss well, the same principles that work for separation anxiety and fears can be put to good use. Around age four or five you may either see at home or hear from the teacher that your child tends to blame others or is provocative and mischievous when faced with loss, whether it is not getting the toy she wants or, more seriously, a beloved babysitter leaving. Perhaps she even has a temper tantrum because she can't accept the feelings that accompany loss. At this age, her temper tantrums may be expressions of a hidden sense of power. The child is saying, "I control everything, and if I control everything I will never accept that I can't have what I want. I am not getting what I want because either you are mean or I am bad." Behind that is her inability to accept any kind of loss. An acceptance of loss means, in part, accepting one's own limitations, whether it's not being able to have a special toy, the friend you want, or to see Grandfather again.

To help children deal with expectable losses, it is important for parents to empathize with the feelings of loss and the associated feelings of helplessness, frustration, anger, and resignation. More difficult is to tolerate and have empathy for that hollow, lonely feeling that is so hard for most adults to cope with in themselves. The tendency is to encourage children to deny or ignore loss. "Come on, cheer up!" We say, "Don't miss your Grandfather," rather than, "Let's think together of all the wonderful things you and Grandfather did together. Boy, we miss him." With the loss of a friend, all too quickly it becomes "Let's find a new friend," rather than, "Let's see what was special about David, what you miss about him." Later on, after the sense of "missing" is clear, you can encourage your child to find other friends who have the qualities he likes.

You can begin to help by providing extra security in some of the ways mentioned before. In make-believe play you can provide opportunities for seeing how the dolls feel when they don't get their way or when there's an illness. You can begin to wonder aloud about what makes it scary to feel that there are sometimes things that no one can control, that things can happen that make us feel bad. You can work on and nurture the ability to feel loss. Keep in mind that it is a developmental accomplishment. Your child needs to feel that sadness and know you accept it before she can accept the loss and integrate it with her new interests to meet new challenges.

Occasionally, as part of exercising their new intellectual abilities, children talk about concepts such as death and war. Interest in these topics sometimes reflect feelings about a recently deceased relative or an underlying feeling of sadness or worries about injury and destruction. To enable children to figure out all that's on their minds, help them take their interests beyond the initial questions they may have. For example, if they are talking repeatedly about death in war, wonder out loud about how death also happens in families, like with Grandpa two years ago; or about dangers not only in war but in school when kids fight; or how dreams sometimes feel scary or dangerous; or how people sometimes worry that something will happen to them or a member of their family. You could also wonder about separation in the family or about sad or angry feelings.

Obviously one doesn't wonder about too much in each conversation. But over a period of weeks or a month, help your preoccupied child explore his worries.

Ongoing feelings of helplessness, hopelessness, badness ("I am bad"), pervasive negative expectations ("I never get what I want"), and/or a complete lack of joy and pleasure may be signs of a childhood form of depression. The ability to accept and deal with loss often works to help children find a resilient, positive strength within themselves. A need for professional consultation is indicated when negative feelings continue in spite of parental attempts to provide extra security, understanding, exploration of feelings and limits. When parents feel too overwhelmed with marital or family problems to truly focus on the child, professional consultation is particularly important.

Chronic despondency is another serious matter, and has roots in a poor self-image, as discussed in chapter IV. In this case, it's important for parents to try to identify the family issues that are contributing to negative self-esteem. Bear in mind that negative self-esteem can also be a damaging way of avoiding a true sense of loss. Floor time, security, limit setting, and respect for your child's uniqueness may all help overcome this debilitating feeling. If it persists, however, here, too, a professional consultation may be especially helpful.

Rivalry and Competition

Rivalry and competition are often first seen between siblings: who gets more cookies, who gets more of Mommy's or Daddy's attention, who got the biggest present, and the like. When your child enters school, these questions and feelings will become part of his day there as well: who is best at jumping, who is bigger or stronger? Most parents consider rivalry and competition a nuisance, something they wish they didn't have to deal with, especially when it's between older siblings and a new baby. There are ways to minimize it, but do we want to eliminate it? Before we get into that, it's useful to define what competition really is.

There are two types of competition: pseudo-competition and real competition. Let's say two children are very competitive in the classroom. Janey comes home and says, "Sarah is unfair. She doesn't like me." What happened? "I wanted to show the teacher my costume but Sarah showed hers first and the teacher looked at hers. Sarah hates me."

Is this competition? What's really happening here? Two children want center stage; one is being clever and undermining the other. Rather than seeing it as being bested in a competition, she prefers to see it as "If she doesn't let me win, she hates me." Lying below the surface of this idea is the belief that "I'm entitled to be number one in every activity." If that doesn't happen, she deduces that she's either a bad person, or everyone hates her. This is pseudo-competition because Janey sees the issue as "Sarah hates me" or "Sarah likes me" rather than "Sarah competes with me."

True competition is the type that, for example, good tennis rivals engage in: it means trying your best while using the set of fair and expectable maneuvers available to you, and has nothing to do with being hated or bad. In true competition, rivalrous anger can co-exist alongside high regard for yourself and your competitor, just as in true love, love and disappointment can co-exist. If the person you love doesn't do what you want, it doesn't mean you aren't loved. Similarly, if your competitor beats you, it doesn't mean you are hated—or bad. But it is rare for young children to achieve this level of competition. How often do you hear of a child coming home and saying, "That Johnny, he beat me in wrestling today. I'm so frustrated. But I'm going to get him next time. I'm going to practice and beat him tomorrow"? Unfortunately, you're much more likely to hear, "They hate me," or "I'm no good," or "I hate them," rather than "I hate losing and I will try to win next time." Or, "Losing feels bad but I can handle it. Next time I'll try a different way."

SUBSTITUTING REJECTION FOR COMPETITION

Should your child feel rejected or degraded when bested by a competitor, he may need extra practice in two areas—security and rivalry. Your job will be to help him to see competition and loss in their own right, rather than as a potential threat to his self-esteem. To do this, you will need to look for at-home experiences that might teach about competition. How does your family practice competition at home? You don't want to turn your household into a battlefield, but within the bounds of love and security, warmth and nurturance, there has to be a certain amount of muscle flexing in the areas of rivalry and competition. These are skills like any others.

Competing with Mom or Dad or a brother or sister while love and security remain constant teaches your child about true competition. For example, Harold and his dad loved to compete in checkers and wrestling. Harold even set up his own handicapping system: Dad could only wrestle with one hand and had to take only two seconds for each checkers move. By giving Harold an opportunity to win—and lose—in the security of his own home under his own set of rules, Dad helped Harold experience and master the feelings associated with competition. If you find such extra opportunities at home, when your child gets to school and finds he's not first in everything, he won't assume that his rivals don't value him. He will be able to see competition for what it is.

HATRED AND COMPETITION

A youngster who asserts, "I hate them," referring to his competitors, most often believes that "the other guy" has been mean or unfair. Whether this is actually true or not is not as important as recognizing that the hatred is about meanness or unfairness, not competition. Your child may not have yet gotten the idea that two people, both wanting the same thing, can't both get there first. Once he understands the real reason for his feelings, he'll slowly begin to appreciate competition as a human endeavor within which relationships survive.

Competition is a fairly high-level construct. The ability to accept it depends on a strong sense of inner security and the knowledge that a relationship based on positive feelings can survive anger and negative feelings. It means that when we go nose to nose in competition for a teacher's attention or Mommy or Daddy's attention, one of us is going to lose, and maybe tomorrow, or next year, or even ten years from now the balance will shift, but the relationship goes on in spite of it. A competition is only that: you're seeing who's better at something. It doesn't have to do with love or rejection, meanness or niceness.

In an adult relationship, presumably, if there is competition it is separate from meanness or rejection. But, often, married couples have the same problem with competition that children do. They compete with each other, but don't see it as a competition for who is better, smarter, or who is going to control the marriage. They see it as a partner who is mean, unfair, rejecting, or, most often "bossy and overcontrolling." In assessing your child's reaction to competition, it may be useful to examine the example that you and your family have set.

FLOOR TIME AND COMPETITION

In the course of normal healthy development, at around age four or four-and-a-half, children begin to understand competition. Although parents may encourage "winning," real competitiveness is a feeling we rarely nurture, though we should. Probably the best way to nurture true competitiveness is to help your child understand that competition is different from always winning or from feeling rejection and "meanness" in others. In sibling relationships, you will have to tolerate the rivalry and keep your children from hurting each other. Let them play out their rivalry to a point, and then help them to articulate and understand their feelings.

You can take much the same approach to your child's rivalries in school, pointing out that relationships go on and no one need be rejected, no one need be unfairly mean. Though it's a very sophisticated emotional concept, your child will be ready to accept competition at around age four, and the idea should be nurtured along between four and ten. Most of us, however, as with loss, don't attain it as well as we might.

Let's look at some specific examples of difficulties with rivalry and competition and see how floor time can help.

Remember Janey, the girl who wanted the teacher's attention in order to show her costume? She went on to express her competitive feelings:

JANEY: "I want the best costume. It's unfair for anyone else to try to have a better one. If they do, they must hate me."

DADDY: "Gee, I can tell you want to have the best costume and that no one should even try to challenge you."

Daddy is not necessarily saying Janey is either correct or incorrect, he's only saying that he can understand her perspective. It's very different from saying, "You mean you want to be the best all the time? What makes you think you're entitled to be the best all the time?" If Daddy had taken that approach, in all likelihood Janey would have said, "I didn't want that, you don't understand!" Daddy would have undermined Janey's ability to verbalize or conceptualize because Janey, feeling his criticism, wouldn't want to acknowledge, even to herself, that that's what she in fact wants. The first step in helping Janey acknowledge her wish is Daddy's empathy for and alignment with her, without necessarily agreeing with her. He can then take it a step further.

DADDY: "I understand what you want, but I can also understand when someone else wants the same thing. What do we have here? We have two children who both want the same thing. What's going to happen with you two?"

JANEY: "But she wants what I want. That's not fair!"

DADDY: "I know how it feels. What do you do when you both want the same thing?"

JANEY: "Share? Well, maybe I'll think about it next time."

This is a useful first step. Dad has helped Janey think about her sense of entitlement without being critical.

LIMIT SETTING AND COMPETITION

Competition frequently announces itself in the guise of the struggle for power. There are few parents who haven't found themselves in the following situation at some point.

You want your child to pick up his toys, his clothes, his books. He doesn't want to. You feel it's competitiveness—who's going to rule the roost. You're a reasonable Mommy or Daddy and you want to be able to lay down the law when necessary. But your child says, "No way, I'm the boss all of the time." He won't see this interchange as an expression of competition, of course; he'll see it as your being mean or rejecting, or as making him depressed or giving him a headache or tummyache.

What do you do? If you are comfortable with competition, you will see it as a power struggle. Whose muscles are bigger? If you feel that you are making a reasonable request and are not unusually irritable that day, you will insist and use whatever means to get this across, from talking to sanctions. It's surprising, however, how many parents are not comfortable winning the battle over who's going to pick up the toys.

Children can smell when their parents have resolve. They know, except for those kids who really believe they rule the roost, when parents feel secure and confident in limit setting and when they are equivocal. It's important for you to be aware of the areas that mean less to you. It's not bad for children to win some of the time. It's not bad either to have a protracted power struggle:

YOU: "Pick it up, please."

YOUR CHILD: "No, you pick it up."

YOU: "I'll pick one up and you pick one up."

YOUR CHILD: "I picked it up yesterday."

Power struggles often result in highly legalistic discussions in which your child is practicing logic and effective arguing and bargaining—good things to learn. It's not bad to have a few gray areas that are subject to negotiation, areas in which you lose and your child knows he can sometimes win. It's also not bad to have areas where you are strict and unmoving. Your child will sense the difference.

If you're irritable (you need to be honest) and have been preoccupied with neatness all day long, for example, you may have to remind yourself to give way a little. (Even if you're irritable but still think your request is reasonable, by all means stick to your guns.) Sometimes you can just be in a bad mood and lack the introspective ability to say, "I'm being pretty unfair today and more rigid than usual." Acknowledging your feelings doesn't mean you have to change them right then, but you will want to try to spend a little more time the next day to achieve a balance. This doesn't necessarily mean you should give your child cake and candy, but you should give her your interest. Show your child you can be more relaxed, move to a different rhythm. She will learn to adjust. Whether or not acknowledging that your own mood and feelings affect the relationship between you and your child changes how you act, it's still good to be honest with yourself and know what's motivating you.

AVOIDING COMPETITION

Avoidance is no solution to the problem of competition. Some children are so competitive they avoid it altogether. This common situation calls for rather careful handling and requires extra practice with competition in particular. Chances are, if he's so scared of competitive and rivalrous feelings that he won't get into competitive situations, his feelings are too intense. Start out by offering practice in fairly low doses. Situations in which he's fairly competent and has good self-esteem are best. Then give him some extra practice while you also introduce a little competition into the activity. Keep the situation adult-to-child initially since you can retain better control than with peer-to-peer activities. (Peers never make it easy if they can help it.) You're now giving him the opportunity to practice in a secure, non-threatening environment.

Again, it's important to increase "security time," the warm, engaging time you spend with your child. Many busy families pass each other by—there's hardly a half-hour for warm, nurturing engagement. Remember, also, the difference between passive and active engagement. You may read or sing to your four- or five-year-old, or listen to music together, all of which is good for relaxing the child before bedtime, for example. But nothing takes the place of chitchat or pretend play when the quality of active engagement is present. Then you can use the secure activity as a transitional experience, introducing the practice of competition little by little. Let's look at how one family used bike riding in this way.

Tanya, at age four-and-a-half, was unsuccessful in dealing with rivalry, but avidly learned to ride her bike. Mother began her attempts to introduce some competition into areas where Tanya felt secure by playing "Follow-the-Leader," first letting Tanya lead and then asking for a turn. Tanya pulled away. The next time, Mother suggested Tanya lead and Mother just followed. After a few more times, Tanya let Mother be the leader. Not long after, they were taking turns, challenging each other, and laughing as they invented different routes on the driveway.

Renny, at five, was very anxious about competition, and so was his father. When they played "Go Fish" together, Father got frustrated because Renny insisted on winning. When Father guessed some cards correctly, Renny would walk away—end of game. Father's attitude was "I'm not going to let him get a false sense of his abilities." They were able to overcome their difficulty in the following way:

We let Renny set the rules for the game, which he naturally structured so he would surely win. Father went along in the interest of creating extra security. As Renny won over and over and felt more and more secure, Father was encouraged occasionally, in a teasing way, to begin taking some of Renny's cards. Sometimes Renny would run away and sometimes Father could woo him back, until gradually the theme of competition came out into the open and Renny became aware that every time Father took his card he wanted to leave the game because he so fiercely wanted to win. Slowly Renny learned to enjoy the give and take of the game and was able to play "Go Fish" with friends also.

Father, to his credit, and in spite of his initial attitude, was able to increase security, lower the stakes, and realize that he had to play catch-up. He first had to show his son that competition didn't have to be scary, and then to slowly increase the stakes until Renny was ready to compete with the kids who were not going to take it easy. The parent-child relationship is the model place for learning about competition, as long as the parent is willing to do what's best for the child.

DECREASING THE NEED TO WIN

Often this question is asked by parents: "Can we help our children feel good about playing a game well, and not be so concerned about winning and losing?"

We can all get to the level, although its always relative, where the joy is in playing the game and making one's best effort. However, we all need first to go through competitive striving. People who get to this higher level of self-regard—and not many adults do—have gotten there by first being comfortable with competition and then, with the help of self-confidence, going beyond competition to the point that lets them simply enjoy their pursuits. The mistake most often made is trying to get to the last step without having gone through the others. The result of sidestepping a normal segment of the developmental pathway may be misunderstanding the true nature of competition. We must keep in mind that there is a normal amount of rivalry and competition between siblings and that children of certain ages must attain comfort with a certain amount of rivalry before they can get beyond it.

We have seen in this section that so-called negative emotions are an important part of development. While unpleasant at times, they serve an important human function: they alert us to our *needs* (separation anxiety), our *limitations* (loss, sadness), our *vulnerabilities* (fears), and our *potentials* (competition).

VIII

Intelligence, Perception, and Movement

Three-year-old Tommy has an undetected difficulty with so-called receptive language, which means that he has trouble understanding what is being said to him. Daddy says, "Tommy, pick your socks up, put them in the laundry, then come down to dinner immediately." Tommy, confused and non-responsive, appears to Mom and Dad to be either belligerent or negative. Typically, a parent in such a situation may shout, "Put your socks in the laundry and come down to dinner. And I mean *now!*" Tommy responds by throwing things around the room. He is actually feeling frightened, but on the surface appears even more provocative and belligerent. Finally, Tommy gets punished, which precipitates a temper tantrum.

Now, in some instances this may be just what it seems to be—Tommy is going to do things "his way" and refuses to listen to Mommy or Daddy. At other times, however, Tommy's problem, like those of Jessica and Robert in earlier chapters, may be that he does not understand the nature of the command; there are too many words strung together too quickly. Even though most three-year-olds can receive and understand such a communication, Tommy has difficulty processing verbal information. He needs to hear the words slowly and only a few at a time. He may, for example, be able to comprehend, "Pick up your socks." Once he does that, he may be able to understand, "Now, put them in the laundry." But if you string together, "Pick up your socks, put them in the laundry, and come to dinner," he is overwhelmed and confused. What appears to be belligerency and negativism is instead a problem with receptive language. If you show him what you want him to do by allowing him to mimic you—by taking the socks and putting them in the drawer, and then showing him that you want him to go downstairs, or by drawing a series of illustrative pictures—he may understand perfectly. So, his visual perception and comprehension may be fine, but his auditory-verbal skills are lagging. Tommy clearly needs to have his situation recognized.

Understanding some of the physical foundations for the emotional, social, and intellectual development of your baby and child will mitigate many of the challenges of parenthood. Especially important are difficulties relating to your child's understanding of what he sees and hears, his overall reaction to sights, sounds, touch, smell and his own movement patterns including his muscle tone, and his ability to plan and initiate organized movement. By becoming aware of all these areas, you will be more prepared to handle some of the more common challenges of child rearing.

All children mature at different rates in terms of brain growth. Some children are slower at learning to process and decode (that is, understand) sounds and words, and better at deciphering what they see. For others it's just the opposite—they readily understand what they hear but are a little slower to comprehend what they see. Some children are strong in all areas and some are slower in all areas. Visual and auditory capabilities are two of the areas that highlight the vital importance of understanding the physical or neurological foundations of your child's social and emotional patterns. Such an understanding may change how you respond to your child.

It's obvious that if a child, like Tommy, is having difficulty understanding you, your approach will be very different than if he's simply being belligerent and stubborn, or if he is tuning you out because you are too intrusive. If he can't understand what you say, you might break your request into simpler units and give him extra practice in listening and comprehending. And in practicing, as in any other educational endeavor, you will start where your child is comfortable, with something he can grasp and slowly add to with more and more practice. Trying to teach calculus to a child who can't add is an endeavor doomed to failure and frustration. A similar fate awaits you if you give a complicated command to a child who can only grasp a simple one.

If, on the other hand, your child is simply being negative, you will have to set limits on her, and at the same time try to understand the basis for her anger and why it is expressed in stubbornness.

Now let's look at additional areas of development.

MOTOR ABILITIES

Your child's ability to use his motor system—that is, to reach out and grab things, to take a crayon and scribble, to walk or run, go upstairs, and to speak—is just as important as his ability to interpret sights and sounds. We know that children's abilities to organize their muscles in order to do all these things vary considerably with their rates of physical maturation.

The motor system is divided into gross motor capabilities (those activities that involve large muscle groups such as running, walking, or kicking), and fine motor capabilities (involving small manipulative movements such as drawing, tying a shoe, or, for an eight-month-old, picking up a Cheerio between thumb and forefinger). No doubt, you are alert to both of these and are carefully watching their progress, worrying that your child may be slow (even though you know that the range of differences in normal patterns is enormous). Slowness and other problems are related to important regulatory and control features to which you can sensitize yourself as you pay attention to larger motor milestones, such as sitting or walking.

MUSCLE TONE

Some children seem very loose, and when you move their arms and legs, even at five or six months of age, they feel limp. (It is normal for some babies to be loose until four months.) Other children, at the same time, feel quite tight. It's hard to move their arms and legs. They have great physical resistance to even a fun game in which Mommy or Daddy bicycles their arms and legs for them.

From a neurological perspective, remember, the range considered normal is enormous. But the issue of muscle tone is not unimportant, because it does play a role in your child's emotions and behavior. What you are seeing is literally a difference in the balance between the child's flexor muscles (the muscles used to bend knees, bend at the waist, pull the neck forward—the extreme of which would be your baby's fetal position), and his extensor muscles (the muscles used to help us stand erect—the extreme being to lie on the floor on your stomach with back arched, legs off the ground, and chin in the air). Normally, the brain keeps a nice balance between the extensor and flexor muscle tones that helps walking, standing, and balance. Your muscles always have some tone, so without consciously trying, you can stand and with minimal effort, walk and keep your head up. But if either tone is naturally a little high or low, simple tasks such as learning to hold your head up or learning to sit without falling, or crawl or walk, may take a little longer and be more difficult.

The baby with low tone, for example, tends to have to work much harder to crawl. Often, she appears lazy, has a slumped posture, and is slow in initiating movements. Motor milestones may be slow as well. But she may be great at tasks requiring muscle flexibility. This is especially important to keep in mind when helping your baby learn to sit up, crawl, and walk.

Whether a baby has slightly high or low tone, working with his muscles will help him in a most fundamental way. *The ability to fine-tune and regulate the body is the foundation upon which other regulatory abilities, including regulating thoughts and emotions, are built.* This is true for two reasons: (1) your baby's body becomes his base for interaction which is, in turn, the basis for thought and emotion; and (2) the confidence developed in regulating his body will often translate into confidence in regulating thought and emotion. Keep in mind, however, that the converse is also true. If you are unsure of yourself at the level of your body, you may be even more unsure of yourself at the level of thought and feeling.

Herbie was a very passive thirty-month-old. He tended to be cautious in his approach to other children, to new games, and even to playful wrestling with his daddy on the floor. It seemed that even when he wanted to ask for a cookie (and he certainly knew the word "cookie" because he mentioned it four or five times a day), he would have to look at his mommy, waiting to make sure she would smile at him and ask, "Herbie, what can I get for you?" Finally, he would say, "Cookie." Even with a child he knew well, he would often wait for as much as half an hour before warming up and rolling a truck back and forth. When frustrated and angry, he would pout, sitting very still with a solemn look on his face. Mommy would have to tease out of him that he was mad because he didn't get to watch his favorite cartoon. By the time his parents' concern led to a consultation, he was beginning to avoid other children.

Among other things, the evaluation found that Herbie had a slight motor problem. It was harder for him to do things such as jump or climb because his poor balance and coordination made such activities extra work. To counter this, the evaluation recommended that Herbie do specific exercises to strengthen his overall tone. One was running and stopping (as in "Mother May I?"), as opposed to just running. Another exercise was to lie on his tummy and pretend to be a boat, rocking back and forth. With Daddy, he played airplane, his legs around Daddy's middle while he faced the floor and tried to hold himself up, Daddy holding him firmly around the legs and tummy. After a few months of these games and others like them, Herbie's motor tone improved, as did his ability to coordinate his actions. Confident in his body, he became more assertive. He spoke louder, played with new friends more easily, went on slides and swings more readily, enjoyed rough-and-tumble play with his father, and argued like an assertive lawyer with his mother.

Herbie's parents were impressed with how physical exercises

could help emotional and behavioral issues. They realized that his growing physical confidence was making him more secure in other ways. He was no longer afraid that his body would be uncontrollable.

When a child is very tentative or cautious, family patterns and emotional feelings that are already a part of the youngster need to be taken into account. In cases like Herbie's, however, focusing on the child's motor tone is an essential part of the program and sometimes, when all else is working well, it may be the critical ingredient in the overall plan to increase his confidence. With so many excellent occupational therapists experienced in helping to regulate muscle tone, it's an ingredient that is relatively simply to add. (Consult your pediatrician about this.)

MOTOR PLANNING

In addition to your baby and child's muscle tone, you will also want to be aware of her ability to carry out a series of complex motor acts, known as motor planning. Motor planning is intregal to learning to crawl, sit, skip, button, or cut with scissors—in short, anything that involves sequencing a series of motor acts into a pattern. There's little activity that doesn't involve some motor planning. The eight-month-old who crawls from one spot to another and under furniture, or the ten-year-old who is building a model airplane, or the adult doing carpentry in the yard all use motor planning to accomplish their aims.

Children who experience difficulty in motor planning need extra help in learning to negotiate successive stages in their emotional development—because each stage involves planning increasingly complicated motor activity: gesturing, talking, and interacting all involve the motor system.

For example, eight-month-old Priscilla, who had some difficulty in motor planning, found it hard to let her parents know her needs. When she wanted to be picked up, she would bang on the floor rather than reach out to her parents and call for them. Because coordinating her arm movements with her vocalizations seemed to be difficult for her, Priscilla's parents were left guessing as to when she wanted to be picked up. Similarly, her gestures didn't convey when she was angry. Instead of making a fist or looking angry, she might again just bang on the floor.

As her parents realized her difficulty in sequencing her motor acts, they tried to tune into the gestures she was capable of making, so that her social communication wouldn't lag behind. They learned that when she began to play with her hair, she was asking for closeness. In other words, Priscilla found it easier to play with a part of her body than to combine two gestures, such as reaching out and vocalizing, which other eight-month-olds might be able to do. By responding to her signal and saying, "Oh, you want a big hug" (at which Priscilla would smile), her parents were tuning into Priscilla's wants and needs. Her emotional development did not have to lag behind just because her motor-planning abilities needed more practice.

Another example was Michael, who would frequently knock things over. Glasses would topple, plates would fly. His parents thought he was just being belligerent and would frequently yell and shout at him. After an evaluation, it became clear that he had trouble sequencing simple motor acts. When asked to copy a motor sequence—patting himself on his head, then putting his hand to his mouth—he would get confused.

For Michael, a very bright youngster, his physical problems resulted in expectable stubbornness. He felt confused, unfairly blamed, and had begun to act as though he didn't care (as a way of coping with his frustration). To counteract this, we evolved a series of games involving sequential movement, such as animal walks, obstacle courses, and skip-hop sequences, to give him extra practice avoiding banging into things when he was moving rapidly. Limit setting and scolding without extra practice would not have worked. Limits with encouragement and extra practice of motor-planning skills, however, resulted in his behavior becoming more and more organized.

PATTERNS OF SENSORY REACTIVITY

Some children have difficulties reacting to routine stimuli. For example, many are overly sensitive to touch—babies may stiffen, older children will jerk away, perhaps yell, scream, or cry when touched. This sensitivity may also manifest itself in discomfort in bathing, in having hair or teeth brushed, in changing clothes—even eating can be a difficulty for such a child. Other children may be sensitive to high-pitched noises, odors, or particular types of patterns (being picked up and spun, for example).

For each sense, children can be hyperreactive (like those above), or hyporeactive, that is, requiring lots of input to get the normal amount of reaction. For instance, hyporeactive children require a great deal of sound before they take notice, large amounts of touch before they experience pleasure, lots of movement in space before they feel a thrill. It's often confusing for parents to realize that some of their children's behavioral "problems" actually have a physical basis.

Probably most perplexing to parents are the children who have a sensitivity to physical touch. The parents of a two-and-a-half-year-old may say, "He won't eat, won't let us bathe him, won't put on his socks. He's finicky. He cries at the slightest provocation." In the office, the child often appears smiling, angelic, intellectually adept. When this same child is three-and-a-half or four and can talk about his experiences, he reports that he doesn't like his hair brushed because it hurts, that when people touch him he becomes uncomfortable—even getting dressed can be an ordeal. But once he takes control of getting dressed, for example, and does it carefully and slowly, he doesn't mind it so much.

What usually works with this type of child is to give him as much of a role as possible, as early as possible, in being the co-director of his care. He needs to work out a partnership with his parents so that things are taken slowly and deliberately. When they are late for an appointment and have to rush out of the house, parents must be prepared for the irritability and tantrums associated with this type of sensitivity. If they know what to expect and are aware of their child's physical discomfort, they can then soothe him. However, if parents feel that their rightful responsibility to dress their child has been undermined by a little tyrant, then there will be no relief from the power struggle that ensues. Children like this require extraordinary patience and a philosophy that encourages participation in their own care.

Many adults also have sensitivities, touch being the most notable. They, too, have the same tendencies as children and once it is understood that the source of the difficulty is physical rather than emotional, these people can pursue those experiences that are most pleasurable to them.

How do muscle tone, motor-planning ability, patterns of sensory reactivity, or your baby and child's ability to understand what he sees and hears affect his emotional development? Probably the best way to begin to understand the impact of the physical on your baby's emotional development is by simple, non-judgmental observation during the various stages of development, beginning with infancy.

Stage One:
Regulation and Interest in the World
(0 to 3 Months)

Often within her first four months of life, you can observe the degree to which your infant is very sensitive, fairly sensitive, or not so sensitive to physical stimuli. Does she require a good deal of vocal input before you gain her attention? Do you have to "warm her up" with lots of stroking or rubbing before she'll look and smile at you? Does she enjoy a close cuddle, or would she rather have a little space around her? Do her limbs seem floppy or tense? Changes in temperature when she is bathed, the kinds of clothing she seems most comfortable in, voice qualities she responds best to, and kinds of movement patterns she enjoys, whether she likes to be bounced in your arms or held overhead are all clues to her uniqueness. By experimenting with these patterns in the first four months of life, you will get a picture of what helps your baby enjoy and become attentive to the world.

FLOOR TIME

It's important in these early months to figure out which sensations your baby enjoys and what level of activity will encourage him to organize his actions and focus first upon you and then upon the world.

To help you make your observations, you may want to observe how your baby enjoys or organizes:

1. *Touch,* including light stroking and gentle pressure to each part of the body. Provide the pattern that helps calm your baby, thus helping her attend to her new and wonderful world. Also, give your baby different textures to touch— soft and cuddly, smooth and hard.

2. *Sounds.* See what pitch—high, low, or medium—and how loud a sound your baby enjoys and focuses upon. See what rhythm your baby is interested in; is it one sound (ta), two (ta-ta), three in a row (ta-ta-ta), or an even more complex combination?

3. *Sights.* Does your baby like lights or colors that are dull or those that are bright? Which of your funny faces does she like the best? Does she like you to repeat the same expression or change it?

4. *Movement.* What position does your baby like? How quickly does he like to be moved up or down, or from side to side? What's his favorite dance with you? His favorite cuddle position?

5. *Muscle Tone.* What's the best way to help your baby cuddle? What encourages her to look around? How much head and body support does she enjoy?

6. *Motor Planning.* How much help does your baby need in learning to put his hand in his mouth?

Remember, the goal of this stage is to foster your child's interest in the world. Help your baby by knowing his or her special capacities.

Stage Two:
Falling in Love (3 to 7 Months)

Your baby's ability to decode information, to take it in, and understand it, affects the way he relates to you—and the pattern of love he enjoys. You can observe how well your baby decodes information through each of his senses, and use this information to make falling in love easier.

FLOOR TIME

For example, by three or four months, most babies can recognize a simple verbal pattern. If Mommy or Daddy says, "Da-Da" (a two-unit sequence), you'll see calm, alert attentiveness. Your baby hangs on each sound, waiting for the next in the sequence. If you introduce a little novelty (accent a different syllable, for example), your baby will look a little surprised. A look of surprise and pleasure in novelty is based on the ability to identify the prior pattern and then be surprised by the next one. In this way you can test his ability to encode the different sounds. But, should you begin with "Da-Da-Da-Da" (a four-unit pattern), or its equivalent in words, you may get a confused look. This pattern may be too long for a baby to understand. Seeing this, if you then say, "Da-Da," baby may very well brighten up and become alert again. *Then* introduce, "Da-Da-Da." He may look surprised because he again recognizes the first two sounds but experiences the third as unusual.

By doing this and similar exercises with the various senses, you will begin to comprehend your baby's earliest abilities to deal with information—some of which have an important physical basis. Don't forget that emotion plays a large part in decoding as well; some babies in very chaotic and overwhelming environments may, because of environmental pressures, not be able to process or decode the patterns. In many instances, however, your baby's behavior is simply a product of the different rates at which his nervous system matures.

As you look at your baby's ability to interpret information, you'll probably detect differences among his senses, and you will almost certainly detect differences between him and another baby. Some babies who are slower with verbal information will be very responsive to facial expressions. Such a baby understands much of the visual world he encounters, even though he may have a harder time figuring out the differences between sounds.

At present, it is difficult, from a technical point of view (although we are working on it), to reliably test a baby's relative strengths and vulnerabilities in terms of each sense. Parents are often best at figuring out these differences once they become intellectually aware of what they are doing intuitively. For example, I normally have very little difficulty when I ask the mother of a four- or seven-month-old, "Does your baby respond more when you talk to him or when you make interesting faces at him?" Many mothers can quickly tell me, "I've noticed that he responds much more when I'm making interesting facial expressions." Another will say, "You know, he responds much more when I talk to him." To be sure, some of this may be a reflection of the mother's preference, but in many instances, after I have had a chance to interact with the baby, my own impression is similar to hers. Parents who interact with their children often get an intuitive sense of what works and begin doing more and more of it.

As early as when your baby is four months old, you can begin playing to his strengths—that is, offering lots of animated facial expressions if that is your baby's orientation—but at the same time, you can consciously combine this with extra practice in words and sounds. Your natural tendency might be to use animation, staying away from words and sounds because they don't "work" as well. But because you want the baby to be just as good at listening as at looking, you want to play to his strengths first so he knows and responds to you, then give him extra practice in listening to sounds. You might accomplish your goal by beginning with simple rhythms that slowly become more complex—a "Da-Da" becoming a "Da-Duh-Da." By combining looking with listening, you are helping your baby use his strength to build himself up where he is weaker.

Babies most often love extra practice in the developmental areas where they need it. For them, it means that you are attending to them, interested, aware, and involved. The only time babies and children resent extra practice is when the practice takes on a nonplayful, anxious, or obligatory tone, or if the challenges you offer cannot be met because they are too far above their abilities.

Once again, if you approach your child with respect for his individuality and sensitivity to the way he learns best, you'll not only spend your floor time helping him with various aspects of his intellectual development but you'll also be working on an aspect of your lives of even greater importance—your relationship.

DIFFERENCES IN MOTOR PATTERNS

Let's look at Jane in the early stage of developing an interest in the world. She has slightly low muscle tone and is having a hard time holding her head up and taking an interest in Mommy's or Daddy's sounds. Attending is hard work for Jane and she tires easily—sometimes after only a few seconds. Mommy and Daddy need to support the back of her neck and be more animated and arousing in order to provoke greater interest.

Sometimes Daddy plays a game where Jane sits on his lap and he holds her at the shoulders. Gently, he lowers her down and then up, slowly engaging her with his sounds and facial expressions. Here, Daddy combines attending with using important muscle groups.

By four months, when Jane is really ripe to fall in love, she may need extra wooing to keep her interest. Remember, she has to work harder to give Mommy and Daddy that big smile. (Smiling, after all, involves muscle control of the face and requires effort.) Mommy and Daddy may become discouraged and feel, "My baby doesn't love me." This would be a mistake in any case, but especially in the case of the baby who simply has to work harder to show she loves you through her movements. In fact, your hardworking baby should be praised even more for that little smile and later on for each of the succeeding emotional milestones that require a greater effort.

When it comes to smiling and falling in love, the high-muscletone baby (whose muscles are tight) may look at Mommy, but may overshoot the mark. He may end up gazing somewhere beyond or to the side of her, or arch his neck in an effort to gaze at her. Mommy needs to move to capture his glance or help him to hold a better body position. From here, she can show him that he can achieve joyful synchrony and harmony, even though his muscles aren't doing exactly what he wants them to. With extra practice in engaging and enjoying Mommy's patient smile and joy, this baby will learn to "tune in" more quickly.

If your baby is "tight," you'll need to help him achieve a little more flexibility. When you're carrying him around, help him relax, encourage him to bend at the knees and at the waist.

Passing the emotional milestone of falling in love has immediate, obvious, and satisfying results for both baby and you. The basis for your baby's future relationship with you and with the world is now established.

Stage Three:
Purposeful Communication
(4 to 10 Months)

When your baby has become an accomplished observer of the world and is hopelessly in love with you, she then begins to learn purposeful communication. Baby vocalizes and Mother vocalizes back. Mommy looks at baby and baby looks back. Baby makes a face and Mommy makes a face back. You will begin to see that her ability to take in visual and auditory information forms the basis for purposeful interaction. Accordingly, your own responses need to be as intentional and purposeful as your child's.

FLOOR TIME

During any stage, but especially important in this one, is your baby's attention. If you notice that the baby seems distractable, withdrawn, or inattentive, it will be difficult for him to take in information and respond to your overtures. Ask yourself, "How well is my baby attending?" After answering this, ask, "Am I offering information in a way that my baby can understand?"

Attention is one of the easiest and most important things to follow in your baby. A baby who can't pay attention will be limited in what he can learn and how he relates to you and the world. By the stage of intentional communication (between four to five months and nine to ten months of age), you should have a clear picture of your baby's capacities to attend and concentrate. He should be able to "hook in" to your sounds or sight or to interesting objects that you make available to him. There's a difference between the baby who fleetingly tunes into you, then looks to the left, right, up, down, all for two to three seconds each, and the baby who pays attention to your face for 10 to 20 seconds or so before looking away for a second or two and then tuning in again for another 20 to 30 seconds.

My clinical impression is that babies who are having a tough time attending usually show fleeting interest in all things—their attention in any one direction will last for only a few seconds. Fleeting attention should serve as an early warning that something is making it hard for your baby to focus—he may need extra practice. To figure out what that "something" is, you can ask yourself "Am I providing sensations in a way that is overwhelming or not sufficiently interesting?" (particularly for babies who tend either to be hypo- or hyperreactive), and "Am I providing too much that is confusing my baby's ability to decode?"

The challenge is to work toward increasing your baby's attention slowly. Don't be greedy. Don't try to get the 20 seconds right away or both you and your baby will give up. Each second, even if it takes two weeks to get from one second to the next, will be an important milestone. Twenty seconds is usually enough time for the baby to decide if he's interested in what is offered to him. The baby who can attend for only two or three seconds may not get enough information to make that decision. Your patience will help him build his capacities slowly and surely.

Stay aware of your progress in communication. Ask yourself, "Is my baby using sounds to communicate to me? How do I respond to them? How many distinct ones are there? Does my baby use gestures?" (e.g., reaching out to be picked up or pointing to what he wants). Now is the time for giving and receiving information and for making sure that what you offer is received. Slow down, simplify, or speed up—depending on what your baby requires.

MOTOR PATTERNS

Your baby is just learning how to muster her forces and negotiate interaction with an aim or purpose. Many influences will determine the extent to which she is successful. Let's take a baby's capacity for assertiveness and competence and see how it develops in a low-muscle-tone eight-month-old.

Cindy wants to reach out and explore her daddy's mouth, but finds it difficult to get her hand in there. She makes a tentative movement toward his mouth, then quits, discouraged. Daddy positions his face closer to her hand to give her some help. He then opens his mouth wide. Cindy makes the effort and gets her hand inside. Daddy, looking delighted, then makes an animal noise— a cow, a cat, dog, or lion—and Cindy is gleeful. She puts her hand into Daddy's mouth again and again to hear the noise he will make next. Cindy is learning, with Daddy's help, that she can have an impact on the world, a delightful one. She is willing to expend the effort if Daddy joins and shares in it to some degree. Even a solitary effort, like spending time on her tummy trying to get on all fours in preparation for crawling, will be practiced more often with encouragement and involvement from Mommy or Daddy.

Eight-month-old Greg had the opposite problem. Having high muscle tone meant he seemed destructive and aggressive when his actual intention was to find out what things were and how they felt. His daddy would get annoyed, "Don't mess things up! You're being bad!" but what Greg needed was extra practice, not criticism. Greg also felt stiff in Mommy's arms. It wasn't that he didn't want a cuddle, any more than Cindy's spaghetti-like posture signaled her disinterest. What it did mean is that parents of children like Cindy and Greg need to provide understanding, support, and lots of floor time in order to help them learn to be intentional.

Around this age, many parents have been tempted to teach their children rote learning tasks such as responding to shapes (pre-reading skills) or doing baby exercises. Remember the best lessons at this age involve *active* discovery—in which your baby makes something happen to his world—and *interactions among people*—in which he communicates to you and you communicate back. Crawling to you and finding the ball you have halfway hidden in your hand or pulling on your nose or finger to get a "bow-wow" sound are great "exercises" for a baby because they are active discoveries that use motor, cognitive, and emotional abilities, and involve *you.*

Stage Four:
The Sense of Self (9 to 18 Months)

By the time your baby is a toddler, he has a lot on his mind. He is not only trying to stand, walk, and get into as much trouble as he possibly can, but he is trying to organize his sense of himself and attempt to balance many of his needs—including the need for closeness and the need for independence. He is piecing together feelings such as love and hate, passivity and activity. During this stage, too, he is trying to see the forest for the trees, that is, trying to understand patterns. He wants to know how the world fits together, not just his own little self, but how the larger world fits together—what makes Mommy and Daddy tick, how the house is also a series of rooms that fit together. Your toddler is beginning to develop what may be called his conceptual attitude. As part of this, your child's *attention* should increase—he now can focus for at least a few minutes on an activity, interaction, or game with you. If this is not occurring, it may relate to his having trouble figuring out "how the pieces fit together."

FLOOR TIME

So far you've had many opportunities to observe your child's reaction to information. This reaction is based on his sensory processing, which includes not only taking in information but also putting it together, or integrating it into some understanding of himself and the world. For example, your baby may be able to look to a person gesturing to him on the left, look to a person gesturing on the right, and then look back at you in the middle. He may be able to take into account and respond to interesting or inviting sounds from the left and right, and then return to his starting point—you. Another child may quickly become distracted and either stay focused on the person to the right or left. Or she may, in fact, become disorganized and begin looking frantically-around the room, or may seem to tune in and out, looking aimlessly about without really focusing. The disorganized or aimless child has trouble integrating and dealing with the whole pattern—in other words, she can't put all the pieces together.

Developing the capacity to put the pieces together has to do in part with integrating what is seen and what is heard. One can think in terms of "listening" space and "looking" space. Using "listening" space is being able to take in sounds from all over and then to return to some central point. Using "looking" space is being able to take in sights from all over and then return to some central point. Both demand that the child formulate a coherent picture of his immediate surroundings—a process with broad implications for his cognitive abilities.

Everyone operates in a world of confusing sensation. We're constantly striving to figure out what other people mean and how the parts of what we are experiencing all fit together. For the child who has difficulty taking in new information and getting back to her "central point," extra practice during floor time in being flexible, moving from one thing to another and back again to the beginning can help her in her struggle to "put it all together" for herself.

For example, Stephanie tended to simply fix on whatever was on the periphery of her vision while Mommy and Daddy were trying to engage her in play with the Jack-in-the-box in front of her. Stephanie would look to the left and get stuck on the light in the distance or a picture on the wall. They would have to literally scream at her to get her to look back at what they were doing.

Jeff had just the opposite pattern. When his parents tried to engage him in play, building a tower with three blocks, for example, he would look around continually—to the left, to the right, up and down, endlessly shifting in a sleepy way. His parents wanted him to focus on them or on the game they were trying to play.

In both circumstances the children had difficulty integrating their "looking" space. Similar patterns occurred with both of these children in regard to sounds. One would get locked in on sounds to the left or right, the other would shift from sound to sound, unable to tune out peripheral sounds and focus on what his parents were saying. Jeff and Stephanie's difficulties with looking and listening space were very discouraging to their parents.

Both sets of parents had to realize that their children's difficulty was related in part to maturational or physical factors. But extra practice in navigating looking and listening space can help even when physical factors contribute. The mind is always working to find new ways to do things.

We introduced some games in which Stephanie was encouraged to look around and return to a starting point. Instead of reducing learning opportunities by avoiding situations where she would be distracted, interesting pictures were placed around her. When her focus became fixed, her parents would move with her focus and make interesting faces to regain her attention. They would use themselves to draw her attention back to the Jack-in-the-box. This was done repeatedly so that she wouldn't lock into things that were separate from the challenge and task at hand. Nor was she forced to give up her interest in the periphery, but she was helped—almost wooed—back to the middle.

All of this was done lightheartedly and good-naturedly; her parents did not precipitate a power struggle that would have added negativism and belligerency to her tendency to focus on peripheral elements. Pleasurable and self-motivating experiences—Mommy and Daddy regaining her focus by combining their faces with the light or picture she was staring at—brought Stephanie back.

Jeff was more of a challenge in some respects. It was hard to get his attention at all. His focus would float away from a face being made to interest him or sounds being made to engage him. An even more patient approach was required here. His parents found they could get his attention for two seconds if they moved with him. With enormous but patient and relaxed efforts at providing interesting facial expressions, sounds, and interesting objects, his parents could involve him for three or four seconds. Using this approach during floor time, where each extra second was greatly appreciated by his parents, Jeff's attention began to increase gradually. The key was the combination of interesting sights or sounds coupled with persistence and patience. He eventually became a good concentrator, able to attend to something for a few minutes before tuning out. This was a great and satisfying achievement for all involved.

FEELING CLOSE FROM AFAR

Let's take one feature of a toddler's conceptual attitude, the balance between dependence and independence, and discuss it with respect to perceptual problems.

Across the room building her tower, seventeen-month-old Candace looks over at Mommy and Mommy says with quick words, no gestures, "Candace, that's terrific!" Candace, however, can't figure out what Mommy is saying because she can't "encode" the information. She doesn't yet have the ability to figure out that this pattern of words means approval, even though most seventeen-month-olds are able to. So Candace runs back to Mommy, grabs her leg, and looks up at her questioning.

Now, if Mommy is unaware that Candace is having some trouble figuring out what she's just said, Mommy might become impatient—she is busy with other things. She also might begin thinking of Candace as a "clinger." As Mommy tries to withdraw from her daughter's grasp, Candace becomes more adamant, and they find themselves in the middle of a power struggle. Candace cries and holds onto Mommy's leg; Mommy feels tyrannized by her daughter, wanting a moment of peace and freedom. Once Candace senses that Mommy wants to get away, Candace, if she is worth her salt as a toddler, is going to persist. (One of the most common complaints I hear from mothers of toddlers is, "My baby is tyrannizing me. I can't breathe for a second. I can't even go to the bathroom alone!")

If Mother knows that Candace is having difficulty figuring out what she is telling her, she can repeat it more slowly when Candace comes back to grab her leg and say, "Great!," and point to the tower. She can then go with Candace to the tower and point again, using animated facial expressions and hand gestures which suggest to Candace that it's the best tower Mommy has ever seen. If necessary, Mommy can then repeat the words again, "This is terrific!" very slowly. If Mommy does this for a few weeks, pretty soon Candace, even though she still has little comprehension of the words, will understand what Mommy means. Within a few weeks when Mommy looks at Candace with specially animated facial expressions, exaggerated hand gestures, and the right words, "That is terrific, Candace!," Candace will smile and nod, and go back to building her tower.

By giving Candace a little extra practice, by combining the words with facial expressions and hand gestures, by walking over with Candace to her tower, and repeating the lesson again, rather than getting into a power struggle, Mother is giving Candace valuable help.

Candace learns that she can communicate with Mommy across space, because to communicate across space includes facial and hand gestures, not just words. Candace, who is slower in terms of receptive language (figuring out the pattern of sound or words), is going to have a better chance at catching up because Mommy is now providing a multisensory approach to communication across space. In addition, Mother's patience, based on her understanding of Candace's difficulty in deciphering her message, helps Candace feel more secure. This is far better than having the interaction degenerate into a power struggle in which Mother feels tyrannized and Candace gets no practice in her receptive language ability. Rather, Mother gets to feel pride in Candace's accomplishment— plus a little breathing room.

You may see another difficulty emerge if your child is very good at discriminating sounds, but not so good at figuring out his environment through sight. This doesn't mean that your child won't recognize you. The difficulty will be more subtle. As your child is most likely crawling well or walking by now, his ability to negotiate space will be tested. He can toddle around the house, exploring different rooms. What happens to little David, let's say, who doesn't have a great sense of geography?

Most toddlers, by seventeen or eighteen months, have figured out how all the rooms of their house or apartment connect to one another. When Mommy is in the kitchen and baby is in the playroom, he knows how to get to the kitchen. If he happens to wander into the living room, he knows where that is in relation to the playroom or kitchen or even how it relates to his bedroom, whether up or downstairs. So, he has an internal map of his surroundings pretty well in his grasp. But, as we adults know, not everyone is equally gifted at creating these internal spatial maps.

Let's return to David, who is sitting alone in the living room. Because he does not have an internal map enabling him to locate Mommy when she is not in sight, he may very well become frightened and start crying for her to come and get him. Should Mommy not realize that he actually *can't* walk into the kitchen and find her, she may assume he's acting "spoiled" and "whiney" and ignore him. What David needs is a few extra tours of the house. This may be especially hard to perceive if David happens to be verbally adept and is talking in short sentences. But before you reach conclusions about your own child, listen to your intuition, particularly if your child "always" runs amok in certain situations.

David's mother remembered that his older sister, Rachel, at seventeen months, learned quickly how to get from one room to another in a new environment. She recalled that when they were at their cousin's two weeks ago, David kept getting lost and then cried to be rescued. At home, when David was in the playroom and Mother was within visual range, in the kitchen, David didn't seem to need her around all the time. Thus she correctly surmised that he liked to play independently. It finally clicked that David seemed to suddenly get very dependent and needy whenever he felt "lost." Mother remedied this by giving him extra tours of the house, reinforcing where they were verbally, and showing him specific salient landmarks in each room and how one room led to the next. Each day they would walk into and play in a different room. Daddy helped in the evening by playing hide-and-seek games throughout the house, initially in one room, then two, then three, so that David wasn't overwhelmed. Also when David couldn't see Mommy or Daddy because they were in a different room, they tried to talk to him so he could hear, and perhaps follow, their voices. Gradually David became much better at negotiating space and creating his own internal maps.

Even at the toddler stage, being fine-tuned to your child's abilities to discriminate over sights and sounds can create unusual learning opportunities for children and unusual teaching opportunities for parents.

MOTOR DIFFICULTIES

By seventeen or eighteen months of age, experimenting with assertiveness and aggression for the low-muscle-tone baby will be hard. Simply banging the floor, squeezing a doll, or trying to push something creates more difficulty and frustration for this baby. It's harder to make things happen. Your empathy for your child's ability to assert his will and initiate activity will give him a sense of competence, even though he has to work much harder to get it. Doing too much for him, because he's "slow" or you're impatient, will only encourage his passivity and, ultimately, more frustration and fearfulness. However long it takes, your child needs to experiment with assertiveness and his own initiative. Support and encouragement here, rather than doing for him, is critical.

Ricky was passive and liked to sit and do puzzles. He would not explore or run. Ricky's parents played hide-and-seek games to help him walk, run, and discover. They had to become really animated, and sometimes even provide new toys, so that Ricky would be willing to toddle around the house—but it worked.

At fifteen and sixteen months, the baby with high muscle tone may be distractable, hyperactive, and slow to imitate movement. He may need extra practice in concentrating and focusing. Specially designed games can be a tremendous help at this point. Using his senses to help him relax and control his muscles, as well as exercises that require lots of relaxation, can be immensely important.

For example, Charles benefited from games where he could run, stop, and focus, run, stop, and focus, to help him control his activity level. He loved to imitate Dad. Dad would pretend to be a horse who ran and then said "Whoa," then looked for grass to eat. Although Charles didn't understand the elements of the game, he enjoyed and benefited from the practice.

PERCEPTUAL PROBLEMS AND
LIMIT SETTING

Limit setting is most important during this phase of development. Children who have difficulty either with muscle tone, or with figuring out sights or sounds, will have more difficulty knowing how to control their behavior and impulses. Normally at this age children are learning to respond to their parents' verbal cues as well as facial and body gestures. When Mommy says, "Stop!" with an angry look and pointed finger, little Johnny should know he'd better reconsider what he's about to do. But when this same youngster doesn't understand the "Stop!" and can't figure out the pointing or angry look, he's at a decided disadvantage. It's as though he's saying, "What was that again?" as his fingers continue to reach for the socket. When his lack of understanding becomes the basis of a power struggle with his parents, he may pretend not to "understand" even when he does. Thus a lack of understanding becomes willfully engrained. To counteract this, his parents need to give him innovative practice with lots of gesturing and words coupled with physical restraint when necessary.

Your baby with high or low muscle tone may find it difficult to learn limits. Because the child can't control his muscles well, he finds it hard to respond to what you say even though he understands it. This leads to frustration and he decides, "Why try?" By making your limits appropriate to what he can do, he can satisfy your request without getting frustrated.

The child with motor-planning difficulties especially needs extra practice. If you want your eighteen-month-old child, who has trouble sequencing motor acts, to learn to put a toy into her toy box, you can't say, "Pick up your toy, put it in the box, and close the box." Rather you should say, "Let's pick up your toy now." After this is done, "Now let's put it into the box." Once that is done, "Okay, let's close the box." Three separate commands are much more likely to lead to three separate successes and will also help her learn to plan motor activities. It's essential to recognize that setting limits is an important goal for this stage and needs to be dealt with in the context of your child's emerging abilities.

Emotional Ideas (18 to 30 Months)
and Emotional Thinking
(30 to 48 Months)

The world of emotional ideas lies waiting to be discovered by your child. She is capable now of constructing her own wonderful images of the world. These images are made by combining information from her senses; they are things that she sees and hears and they have to do with words as well as pictorial configurations. How much more she can understand with the help of her newly constructed, multisensory images! Mommy and Daddy are what they look like, what they sound like, and what they smell like, as well as the feeling they engender in her. With this wonderful new tool for imagination, she can picture in her mind's eyes all kinds of interesting things.

Parents will find it fascinating to observe how a child can practice and show how she deals with visual space, words, and motor patterns in her special play time or floor time. As she grows, her ability to mentally recreate her world will enable her to organize her experiences into categories and use them in tandem to further her understanding of the world. She will be able, for example, to expand her play and use of language into many emotional areas, including closeness or dependency, pleasure, assertiveness, curiosity, and even anger. She will be able to figure out the differences between her world of "pretend" or fantasy and the world of reality.

Let's watch three-year-old Will playing with his warrior and soldier dolls. He gives a beautiful verbal description of how the good guys are capturing the bad guys and putting them in jail for being mean. Then, the doctor helps one of the bad guys who has been wounded in the fight. From the way in which space is organized into a jail and a separate battlefield, we know that Will has a good eye for visual detail. At the same time, by his selective use of words that describe the action, we know he can use words to communicate what he's already seeing in his imagination. He also understands Daddy's part of the make-believe drama, demonstrated when Daddy suggests to Will that the wounded soldier needs help and Will gets the doctor kit and brings it over. He shows a good receptive understanding of words and integrates language into his make-believe world. As he moves around the room and delicately moves the dolls and figures around, we see his motor abilities coordinated with his ideas.

It's a pleasure to watch Will play. His development is the ideal. As he gets closer to age four, we will see him tell Daddy to play the bad guy a certain way: "Hold him over there and have him say, 'We got you.' " When Daddy gets too enthusiastic, he may say, "Look, it's only pretend."

DIFFICULTIES

At the beginning of the chapter, we showed how Tommy had trouble with receptive language. If he had been playing good guys–bad guys with his dad, he would not have understood about getting the doctor. Now let's watch three-year-old Sally. She has a slight difficulty with expressive language or her ability to put her ideas into words. She hears that the doll needs a doctor and goes to the doctor kit—an indication that she understands—but she rarely speaks as she plays because she can't find or articulate the words to describe what is going on. The organization of her play tells us that she has reached the level of emotional ideas— she's playing out all manner of complicated dramas with tea parties, dancing school, and restaurants. It's her lack of verbal interaction and description that helps us realize she has trouble putting her ideas into words.

Floor-time practice from Mommy or Daddy, repetition, simplification, and the use of gestures all help Sally to understand words. Helping her put her ideas into a logical structure will facilitate her finding the right word. For example, Sally cannot recall the word "tomorrow." Rather than just telling it to her, have some fun and help her figure out what comes two days after yesterday. She will have an easier time retrieving the correct words when it's not only a memory task but also a logic task. Spontaneous play will gradually encourage her to use words more and more. Sally will slowly but surely progress in understanding and/or expressing her thoughts and ideas in language.

Adults often experience a mild form of this *word retrieval* challenge. I'm sure that most people—at one time or another—have experienced the embarrassment of forgetting someone's name in the midst of introductions. Children who can't find the words to describe what they did at school, how they felt, or what they want may seem vague, private, negative, or just simply uncommunicative when they are actually warm, engaging, bright children in need of extra patience and helpful cues to facilitate communication.

Different from word retrieval difficulties are problems making the sounds for a word you know quite well. Children with this type of problem—which responds very well to speech therapy—can benefit from extra floor time.

ATTENTION PROBLEMS

Not infrequently during this stage, parents express concern that their child is "inattentive" to either Mommy or Daddy, or the pictures in books, for example. Sometimes the labels "hyperactive" or "distractable" are used by nursery school teachers or by parents themselves. Before these catch-all labels are used, or before you are tempted to take the label as the explanation, look at your child carefully to discover the basis for her lack of attentiveness. Family stresses and tensions, overstimulation or fear of nightmares, can all certainly play a role; but if these don't prove to be the basic cause, or are only a part of the picture, look for difficulties or delays in cognitive, motor, or language development.

Sabrina, age three-and-a-half, often couldn't figure out what Mommy said. As a result she understandably started to tune into her own internal rhythm. She was described as "spacey" and was highly distractable most of the time. As discussed earlier, she had a receptive language problem, but instead of responding with belligerent or clingy behavior, like our earlier examples, Sabrina tuned out. She needed to be talked to in simple terms with great perseverance.

Consider her situation. Mommy was an energetic woman who liked to talk very quickly and who liked to get things done. Sabrina's older brother, Jonathan, was verbally gifted. When he was three and a half, Mommy could give him six commands in a row and he would either carry them out easily or argue with her about why he didn't want to. She knew he was involved and engaged, which fit right in with her very alert and attentive, high-energy style.

Her daughter, however, was slower to develop in this area and was often left confused, even stunned, by Mother's quick barrage of requests and commands. Sabrina, who was an adorable little girl, wanted to please, but began withdrawing to avoid having to see the look of disappointment in her mother's eyes. In turn, Mommy was increasing the pace at which she issued her commands due to her own frustration. This was also understandable, given her own upbringing and the success that talking quickly and energetically had previously brought her in both her professional and her family lives. That a new strategy was now necessary for Sabrina was not intuitively obvious to her. It seemed to her that Sabrina was just more and more withdrawn and overwhelmed and that the reason was predominantly psychological.

On closer inspection, however, it became clear that there were other causes—particularly when we played a simple "Simon Says" game. To the command, "Touch your nose," Sabrina did just that, accompanied by a big smile and her rapt attention. To "Touch your nose, touch your head, put your hands on your hips," she quickly became distractable, "spacey," unfocused, and provocative when pressed.

Once Mother became aware of the connection between Sabrina's inability to understand rapid-fire commands and her difficult behavior, she was able to use her considerable energy and dedication to build from a more basic foundation: simple commands. As it turned out, Sabrina was gifted visually and, by using extra animated gestures of face, body, and particularly of hands, Mother was able to communicate effectively with her. Gradually, as Mother helped Sabrina work on her difficulty with receptive language, Sabrina became more relaxed and less distractable. Mother did not have to tone down her energy level, but she did have to learn to channel her energy in a different way.

At almost any age, when a child gets confused or overwhelmed, she will suddenly indicate, "I don't want to do this any more." I've seen this in my office with children from age two on up. As soon as the task becomes something that's a little bit beyond their ability, they decide that they want to go out and see Mommy, or they want to pull the phone out of its socket or scatter the papers on my desk. As soon as I go back to something that they feel comfortable doing, their provocativeness seems to cease. Children have an uncanny ability to know when something is "over their heads," and that's when they get the most distractable, provocative, or withdrawn.

ORGANIZING IDEAS (CLOSING THE CIRCLE)

Sometimes children have difficulty comprehending what other people are saying because it's hard for them to hold the sequence of sounds or words in their minds. They may tend to have a hard time in organizing ideas and "closing the circles" (as described earlier in chapter III). In other words, they have difficulty completing their thoughts or responding to the information someone else offers. This may be present even when there is no difficulty with receptive language. Let's look at how this manifests itself.

Joel had a very good imagination which he used in his play. He could also hold marvelous conversations as long as they were mainly one-sided—his side. He was adept at reasoning and could argue with great conviction for his younger sister's removal from the house, preferably to Siberia. But there also existed a subtle challenge his parents were beginning to notice. Every time their otherwise verbal and sophisticated three-and-a-half-year-old would enter into conversation with them, he never seemed to respond to their part of the argument. He would frequently return to his own point of view without taking in their information. At times he seemed to ramble, his verbiage obscuring the point they were discussing.

One such instance occurred when Joel was given the choice of three playmates he could invite to his house. He talked about playing with his rocket ship. Mother tried to bring him back to the topic of playmates. Joel looked puzzled as he pretended to fly his rocket ship all around the room. "Well, who do you want to invite?" Joel handed Mother one of his action figures and suggested she put him into the rocket ship. They seemed to be talking past each other.

In other situations Mother noticed that it was hard for Joel to shift between the world of make-believe and the world of reality. If he had to make the transition between a pretend drama and putting his shoes on in order to go outside, Mother would have to begin putting the shoes on his feet for him. Even in school, though he was verbal and interesting, his teacher characterized him as "out of sync" with the rest of the class.

Eventually everyone began to get a little worried about Joel, but there didn't appear to be any apparent reason for his difficulty. When spoken to, he wanted only to play out his own agendas. Follow-up questions to what he did want to talk about were similarly ignored. When Joel came to see me and I asked why Frankie, a not-so-liked friend of his, made him mad, he began talking about Judd, whom he did like. Finally, after asking him for the third time and then pointing out that he hadn't answered my question, I asked him why he didn't want to. He concentrated and was able to tell me a few things about Frankie. The fact that he could cooperate with me made me wonder whether he had a hard time taking in the information I had to offer and *completing the circle*. Perhaps he couldn't, in a conversation, have his own ideas, listen to your ideas, and then close the circle by responding to your ideas. A child must be able to respond in a logical and reality-based way to what you are saying. If your child initiates a conversation, then you say something to elaborate on that, and the child follows with something related to what you said, your child is "closing the circle."

What should one do in a situation such as Joel's? First, the situation can be related to the difficulty the child has in understanding and attending to what you and others say. There may be other factors involved, which we won't go into at this point. What is important is that there are exercises and games that can help your child learn to "close his circles"—or be more logical and reality-based.

The exercise we designed for Joel and for children like him is as follows.

Parents are asked to try to close the circle (as described in chapter III) as many times as possible, either in pretend play or in daily conversation. Even a negative answer ("Be quiet, I'll tell you when I'm ready!") counts as closing the circle, as long as it responds to your comment rather than ignoring it. "Never ignore what a child says" is axiomatic to this approach. Parents need to repeat their questions in a gentle, supportive way ("What you're saying is very interesting, but you forgot to answer my question"), or to rephrase the question in simpler and simpler ways. I've seen very bright parents talking with their equally bright children and, in a 15-minute conversation, only one or two circles are closed. Parents and children tended to talk past each other, even when discussing the same general topic. As the child begins to close one or two circles with you, he'll soon be having normal conversations. One circle leads to another and another.

So if Joel can answer his mother's request to name a playmate to invite and he can answer, "Andrew," then Mother can continue. "Would you like him to come over before or after lunch?" and Joel can say, "I'd like us to eat lunch together." Then the discussion of what to have for lunch can follow. This is much different from the earlier conversation where playmates and spaceships weren't connecting in space or anywhere else.

It's a mistake for parents to assume that not "closing the circle" is a willful act of evasion. Some children just need extra practice to be able to do this. Parents of very bright, imaginative children who are hesitant to interfere with their child's creative process are making a mistake in not helping the child—even in pretending— to close the circle. Closing the circle is essential to learning about reality, and especially important for children who have difficulty taking in what another person is saying.

LAWYER-TO-LAWYER TALK

Besides closing the circle, there's another tactic that helps children develop the capacity for logical thinking—the lawyer-to-lawyer talk. Your child may argue about why the spoon should be to the left of her or why she wants this cereal rather than that cereal. The temptation, when one is in a hurry, is to simply say, "Do it my way." End of conversation.

Logical thinking and articulation, however, should be encouraged when you enter into such a contest of wills. You can still pull rank at the end of the conversation and, while respecting and understanding the child's point of view, explain why you have decided that things are to be done your way. He may still throw a fit, causing you to have to set limits and be firm, but in the meantime you have encouraged his logical thinking. There's no substitute for a motivated child who is trying to convince you of his point of view and an interested parent who will let the child say his piece. Even if you turn him down, at least he knows he's gotten a fair shot at convincing you that he's correct. Enjoying rather than fearing or avoiding competition is essential to a hearty legal debate.

Lawyer-to-lawyer talk is one of the best ways for your child to practice receptive language (taking into account your objections), expressive language (giving you complex sentences in return), and action-oriented logical thinking. This will make him an action-oriented, intelligent person later in life. If there was ever an opportunity to learn to think on your feet—one of the main ingredients of successful adult functioning—it's the lawyer-to-lawyer conversations of early childhood. This also provides a nice balance to the pretend, creative thinking your child does in fantasy play, and it's especially valuable for children with receptive or expressive language difficulties or for those who are shy and passive.

MOTOR CHALLENGES

By the time your child hits the two- to four-year-old range and is capable of make-believe play, group games, and active outdoors play, a great help for the child with low muscle tone is to engage her in special games and exercises that will increase tone. Just as we discussed for the toddler, the airplane game is a good example. Only now this game and others can be part of a group of games called "Let's see who can fly the farthest" or part of pretend, "Okay, if we're visiting Aunt Milly in California let's become an airplane." Have your child put her legs around your waist and face downward while you support her at the waist. She will arch her back and put her arms out while you either go around and around or run forward, imitating an airplane, of course. This will give her practice that will increase her motor tone.

Here's another example. When your child is learning to run,

playing chase games in which she has to change directions frequently rather than run in a straight line will help her use her extensor muscles. Now a game of tag can help your child also learn about rules and organized games. The boat game is another. Lie on the floor on your stomach and rock back and forth, lifting legs and extending arms in front of you. Have your child imitate you. It's good exercise for both of you, and the boat can go any place in the world your imagination takes you. Once you have the principle down, you can be sensitive to your child's need to learn to master her body and give her practice where she needs it.

As your child exercises more and more, you will see that, along with her increase in muscle tone, her general sense of her physical ability will improve and she'll enjoy physical exercise more—especially as it becomes part of games and pretend play. I've seen children who were relatively inactive, labeled by their parents as passive, unassertive, and fearful of aggression, take joy in robust physical activity once they become more comfortable with their bodies and more confident in their ability to experiment with aggressions. With greater confidence in one's body at this age, we see how self-image in terms of "ideas" also changes. Frequently a child whose action figures "felt scared" and whose buildings were knocked over by storms will change his play to reflect his new confidence. Now the buildings will stand up to the storms and the action figures will not be afraid.

The high-muscle-tone child, to whom emotional ideas are becoming important, is beginning, as with all children at this stage, to have an image of her body. Related to this image is whether she is an aggressive person or a loving person, for example. She will get a sense of herself from how she behaves or by how she uses her muscles. Interactions with peers are becoming important, too. Learning how to control her body vis-à-vis another person will help her achieve a basic sense of security in handling assertiveness, aggression, and curiosity, and will, in part, determine the "ideas" she has of herself.

Children with motor-planning difficulty need extra practice just as do those with low or high muscle tone. An act like tying a shoelace or trying to draw, or playing a game requiring a sequence of movements, may be difficult for the child who has trouble putting together two or three motor acts. These children may appear clumsy. If you identify a problem (it's easy to do this by playing "Simon Says" or another imitative game with your three- to four-year-old child), then the child should receive support, extra security, and extra practice.

For example, a child has difficulty taking his glass from the table, pouring his drink into the sink, rinsing the glass, and putting it in the dishwasher. You will need to play a game with him, taking each act by itself. "Cooking" or "tea party" will involve lots of these motor patterns as a part of pretend play. Once he's gotten one part down, you can proceed to the next and the next. Special games using large and fine motor coordination as well can be devised, such as fitting block pieces together to make the "good guy's house" or riding to "He-Man-Land" in a hammock and throwing bean bags at various targets who happen to be the "bad guys." Your child doesn't know he has a motor-planning problem; he just knows some things are hard. They become less hard when they're broken down into smaller parts, and they can be fun when put into games and pretend play.

Children with motor-planning problems require not only extra practice but extra focus in breaking down motor challenges into small steps. They also require that parents provide them with enough emotional respect to let them struggle on their own with you cheering them on from the sidelines. One mother recently told me that her four-year-old still wasn't dressing himself. "Finally, I went over the steps with him and broke it down bit by bit. For the first week we only worked on his pulling on his pants, but I had to let him struggle. I encouraged him, but didn't do it for him. He moaned and threw his pants down many times. I demonstrated how to do it on myself so he could copy, but that didn't do it for him. Finally, he did it on his own. It was a great day. In the past, I would have moved in and done it for him. I didn't realize that he needed much more time than my other children to struggle and finally succeed. He got mad at me, saying he thought we didn't love him. But we did extra floor time at other times to make sure he knew we cared. He was so pleased with himself when he succeeded."

This vignette says it all in relation to motor problems and motor planning. The principles are (1) break down the task into doable steps; (2) practice each step; and (3) get out of your child's way. Don't overprotect or overdo. Cheer from the sidelines and let him struggle it through—even temper tantrums can simply be an expression of his struggle.

In a study of children with serious motor delays, we noticed that most parents tended to be overprotective and hover over their children too much. When we, as part of a game, asked parents to give the children only visual and vocal support from the sidelines, rather than physical assistance, a remarkable thing happened. Some of the children began to use motor skills four to six months beyond what they were doing when their parents were overdoing for them. One child, who couldn't sit up without support, rolled out of his chair onto a mat, rolled over to a game, positioned the game, and then, using his hands, banged down on a key to get a special animal to pop up. No one would have dreamed he was capable of this feat of motor skill and logic.

The best activities for children with motor tone or motor-planning difficulties are those that combine physical activity with pretend and imagination. It's best if you follow and build on your child's interests. For example, playing "spaceman"—going to visit the planets—can involve running to the spaceship, fine motor actitivies to control the space ship, and drawing a secret message that must be sent. As you interact with the Martians, you can see how your child feels about himself—are the Earthlings overwhelmed by the Martians? Are the Martians friendly and nurturing? Mean and evil? The pretend drama is a way to help your child practice motor activities and deal with his feelings all at once.

Goals for Parents

As parents, you need to work toward highly individualistic ways of monitoring your child's sensory, motor, and language development. We have seen how the reactivity of the senses, visual and spatial abilities, receptive language capacity, muscle tone, and motor planning all can play a role in your child's emotional and intellectual development. To foster emotional and intellectual growth, each child requires admiration for his or her unique strengths, and each child must be offered practice in areas that need extra work. The key for understanding your child is to discover these.

Some children are strong in conventional ways. When they grow to be school age, they are good in reading or arithmetic and can run around the school grounds with minimal effort. But other children have strengths in ways that are not as obvious. Your child may be good at art or may have a novel way of seeing the world. What adult have you ever known whose success is based on reading ability or the ability to do arithmetic? By and large we attribute success to an ability to make decisions, or to think quickly, or to be creative, a leader, energetic, or to see things from a novel angle. Or we may tout someone's delicacy and gentleness, or his combination of sensitivity and assertiveness, or his ability to organize people and things and see how all the pieces work together. What might this mean to you as you look at your own child?

In our current educational system, certain skills are valued at early ages which may have little relationship to the skills that are valued at later ages and grades. For example, in the first few grades reading and language skills are most valued, more so than arithmetic skills, problem-solving skills, and originality, creativity, or social skills. Typical report cards of first or second graders contain six or seven categories having to do with reading and language skills, one category for arithmetic, and almost nothing for problem-solving, creativity, and emotional skills. High school report cards reflect a heavy emphasis on abstract reasoning ability, especially science and math. Some of the champion readers of the earlier years may have a hard time with physics or chemistry, algebra, or geometry. Have they become less smart as they matured? No, they just don't happen to be so great at spatial and abstract reasoning, the skills required for learning science and math. They needed practice in problem solving and abstract reasoning early in their education; they needed to realize that this ability was *not* easy for them and they would have to work hard at it. Now, they need to catch up in order to become as good as they can.

In college, essays demonstrating originality, organization, and the ability to make a point in a logical way win the day. We may

see that students who were a little slower at lea͟
out to be very good at making and supporting th
have logical abilities and are good at abstract reasor.
become smart all of a sudden or were their abstr͟
skills and problem-solving abilities just not worked wit͟
We always hear of the brilliant scientist who was a sl͟
But how many great problem solvers "gave up" or thou͟
were "stupid" because they were slow readers and spelle͟

We are locked into narrow values and emphasize what ͟
sidered important at the moment, without seeing it in the co͟.
of a life-span. We should be building skills that both help us t͟
in and give out information, such as reading, writing, and spea͟
ing, as well as the more general "processing" skills of abstract
reasoning, creativity, action-oriented problem solving, leadership,
and social interaction. If we lose sight of the fact that the traditional fundamentals are simply tools for higher-level tasks, then
we do our children a great disservice.

Skills for taking in information depend heavily on the timing
and maturation of the nervous system. Some children will need
as much as a couple of years longer to master reading, writing
and numbers. It's better to recognize this fact and give those
children the extra time and practice they need. At the same time,
those children will profit from work in areas in which they are
gifted. Creative problem-solving tasks should not depend solely
upon reading during this time, but on verbal, dramatic, spatial,
artistic, or other skills. Their self-esteem will remain intact and
their originality or ability to reason abstractly won't stagnate. Don't
let your gifted reader who is less able to "see the forest for the
trees" develop a false sense of security about his "spatial" and
problem-solving skills, only to be surprised later. A balanced approach will respect both sets of skills and help place academic
abilities in the context of emotional and social development.

IX

Peer and Group Relationships

As your child grows, the intimacy of his partnership with you—and all that he has learned through it—becomes part of a life-long drama as he ventures out into peer and group relationships. His horizons now expand: he must gradually balance his interest in his family with that of peer and larger groups, and how well he does this will depend on the strength and pattern of your partnership.

Peer Relationships

Surprisingly, babies can enjoy interacting in groups at a far younger age than anyone has imagined. Even ten-month-olds will exchange toys or examine a toy together. By fourteen months, toddlers are curious about each other's hair and clothing and size each other up. At eighteen months, they are giggling and laughing together over a silly face or a spilled glass of water. Twenty-month-olds will exclude children who are not their preferred friends. By twenty-four to thirty months, children can begin sharing meanings together by participating in a drama, like setting up the tea party or crashing the battle trucks together. And by thirty to forty months, self-assigned roles in pretend play and rules of social interaction, such as sharing or everything is mine, are well established.

Developing healthy peer relationships—enjoying one another—requires children to use their new abilities for interacting and thinking. Intimacy, sharing, power struggles, fights, and even tantrums gradually become part of peer relationships, just as they are part of parent-child patterns. And just like parent-child relationships, children need opportunities to apply their emotional skills to peer relationships.

There is enormous variation in the age that children begin to form true friendships. Depending partly on the accessibility and availability of other children, their comfort with peers gradually increases, until sometime between the ages of three and four a clear preference emerges for playing with children rather than "boring" adults. Children who don't show this preference and are reluctant to interact with peers require extra practice, including parents' joining the "peer group" to monitor aggression or to promote longer and more pleasurable interactions.

Play groups are a perfect opportunity for your participation. While play groups often free a parent up to pursue his/her own peer relationships, they also allow the parent to buffer the child so he can master this new terrain of peer relationships. At the same time, they help children learn that they can handle things on their own. Availability and guidance, not overprotectiveness, are what is needed. Children between ages two and four should not be allowed to avoid this developmental opportunity.

Children can find peer relationships challenging for a number of reasons. Here are a few of the most common.

Fearful of being assertive and intimate in the same relationship, Meg tended to "bite the hand that fed her." As soon as another three-year-old took an interest in her and they played for 10 or 15 minutes, Meg would either start throwing things, hit her potential new friend, or wander off for no reason. Needless to say, before very long not too many children wanted to play with Meg.

Meg was eventually referred to treatment and through her play, we learned that she was afraid of combining closeness with the give and take of expectable peer relationships. Just as we earlier discussed the little girl who was fearful of closeness with her mother, Meg often hit or wandered off because she was concerned with being hurt or left herself. With treatment, Meg and her family were able to overcome this challenge.

Scott had a more common problem. He wouldn't share with his fellow three-year-olds. What was his was his and what was theirs was his. He didn't fight or hit; he just borrowed and never returned. He was quite self-sufficient as well. When other children came over to his side of the room, he turned his back and said, "Play alone." If one of the other kids had a new toy, however, he was over on their side of the room, acting like a long-lost cousin. After a few months of this pattern, Scott was enmeshed in continuous power struggles with the other kids who had caught on to his strategy.

Pushed by complaints from the teacher, Mother finally figured out that Scott was doing in school what she wasn't letting him do at home. It seems that Scott had a younger brother. The house rule was that all toys were shared—no exclusive use permitted. Mother realized that Scott's ill-formed lessons were obviously backfiring. To remedy the situation, the rules were changed. Now there would be greater protection of Scott's possessions from his brother; extra floor time with Mom and Dad (who agreed to be home earlier); and sensitivity to themes of sibling rivalry in his pretend play. Special projects with Dad, tough limits on sharing refereed by the teacher, problem-solving discussions about specific sharing problems each evening, and extra practice with having children over and being a good host, all helped Scott find friends and enjoy sharing with them—at least most of the time.

Judy had a different challenge. She insisted that she "loved" Amy, that Amy was special, her best friend. Amy, who was indifferent to Judy, felt pressured by Judy's attention. The more Judy pushed, the faster Amy ran away. Other children who wanted to play with Judy were ignored by her. Mother and teacher were perplexed about what to do.

Parents need to realize that idealization is a normal step in the friendship process—just as idealizing a parent is. Part of the idealization is often related to a child's desire not to experience any disappointment or sense of loss. After all, if your friend is perfect, she can never be less than you want her to be. Feelings of anger and rivalry are also hidden under the guise of perfection—a convenient way for a child to simplify the turbulent waters of intimate friendships. Sensitive parents need to help the child to slowly make the transition from idealization to reality. Awareness of loss, disappointment, and eventual anger—introducing the notion that mixed feelings toward a friend are okay—helps the child balance her wish for a perfect friend with reality.

Some children are so controlling that they insist on playing only their game. Paul would only play with the red truck: he liked transporting rocks from one part of the room to another. When his classmates would suggest other games, he insisted on his way. Needless to say, he spent his time either playing alone or involved in a power struggle.

An ingenious teacher worked with him to incorporate his truck's activities into other games. She suggested that some children building a tower needed some rocks and Paul dutifully brought the rocks. At the same time, she talked with his mother and found that at home Paul was very possessive and controlling. He was jealous of both his older sister and his father, wanting Mother to read to him alone. Mother said, "I give in, because, if I don't, he'll cry." In cooperation with the teacher, Paul's mother shifted her approach, encouraging more involvement with Dad and his sister. Paul slowly became more flexible. There are many different reasons why a preschooler will be over-controlling. Encouraging flexibility while investigating possible causes often helps.

Another common problem with peer relationships involves the very timid child. Here the approach is similar to the one we suggested before: gradual exposure to children with lots of security from an adult when the child is facing new experiences.

Sometimes, timid children are especially sensitive to loud noises, touch, or quick movement patterns. Simple activities like going down a slide may be difficult. A non-demanding, gradual, "Let's do it together" approach with extra security rather than avoidance or overprotectiveness is often helpful.

A very common situation involves the timid child's response to "meanness" and exclusion. Not infrequently, Mary wanted to play with Jane and Nancy, who, being best friends, excluded her without being especially nice. "We're playing here," they would say. Mary felt hurt and for many days didn't reach out to other children. Mother and teacher huddled. At first all that was obvious was Mary's hurt feelings. Special projects with teacher and Mother helped her feel better, but didn't change Mary's insistence on playing only with the two children who continued to shun her. Finally, in exasperation, Mother said to the teacher, "She is so stubborn." "That's it," responded the teacher. "We've been working with Mary as though she is hurt and helpless. We've missed the fact that she is stubborn."

Mother began mentioning to Mary that she seemed to insist on only these two girls. How much she needed to have her own way! Mother reflected that in the family Mary almost always got her way, not by belligerence, but by "hurt feelings" and tenacity. As her mother opened up these feelings for discussion and helped Mary talk about her subtle insistence that she get her own way, a slew of new feelings came out.

In floor time, Mary showed a more aggressive side, knocking down buildings and crashing cars. Mary also began demanding more time with Mother. Armed with this new assertiveness and support and suggestions from her teacher, Mary reached out to other children. One day she said to her mother, "Jane and Nancy are best friends. I'm not their best friend. I'm becoming good friends with Sally." Mother calmly said, "That's great! Do you want to invite Sally over to play?" Mary was learning an important lesson. Frequently children who are always excluded and feel other children are mean have challenges of their own to master.

The nuances of peer relationships are many. The following principles, however, may prove helpful:

1. Provide lots of peer-to-peer opportunities (more than three times per week) for children over two and a half.

2. Provide more, not less, practice with peer play when you see difficulties.

3. Look carefully for signs of pleasure and spontaneity.

4. Look for real interaction (not simply playing alongside

each other) and sharing. Help them along with your active participation, if necessary.

5. Look for signs of assertiveness. Is your child expressing his/her preferences and negotiating his/her interests? If not, look at this quality in your relationship with your child.

6. Look for growing interaction and intimacy with selected children.

7. Look for your child's interactive play to grow more complex, including using language and ideas in pretend, making up rules, or designing new games.

Group Relationships

Just as a child sometimes misses the path to an intimate peer relationship, so a child can do the same with relationships in larger groups. For some children, group activities are very difficult. You may have a child who has warm relationships with children down the street or with family members but becomes aloof and sometimes confused in group settings like school. A child's first experience with ten or fifteen kids could make him feel a little disorganized and cause him to physically or mentally withdraw.

Some of us as adults may experience the same feelings at a large, noisy party or meeting. After a while our one desire becomes to find a quiet corner or to pull a friend over to use as an anchor in the swarming sea. Others can be in the midst of commotion and have no trouble negotiating the waves, even thrive on them.

Adults frequently draw all kinds of conclusions about a child's level of trust, curiosity, or social maturity, based on his interactions in a group. But kids' behavior in a group can be deceptive. A child who is withdrawn or sensitive in a group may give an inaccurate and often negative sense of his social and intellectual abilities. In fact, sensitive children may be great in one-on-one relationships and turn out to be exceptionally empathetic as well as intellectually gifted. The next budding Einstein or Michelangelo may be one of these children who looks "overwhelmed" and confused in large groups.

Problems with groups become more obvious when your child starts school. Then, should there be a problem, you are likely to hear about your son or daughter from the teacher. A typical scenario has little Angela doing just fine at home. While shy and careful, she has always been warm and engaging. She has a friend down the street and they enjoy playing dress up, having a tea party, and watching cartoons. She is sometimes stubborn. She doesn't like to comb her hair or brush her teeth and occasionally has temper tantrums, but Mother assumes that these irritations will be resolved with time.

Angela starts nursery school with the typical anticipatory excitement: she is going to school like the big kids. When Mother's questions about school begin to receive perfunctory answers, Mother doesn't think much about it. Angela's enthusiasm has waned a bit but she is still interested in school.

After four months in the preschool program Angela's teacher announces to Angela's mother that Angela is "spacey" in class— "She doesn't interact with the other kids. She needs me to tell her exactly what to do and often just watches the others from a corner of the room. I think she may need to repeat the year because at this rate she won't be ready for the more demanding class next year. I think she is just immature." Mother is not only upset, she is confused. At home, Angela is gifted verbally and is already interested in sounds and letters. She can even sound out simple words like "cat." The level of the teacher's concern does not add up with Angela's behavior at home.

How do we relate Angela's age-appropriate relationships at home with her behavior in preschool? As indicated earlier, parents need to remember that a child's behavior at home or with one or two friends is more revealing of true emotional competence than the new and challenging situation of a large group. Since you are the observer in the former situations, you are often in the best position to know about your child's overall emotional health. Of course problematic behavior observed only in the group setting shouldn't be ignored, but rather than viewing it as a global problem, accept it as a challenge special to the group relationship. The fact that children are placed in groups at earlier and earlier ages and that judgments about their abilities are made in these settings place a special challenge on parents to form their own opinion.

Now, why are group relationships so challenging for many pre-schoolers? While related to more intimate one-on-one relationships, group relationships are really a separate aspect of development. Being comfortable in groups, in part, relates to dealing with many sensations at once—noise, touch, movement—and the ability to comprehend or "integrate" information in space, that is, a visual-spatial abstracting ability as compared to, let's say, the ability to comprehend words, a verbal abstracting ability. So for young children, funtioning in a group is a new activity that taps new abilities, such as figuring out what's happening with many moving and talking people in a large space. Some children who are great with words have difficulty with spatial abilities, while those who excel at higher-level mathematical abilities sometimes have weaker verbal skills.

We have all been awed by the basketball player who dribbles the ball up the court full speed, looks to his right, takes a step to the left, jumps up in the air, begins passing the ball to a streaking player on his left and, at the last second, flips the ball over his shoulder to the outstretched fingers of a player on his right who dunks it into the basket. Given his uncanny ability to deal with the chaotic activity in a large area, this athlete was unlikely to panic in groups when young.

On the other hand, I frequently hear from frustrated fathers that their Johnny is "just not trying." They describe how, at age seven, Johnny is already a "washed-up athlete" as he stands around the soccer field watching the action instead of participating.

"Why doesn't he go after the ball? He kicks it great with me in the backyard," moans the frustrated father. "He just doesn't want to try."

Johnny is actually highly motivated and extremely hardworking. One-on-one relationships never being a problem, he now has some good friends. But a large group of kids all running and shouting is overwhelming. His mother recalls that Johnny had difficulty in preschool and kindergarten "warming up to the group." Off sitting in a corner, he needed his mother to help him initially interact with the other childen. School is now okay but he is still a little shy with new groups of people.

So as not to be paralyzed by all the commotion and activity, Johnny needed to focus on a simple task. What worked for him was simply to count the number of times he kicked the ball in the direction of the goal and to ignore trying to score, pass, or see how many others were pressing down on the ball. Concentration on just this one objective freed him to become a participant. Suddenly he was moving around the field, getting good solid kicks, and being a valued team member.

If Johnny's father had realized that his son's problem was the group and not his attitude, he would have been far less frustrated and far more helpful to Johnny. Seeing the problem for what it is makes finding a solution much easier.

Four-year-old Adam also became confused in a group of people. It wasn't the noise level, with which he could cope; it was—unlike the gifted basketball player—other people's movements that gave him a rough time. He had trouble figuring out where, physically, he belonged in relationship to everyone else. He consequently became overly active when he tried to join a crowd, and this disorganization then caused him to withdraw. His spatial map of the room and of the people in the room was inadequate.

At school, his teacher recognized this difficulty and let Adam play in his favorite corner, at first with only one other child and herself. Then she added another and another. Over many weeks, she very gradually brought the "group" to him in his secure spot.

When Adam wasn't safely tucked in his corner, he was on the move, chaotically circling the room, feeling overwhelmed. He clearly needed a better sense of his position in the room and vis-à-vis the other children. The teacher found that games involving spatial relationships gave him this sense. Almost from the start he was very excited about the game of "Musical Chairs." It became his vehicle for negotiating space, since figuring out which chair he was supposed to sit in gave him a chance to practice his self-control while also sharpening his sense of where things belonged in space. It also helped him to position himself among other children. At first the game included only two or three children and a few chairs, but before long Adam enjoyed having a whole group to contend with. Games like "Red Rover," in which he had to go from one side of the room to the other, also helped him learn how to organize himself in space among many children, but they had to be introduced gradually.

As another aid in mastering spatial relationships, he and his father built block houses with rooms that interconnected in more and more complicated ways. Adam, at four years old, was talking beautifully and could even read simple words, but he was still a novice when it came to constructing a simple Lego rocket ship or a farm with different corrals for his animals.

When he was older, certain athletic endeavors, like running bases, particularly in irregular patterns—say, from first to home to second—helped Adam not only to become a good baseball player but also a strong base runner who could modulate his speed depending on the skills needed. All kinds of games that had to do with finding his way around in space and varying his level of speed proved helpful. He gradually went from being a distractable child to a very attentive one.

Likewise, little Claire seemed to get confused when there were more than a few children around. And also like the other children we've discussed, she played nicely when she had one or two play-mates and was terrific with Mommy, Daddy, and her little brother. But, as with the other children, the nursery school teacher saw something different—a little girl sitting in a corner.

It wasn't a matter of inventing a complicated psychological cause for Claire's behavior in school, or assuming that she wanted to retreat from the world. Claire's early history clearly showed her sensitivity to noise, commotion, and touch. People knocking into her and brushing past made her feel finicky and want to withdraw.

As with Adam, Claire's teacher began working with her and one other child in a quiet corner of the room, slowly enlarging the group, trying to establish Claire's threshold level. Once the teacher found that more than three children overwhelmed Claire, she spent some time reinforcing her sense of security in a group this size by having the class divide up many of the activities into small groups. Snack was eaten in small groups; puzzles and games were organized likewise. Cooking had rotating groups of those who stirred, those who measured, and those who rinsed. Over a three- or four-month period Claire began to participate in more spontaneous interaction within these small groups.

From her parents she learned to join the group that made her feel the most comfortable. They told her that if she didn't want to hold hands or link arms, all she had to do was explain that it bothered her. Through their guidance, she realized that she could control her environment.

If, in contrast, Claire had been forced into the group to "sink or swim"—a popular method—she might have developed a counter-productive reaction. Claire could very well have gotten more tense, withdrawn, or distracted in school, though she would still have been fine at home. A child's pattern of reaction to basic sensations, which has been present since birth, will continue to play itself out in early childhood but may eventually lessen with the growth of the nervous system. It is an aspect of your child that you will always want to be aware of and attentive to.

As Claire's parents did, it's important to let your child know and understand his reactions. As he grows older he will be helped by realizing that, for example, he's a slow-to-warm-up child. With practice in the early years, he'll be a nine-year-old expert at structuring his own environment to avoid overload. He will learn to enter groups of different sizes and complexity, and most importantly, by learning about his own special sensitivities, he won't attribute his feelings to unrealistic causes like "I'm scared because those kids want to be mean." Instead, he might say to himself, "Those kids are active and noisy. I'd better move in very slowly."

Some principles for the young child with difficulties in a group include the following:

1. Remember that if the child's two-person relationships are going well, the group is probably a special situation, not indicative of general emotional abilities.

2. Create a two-person relationship within the larger group and build on it. For example, encourage Sam to play with Jack in a corner. Mom or teacher may need to be present to serve as an intermediary. Don't worry about indulging. Create a sense of security.

3. Help the two-person relationship develop and become robust. For example, help the child experiment with assertiveness, initiative, and cooperation.

4. When security and robustness are established, add a third child to the little group. Mediate and create the sense of security as needed. Support robustness again.

5. Add a fourth and fifth child, and so on.

6. As Joey tries moving into the larger circle, don't hesitate, if needed, to hold his hand and be his partner or have his "best friend" be his partner. The key is to increase a sense of security during transitional experiences.

7. Engage the child in activities that increase security, exploration, and assertiveness in the larger group. Encourage quiet, peaceful games, snacks, gentle holding of hands, along with running and playing active games. Security teamed with activity helps a child master a new situation and a "new space."

8. Do not make the mistake of assuming Eddie is just immature.

9. Do not make the mistake of "not indulging him" and pushing him too quickly.

10. Remember to increase his sense of security simultaneously with the amount of his time spent practicing new experiences. Take your time. He has many months and even years to master this new challenge. Remember the tale of the tortoise and the hare—the slow tortoise always finishes the race.

11. If specific maturational lags or sensitivities can be identified—such as sensitivities to touch, sound, or bright lights; muscle tone or motor-planning difficulties; auditory, verbal, or visual-spatial processing lags—work with them to strengthen your child's foundation, as described in chapter VIII.

12. Provide extra floor time and problem-solving time to help your child understand his/her special sensitivities, feelings about them and, most importantly, to figure out practical strategies that help him/her to master rather than avoid new challenges.

Should a misguided but well-intentioned adult try to pressure or embarrass the overloaded and cautious child into being too involved with the group too quickly, he could just become more overwhelmed. He then has to guard himself against the adult who has become another overwhelming force in the environment. Remember, all the feelings that characterize family and peer relationships may be experienced quite intensely in groups and may be greatly exaggerated due to a child's special sensitivities or the structure of the group itself.

Peer and group relationships are quite challenging to children, often revealing new areas of competence and vulnerability. When your child moves out into this wider world, you are no less important. As with all new adventures, parents and teachers can work together with children to help them learn from their new challenges and their successes in meeting those challenges depends on the strength and character of their relationship with you.

Conclusion

Your child is born with many qualities and built-in abilities. Most importantly, however, he or she is born into a family with ready-made "essential partnerships." How these partnerships harness his unique characteristics and create learning opportunities will help to determine the type of person he becomes. Tempting though it is to find simple reasons for our children's behavior— "It's genetic," or, "It's part of her temperament"—their most important abilities are fortunately those complex, illusive, human abilities: to trust and love, feel like a "good and worthwhile person," share and empathize with others, create emotional ideas, comprehend reality, solve new problems, and experience the full array of distinctly human feelings as part of ongoing relationships. And these abilities are almost completely learned in the intimacy and complexity of the Essential Partnership.

In this book, we have described the steps and components of the Essential Partnership. We have tried to show how parents can harness their own and their child's potential and together transform challenges and problems into opportunities for even further emotional growth. Children who are feeling negative about themselves can discover their uniqueness and feel optimistic. Children who are aloof or avoid their peers can learn that relationships need not be frightening and, in fact, can provide the security they seek. Children who are negative and stubborn can figure out that they can also be assertive through cooperation and sharing. Children who are overly serious and sullen can learn about joy. Children who are impulsive can learn how to reason out their angry feelings and respect the rights of others. And children who are distractable and easily overwhelmed can learn special ways to concentrate and focus.

Remarkable as it may seem, the parents' and child's ability to form and develop a relationship can be the critical vehicle for early learning. This is because early learning is about the most important human qualities, the very qualities that define the Essential Partnership.

Index